CAPITAL BUDGETING
AND LEASING

Ahmed Riahi-Belkaoui

PREFACE

In writing this book, my goal was to create a text that combines both financial and quantitative techniques on the basis of their usefulness to capital budgeting and leasing decisions.

The first part of the book focuses on capital budgeting. Management must often decide whether to add a product or to buy a new machine. They make many general, nonrecurring investment decision involving fixed assets, or capital budgeting decisions. The techniques presented in this book are intended to facilitate and improve the capital budgeting decisions in a way as to lead to the maximization of owners' wealth.

The second part of the book focuses on an analysis of the lease-or-buy decision. Leasing has become an important source of financing for many types of assets. So, the decision to lease an asset is generally evaluated by comparing it with the borrowing decision necessary for an outright purchase of the same asset. The main purpose of this second part of the book is to explain the leasing arrangements and the main issue in financial leasing, and to provide a methodology for analysis.

No book can be written without the help of numerous individuals and organization. I am indebted to all the people who influenced this book by their reviews and/or comments. A special note of appreciation is extended to my research assistant, Olivia Ellsworth, for her cheerful and intelligent assistance.

Ahmed Riahi-Belkaoui

PART 1- CAPITAL BUDGETING

Chapter 1
Time Value of Money

Introduction
When people must choose between receiving payment immediately or periodically over a number of periods, they show a preference for present satisfaction over future satisfaction. The preference for present payment is motivated by the possibility of either consuming the funds or investing them to provide greater amounts in the future, whereas the choice of receiving money in the future involves the sacrifice of waiting before it can be used. The compensation for waiting is the time value of money, called *interest.* Individuals require interest for postponing consumption.

Compound Value
The *compound value* (CDV) is the future value of funds received today and invested at the prevalent interest rate. For example, assume an investment of $1,000 at 10 percent per year. The compound value at the end of year 1 is computed as follows:

$$CDV_1 = \$1,000(1 + 0.10)^1 = \$1,100$$

Similarly, the compound value at the end of year 2 is computed as follows:

$$CDV_2 = \$1,100(1 + 0.10)^1 = \$1,210$$

or

$$CDV_2 = \$1,000(1 + 0.10)^2 = \$1,210$$

This can be generalized to yield the following formula, which applies to compute the compound value:

$$S_n = P(1 + r)^n,$$

where

S_n = Compound value at the end of year n = $1,210.
P = Beginning amount or present value = $1,000.
r = *Interest* rate or rate of return = 10%.
n = Number of years = 2.

Thus, the future value (FV) of $1, with n corresponding to the number of compounding periods, is

$$FV = (1 + r)^n.$$

The FV can be computed for any interest rate (r) and any number of compounding periods (n). Exhibit 1.1 shows the future value of $1 for a variety of interest rates and compounding periods.

PRESENT VALUE
In the previous example, if $1,000 compound at 10 percent per year becomes $1,210 due at the end of two years, the $1,000 is the present value (PV) of $1,210 due at the end of two years. Finding the present value of a future value involves discounting the future value to the present. Discounting, then, is the opposite of

compounding. The formula for the present value is the same as the formula for the future value, except it solves for P instead of S, which is known. Thus, if

$$S_n = P(1 + r)^n,$$

then

$$P = \frac{S_n}{(1 + r)^n}.$$

Inserting the illustrative numbers yields

$$P = \frac{\$1,210}{(1+0.10)^2} = \$1,000.$$

Thus, the general formula for the present value of $1 is

$$PV = \frac{1}{(1 + r)^n}.$$

Exhibit 1.2 shows the present value of $1 for any interest rate (r) and any number of periods (n).

FUTURE VALUE OF AN ANNUITY IN ARREARS OF $1

An *annuity in arrears* is a series of periodic and equal payments (receipts) to be paid (received) at the end of successive similar periods. Assume, for example, that a firm is to receive annual payments of $1,000 at the end of each year for three years and charges an interest rate of 10 percent. Using Exhibit 1.1, the pattern of compounding is as follows:

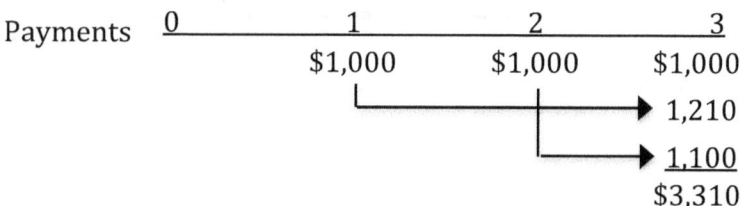

In other words, the future value of an annuity in arrears of $1,000 for three years at 10 percent is equal to

$$1,000(1 + 0.10)^2 + 1,000(1 + 0.10) + 1,000 = \$3,310$$

or

Exhibit 1.1
Future Value of $1 Payable in Period N

Year (N)	1%	2%	3%	4%	5%	6%	7%
1	1.010	1.020	1.030	1.040	1.050	1.060	1.070
2	1.020	1.040	1.061	1.082	1.102	1.124	1.145
3	1.030	1.061	1.093	1.125	1.158	1.191	1.225
4	1.041	1.082	1.126	1.170	1.216	1.262	1.311
5	1.051	1.104	1.159	1.217	1.276	1.338	1.403
6	1.062	1.126	1.194	1.265	1.340	1.419	1.501
7	1.072	1.149	1.230	1.316	1.407	1.504	1.606
8	1.083	1.172	1.267	1.369	1.477	1.594	1.718
9	1.094	1.195	1.305	1.423	1.551	1.689	1.838
10	1.105	1.219	1.344	1.480	1.629	1.791	1.967
11	1.116	1.243	1.384	1.539	1.710	1.898	2.105
12	1.127	1.268	1.426	1.601	1.796	2.012	2.252
13	1.138	1.294	1.469	1.665	1.886	2.133	2.410
14	1.149	1.319	1.513	1.732	1.980	2.261	2.579
15	1.161	1.346	1.558	1.801	2.079	2.397	2.759
16	1.173	1.373	1.605	1.873	2.183	2.540	2.952
17	1.184	1.400	1.653	1.948	2.292	2.693	3.159
18	1.196	1.428	1.702	2.026	2.407	2.854	3.380
19	1.208	1.457	1.754	2.107	2.527	3.026	3.617
20	1.220	1.486	1.806	2.191	2.653	3.207	3.870
25	1.282	1.641	2.094	2.666	3.386	4.292	5.427
30	1.348	1.811	2.427	3.243	4.322	5.743	7.612

Exhibit 1.1 (continued)

Year (N)	8%	9%	10%	12%	14%	15%	16%
1	1.080	1.090	1.100	1.120	1.140	1.150	1.160
2	1.166	1.188	1.210	1.254	1.300	1.323	1.346
3	1.260	1.295	1.331	1.405	1.482	1.521	1.561
4	1.360	1.412	1.464	1.574	1.689	1.749	1.811
5	1.469	1.539	1.611	1.762	1.925	2.011	2.100
6	1.587	1.677	1.772	1.974	2.195	2.313	2.436
7	1.714	1.828	1.949	2.211	2.502	2.660	2.826
8	1.851	1.993	2.144	2.476	2.853	3.059	3.278
9	1.999	2.172	2.358	2.773	3.252	3.518	3.803
10	2.159	2.367	2.594	3.106	3.707	4.046	4.411
11	2.332	2.580	2.853	3.479	4.226	4.652	5.117
12	2.518	2.813	3.138	3.896	4.818	5.350	5.936
13	2.720	3.066	3.452	4.363	5.492	6.153	6.886
14	2.937	3.342	3.797	4.887	6.261	7.076	7.988
15	3.172	3.642	4.177	5.474	7.138	8.137	9.266
16	3.426	3.970	4.595	6.130	8.137	9.358	10.748
17	3.700	4.328	5.054	6.866	9.276	10.761	12.468
18	3.996	4.717	5.560	7.690	10.575	12.375	14.463
19	4.316	5.142	6.116	8.613	12.056	14.232	16.777
20	4.661	5.604	6.727	9.646	13.743	16.367	19.461
25	6.848	8.623	10.835	17.000	26.462	32.919	40.874
30	10.063	13.268	17.449	29.960	50.950	66.212	85.850

$$1{,}000\left[1 + (1 + 0.10) + (1 + 0.10)^2\right] = \$3{,}310$$

Therefore, the future value of an annuity in arrears can be determined from the following basic relationship:

$$S_n = a\left[(1+r)^{n-1} + (1+r)^{n-2} + \cdots + (1+r)^1 + 1\right]$$

or

$$S_n = a\left[\frac{(1+r)^n - 1}{r}\right]$$

where

S_n = The future value to which an annuity in arrears will accumulate.

a = The annuity.

$\dfrac{(1+r)^n - 1}{r}$ = Annuity compound interest factor.

The annuity compound interest factor for an annuity in arrears of $1 can be computed for any interest rate and compounding period, as shown in Exhibit 1.3.

PRESENT VALUE OF AN ANNUITY IN ARREARS OF $1

Assume again that a firm is to receive annual payments of $1,000 at the end of each year for three years. At a 10 percent interest rate, what is the present value of those annual payments? Using Exhibit 1.2, the pattern of discounting is as follows:

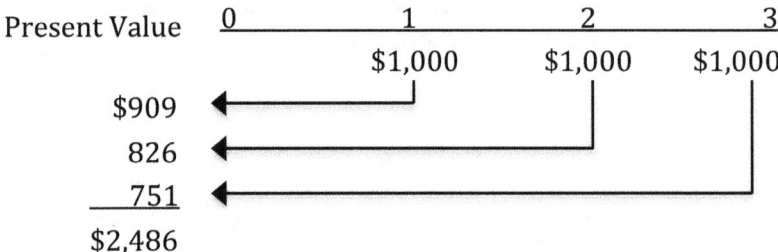

The present value of an annuity in arrears of $1,000 for three years at 10 percent is equal to

$$\$1{,}000\,(1 + 0.10)^{-1} + 1{,}000(1 + 0.10)^{-2} + 1{,}000(1 + 0.10)^{-3} = \$2{,}486$$

or

$$\$1{,}000\left[(1 + 0.10)^{-1} + 1{,}000(1 + 0.10)^{-2} + 1{,}000(1 + 0.10)^{-3}\right]$$

Exhibit 1.2
Present Value of $1 Received at the End of
Period

Years Hence	1%	2%	4%	6%	8%	10%	12%	14%	15%	16%	18%
1	0.990	0.980	0.962	0.943	0.926	0.909	0.893	0.877	0.870	0.862	0.847
2	0.980	0.961	0.925	0.890	0.857	0.826	0.797	0.769	0.756	0.743	0.718
3	0.971	0.942	0.889	0.840	0.794	0.751	0.712	0.675	0.658	0.641	0.609
4	0.961	0.924	0.855	0.792	0.735	0.683	0.636	0.592	0.572	0.552	0.516
5	0.951	0.906	0.822	0.747	0.681	0.621	0.567	0.519	0.497	0.476	0.437
6	0.942	0.888	0.790	0.705	0.630	0.564	0.507	0.456	0.432	0.410	0.370
7	0.933	0.871	0.760	0.665	0.583	0.513	0.452	0.400	0.376	0.354	0.314
8	0.923	0.853	0.731	0.627	0.540	0.467	0.404	0.351	0.327	0.305	0.266
9	0.914	0.837	0.703	0.592	0.500	0.424	0.361	0.308	0.284	0.263	0.225
10	0.905	0.820	0.676	0.558	0.463	0.386	0.322	0.270	0.247	0.227	0.191
11	0.896	0.804	0.650	0.527	0.429	0.350	0.287	0.237	0.215	0.195	0.162
12	0.887	0.788	0.625	0.497	0.397	0.319	0.257	0.208	0.187	0.168	0.137
13	0.879	0.773	0.601	0.469	0.368	0.290	0.229	0.182	0.163	0.145	0.116
14	0.870	0.758	0.577	0.442	0.340	0.263	0.205	0.160	0.141	0.125	0.099
15	0.861	0.743	0.555	0.417	0.315	0.239	0.183	0.140	0.123	0.108	0.084
16	0.853	0.728	0.534	0.394	0.292	0.218	0.163	0.123	0.107	0.093	0.071
17	0.844	0.714	0.513	0.371	0.270	0.198	0.146	0.108	0.093	0.080	0.060
18	0.836	0.700	0.494	0.350	0.250	0.180	0.130	0.095	0.081	0.069	0.051
19	0.828	0.686	0.475	0.331	0.232	0.164	0.116	0.083	0.070	0.060	0.043
20	0.820	0.673	0.456	0.312	0.215	0.149	0.104	0.073	0.061	0.051	0.037
21	0.811	0.660	0.439	0.294	0.199	0.135	0.093	0.064	0.053	0.044	0.031
22	0.803	0.647	0.422	0.278	0.184	0.123	0.083	0.056	0.046	0.038	0.026
23	0.795	0.634	0.406	0.262	0.170	0.112	0.074	0.049	0.040	0.033	0.022
24	0.788	0.622	0.390	0.247	0.158	0.102	0.066	0.043	0.035	0.028	0.019
25	0.780	0.610	0.375	0.233	0.146	0.092	0.059	0.038	0.030	0.024	0.016
26	0.772	0.598	0.361	0.220	0.135	0.084	0.053	0.033	0.026	0.021	0.014
27	0.764	0.586	0.347	0.207	0.125	0.076	0.047	0.029	0.023	0.018	0.011
28	0.757	0.574	0.333	0.196	0.116	0.069	0.042	0.026	0.020	0.016	0.010
29	0.749	0.563	0.321	0.185	0.107	0.063	0.037	0.022	0.017	0.014	0.008
30	0.742	0.552	0.308	0.174	0.099	0.057	0.033	0.020	0.015	0.012	0.007
40	0.672	0.453	0.208	0.097	0.046	0.022	0.011	0.005	0.004	0.003	0.001
50	0.608	0.372	0.141	0.054	0.021	0.009	0.003	0.001	0.001	0.001	

Exhibit 1.2 (continued)

20%	22%	24%	25%	26%	28%	30%	35%	40%	45%	50%
0.833	0.820	0.806	0.800	0.794	0.781	0.769	0.741	0.714	0.690	0.667
0.694	0.672	0.650	0.640	0.630	0.610	0.592	0.549	0.510	0.476	0.444
0.579	0.551	0.524	0.512	0.500	0.477	0.455	0.406	0.364	0.328	0.296
0.482	0.451	0.423	0.410	0.397	0.373	0.350	0.301	0.260	0.226	0.198
0.402	0.370	0.341	0.328	0.315	0.291	0.269	0.223	0.186	0.156	0.132
0.335	0.303	0.275	0.262	0.250	0.227	0.207	0.165	0.133	0.108	0.088
0.279	0.249	0.222	0.210	0.198	0.178	0.159	0.122	0.095	0.074	0.059
0.233	0.204	0.179	0.168	0.157	0.139	0.123	0.091	0.068	0.051	0.039
0.194	0.167	0.144	0.134	0.125	0.108	0.094	0.067	0.048	0.035	0.026
0.162	0.137	0.116	0.107	0.099	0.085	0.073	0.050	0.035	0.024	0.017
0.135	0.112	0.094	0.086	0.079	0.066	0.056	0.037	0.025	0.017	0.012
0.112	0.092	0.076	0.069	0.062	0.052	0.043	0.027	0.018	0.012	0.008
0.093	0.075	0.061	0.055	0.050	0.040	0.033	0.020	0.013	0.008	0.005
0.078	0.062	0.049	0.044	0.039	0.032	0.025	0.015	0.009	0.006	0.003
0.065	0.051	0.040	0.035	0.031	0.025	0.020	0.011	0.006	0.004	0.002
0.054	0.042	0.032	0.028	0.025	0.019	0.015	0.008	0.005	0.003	0.002
0.045	0.034	0.026	0.023	0.020	0.015	0.012	0.006	0.003	0.002	0.001
0.038	0.028	0.021	0.018	0.016	0.012	0.009	0.005	0.002	0.001	0.001
0.031	0.023	0.017	0.014	0.012	0.009	0.007	0.003	0.002	0.001	
0.026	0.019	0.014	0.012	0.010	0.007	0.005	0.002	0.001	0.001	
0.022	0.015	0.011	0.009	0.008	0.006	0.004	0.002	0.001		
0.018	0.013	0.009	0.007	0.006	0.004	0.003	0.001	0.001		
0.015	0.010	0.007	0.006	0.005	0.003	0.002	0.001			
0.013	0.008	0.006	0.005	0.004	0.003	0.002	0.001			
0.010	0.007	0.005	0.004	0.003	0.002	0.001	0.001			
0.009	0.006	0.004	0.003	0.002	0.002	0.001				
0.007	0.005	0.003	0.002	0.002	0.001	0.001				
0.006	0.004	0.002	0.002	0.002	0.001	0.001				
0.005	0.003	0.002	0.002	0.001	0.001	0.001				
0.004	0.003	0.002	0.001	0.001	0.001					
0.001										

Exhibit 1.3
Future Value of Annuity in Arrears of $1 for N Periods

Year (N)	1%	2%	3%	4%	5%	6%
1	1.000	1.000	1.000	1.000	1.000	1.000
2	2.010	2.020	2.030	2.040	2.050	2.060
3	3.030	3.060	3.091	3.122	3.153	3.184
4	4.060	4.122	4.184	4.246	4.310	4.375
5	5.101	5.204	5.309	5.416	5.526	5.637
6	6.152	6.308	6.468	6.633	6.802	6.975
7	7.214	7.434	7.662	7.898	8.142	8.394
8	8.286	8.583	8.892	9.214	9.549	9.897
9	9.369	9.755	10.159	10.583	11.027	11.491
10	10.462	10.950	11.464	12.006	12.578	13.181
11	11.567	12.169	12.808	13.486	14.207	14.972
12	12.683	13.412	14.192	15.026	15.917	16.870
13	13.809	14.680	15.618	16.627	17.713	18.882
14	14.947	15.974	17.086	18.292	19.599	21.015
15	16.097	17.293	18.599	20.024	21.579	23.276
16	17.258	18.639	20.157	21.825	23.657	25.673
17	18.430	20.012	21.762	23.698	25.840	28.213
18	19.615	21.412	23.414	25.645	28.132	30.906
19	20.811	22.841	25.117	27.671	30.539	33.760
20	22.019	24.297	26.870	29.778	33.066	36.786
25	28.243	32.030	36.459	41.646	47.727	54.865
30	34.785	40.568	47.575	56.085	66.439	79.058

Exhibit 1.3 (continued)

Year (N)	7%	8%	9%	10%	12%	14%
1	1.000	1.000	1.000	1.000	1.000	1.000
2	2.070	2.080	2.090	2.100	2.120	2.140
3	3.215	3.246	3.278	3.310	3.374	3.440
4	4.440	4.506	4.573	4.641	4.779	4.921
5	5.751	5.867	5.985	6.105	6.353	6.610
6	7.153	7.336	7.523	7.716	8.115	8.536
7	8.654	8.923	9.200	9.487	10.089	10.730
8	10.260	10.637	11.028	11.436	12.300	13.233
9	11.978	12.488	13.021	13.579	14.776	16.085
10	13.816	14.487	15.193	15.937	17.549	19.337
11	15.784	16.645	17.560	18.531	20.655	23.045
12	17.888	18.977	20.141	21.384	24.133	27.271
13	20.141	21.495	22.953	24.523	28.029	32.089
14	22.550	24.215	26.019	27.975	32.393	37.581
15	25.129	27.152	29.361	31.772	37.280	43.842
16	27.888	30.324	33.003	35.950	42.753	50.980
17	30.840	33.750	36.974	40.545	48.884	59.118
18	33.999	37.450	41.301	45.599	55.750	68.394
19	37.379	41.446	46.018	51.159	63.440	78.969
20	40.995	45.762	51.160	57.275	72.052	91.025
25	63.249	73.106	84.701	98.347	133.334	181.871
30	94.461	113.283	136.308	164.494	241.333	356.787

Exhibit 1.4
Present Value of $1 Received Annuity at the End of Each Period for N Periods

Year (N)	1%	2%	4%	6%	8%	10%	12%	14%	16%
1	0.990	0.980	0.962	0.943	0.926	0.909	0.893	0.877	0.862
2	1.970	1.942	1.886	1.833	1.783	1.736	1.690	1.647	1.605
3	2.941	2.884	2.775	2.673	2.577	2.487	2.402	2.322	2.246
4	3.902	3.808	3.630	3.465	3.312	3.170	3.037	2.914	2.798
5	4.853	4.713	4.452	4.212	3.993	3.791	3.605	3.433	3.274
6	5.795	5.601	5.242	4.917	4.623	4.355	4.111	3.889	3.685
7	6.728	6.472	6.002	5.582	5.206	4.868	4.564	4.288	4.039
8	7.652	7.325	6.733	6.210	5.747	5.335	4.968	4.639	4.344
9	8.566	8.162	7.435	6.802	6.247	5.759	5.328	4.946	4.607
10	9.471	8.983	8.111	7.360	6.710	6.145	5.650	5.216	4.833
11	10.368	9.787	8.760	7.887	7.139	6.495	5.938	5.453	5.029
12	11.255	10.575	9.385	8.384	7.536	6.814	6.194	5.660	5.197
13	12.134	11.348	9.986	8.853	7.904	7.103	6.424	5.842	5.342
14	13.004	12.106	10.563	9.295	8.244	7.367	6.628	6.002	5.468
15	13.865	12.849	11.118	9.712	8.559	7.606	6.811	6.142	5.575
16	14.718	13.578	11.652	10.106	8.851	7.824	6.974	6.265	5.668
17	15.562	14.292	12.166	10.477	9.122	8.022	7.120	6.373	5.749
18	16.398	14.992	12.659	10.828	9.372	8.201	7.250	6.467	5.818
19	17.226	15.678	13.134	11.158	9.604	8.365	7.366	6.550	5.877
20	18.046	16.351	13.590	11.470	9.818	8.514	7.469	6.623	5.929
21	18.857	17.011	14.029	11.764	10.017	8.649	7.562	6.687	5.973
22	19.660	17.658	14.451	12.042	10.201	8.772	7.645	6.743	6.011
23	20.456	18.292	14.857	12.303	10.371	8.883	7.718	6.792	6.044
24	21.243	18.914	15.247	12.550	10.529	8.985	7.784	6.835	6.073
25	22.023	19.523	15.622	12.783	10.675	9.077	7.843	6.873	6.097
26	22.795	20.121	15.983	13.003	10.810	9.161	7.896	6.906	6.118
27	23.560	20.707	16.330	13.211	10.935	9.237	7.943	6.935	6.136
28	24.316	21.281	16.663	13.406	11.051	9.307	7.984	6.961	6.152
29	25.066	21.844	16.984	13.591	11.158	9.370	8.022	6.983	6.166
30	25.808	22.396	17.292	13.765	11.258	9.427	8.055	7.003	6.177
40	32.835	27.355	19.793	15.046	11.925	9.779	8.244	7.105	6.233
50	39.196	31.424	21.482	15.762	12.233	9.915	8.304	7.133	6.246

Exhibit 1.4 (continued)

18%	20%	22%	24%	25%	26%	28%	30%	35%	40%	45%	50%
0.847	0.833	0.820	0.806	0.800	0.794	0.781	0.769	0.741	0.714	0.690	0.667
1.566	1.528	1.492	1.457	1.440	1.424	1.392	1.361	1.289	1.224	1.165	1.111
2.174	2.106	2.042	1.981	1.952	1.923	1.868	1.816	1.696	1.589	1.493	1.407
2.690	2.589	2.494	2.404	2.362	2.320	2.241	2.166	1.997	1.849	1.720	1.605
3.127	2.991	2.864	2.745	2.689	2.635	2.532	2.436	2.220	2.035	1.876	1.737
3.498	3.326	3.167	3.020	2.951	2.885	2.759	2.643	2.385	2.168	1.983	1.824
3.812	3.605	3.416	3.242	3.161	3.083	2.937	2.802	2.508	2.263	2.057	1.883
4.078	3.837	3.619	3.421	3.329	3.241	3.076	2.925	2.598	2.331	2.109	1.922
4.303	4.031	3.786	3.566	3.463	3.366	3.184	3.019	2.665	2.379	2.144	1.948
4.494	4.192	3.923	3.682	3.571	3.465	3.269	3.092	2.715	2.414	2.168	1.965
4.656	4.327	4.035	3.776	3.656	3.543	3.335	3.147	2.752	2.438	2.185	1.977
4.793	4.439	4.127	3.851	3.725	3.606	3.387	3.190	2.779	2.456	2.196	1.985
4.910	4.533	4.203	3.912	3.780	3.656	3.427	3.223	2.799	2.469	2.204	1.990
5.008	4.611	4.265	3.962	3.824	3.695	3.459	3.249	2.814	2.478	2.210	1.993
5.092	4.675	4.315	4.001	3.859	3.726	3.483	3.268	2.825	2.484	2.214	1.995
5.162	4.730	4.357	4.033	3.887	3.751	3.503	3.283	2.834	2.489	2.216	1.997
5.222	4.775	4.391	4.059	3.910	3.771	3.518	3.295	2.840	2.492	2.218	1.998
5.273	4.812	4.419	4.080	3.928	3.786	3.529	3.304	2.844	2.494	2.219	1.999
5.316	4.843	4.442	4.097	3.942	3.799	3.539	3.311	2.848	2.496	2.220	1.999
5.353	4.870	4.460	4.110	3.954	3.808	3.546	3.316	2.850	2.497	2.221	1.999
5.384	4.891	4.476	4.121	3.963	3.816	3.551	3.320	2.852	2.498	2.221	2.000
5.410	4.909	4.488	4.130	3.970	3.822	3.556	3.323	2.853	2.498	2.222	2.000
5.432	4.925	4.499	4.137	3.976	3.827	3.559	3.325	2.854	2.499	2.222	2.000
5.451	4.937	4.507	4.143	3.981	3.831	3.562	3.327	2.855	2.499	2.222	2.000
5.467	4.948	4.514	4.147	3.985	3.834	3.564	3.329	2.856	2.499	2.222	2.000
5.480	4.956	4.520	4.151	3.988	3.837	3.566	3.330	2.856	2.500	2.222	2.000
5.492	4.964	4.524	4.154	3.990	3.839	3.567	3.331	2.856	2.500	2.222	2.000
5.502	4.970	4.528	4.157	3.992	3.840	3.568	3.331	2.857	2.500	2.222	2.000
5.510	4.975	4.531	4.159	3.994	3.841	3.569	3.332	2.857	2.500	2.222	2.000
5.517	4.979	4.534	4.160	3.995	3.842	3.569	3.332	2.857	2.500	2.222	2.000
5.548	4.997	4.544	4.166	3.999	3.846	3.571	3.333	2.857	2.500	2.222	2.000
5.554	4.999	4.545	4.167	4.000	3.846	3.571	3.333	2.857	2.500	2.222	2.000

Therefore, the present value of an annuity in arrears can be generalized by the following formula:

$$P_n = a \left[\frac{1 - \frac{1}{(1+r)^n}}{r} \right].$$

where

P_n = Present value of the annuity in arrears.
a = Amount of the annuity.
r = Interest rate.
n = Number of years.

The annuity discount interest factor,

$$\frac{1 - \frac{1}{(1+r)^n}}{r}$$

can be composed for an annuity of \$1 in arrears for any interest rate and discounting period, as shown in Exhibit 1.4.

Chapter 2
Principles of Capital Budgeting

Introduction

Management must often decide whether to add a product or buy a new machine. They make many general, nonrecurring investment decisions involving fixed assets, or *capital budgeting* decisions. Capital budgeting involves a current outlay or a series of outlays of cash resources in return for anticipated benefits to be received beyond one year in the future. The capital budgeting decision has three distinguishing characteristics: anticipated benefits, a time element, and a degree of risk associated with the realization of the benefits. In general, these characteristics can be described more specifically as anticipated cash benefits, a time lag between the initial capital investment and the realization of the cash benefits, and a degree of risk. Ideally, a firm with a profit maximization motive will seek an investment that will generate large benefits in a short period and with a minimum of risk. However, investments with potentially large benefits are generally possible only with high risk and may require more time than investments with lower benefits.

Given these less-than-ideal relationships between the dimensions of a capital budgeting decision, management should desire a trade-off between these elements in making a capital budgeting decision that will meet their objectives. Although various objective functions may be chosen by firms, the most useful for evaluating capital budgeting decisions is the stockholders' wealth maximization model (SWMM). Despite the fact that it represents a normative model, the SWMM provides a generally acceptable and meaningful criterion for the evaluation of capital budgeting proposals: the maximization of owners' wealth.

Administration of Capital Budgeting

Although the administrative process of capital budgeting may differ from one firm to another, it involves five basic steps. The first step is the planning, or organization and specification, of capital investment. Because capital investments are considered essential to a firm's profitable long-run growth, managers constantly search for new methods processes, plants, and products. These projects usually come from various sources, including the following:

1. New products or markets, and the expansion of existing products or markets.
2. Research and development.
3. Replacement of fixed assets.
4. Other investments to reduce costs; improve the quality of the product; improve morale; or comply with government orders, labor agreements, insurance policy terms, and so forth.

The second step in capital budgeting is the evaluation of the proposed capital investments. Firms differ in their routine for processing capital budgets, but most evaluate and approve the projects at various managerial levels. For example, a request for capital investment made by the production department may be examined, evaluated, and approved by (1) the plant managers, (2) the vice-president of operations, and (3) a capital budget committee or department, which may submit recommendations to the president. The president, after adding recommendations, may submit the project to the board of directors. This routine in often complemented and simplified by a uniform policy and procedure manual presenting in detail the firm's capital budgeting philosophy and techniques.

The third step in capital budgeting is the decision making based on the results of the evaluation process. Depending on the size of the projects, some decisions may be made at a high level, such as the board of directors (if they are large projects), or at a lower level if they are small to medium-sized projects.

The fourth step is control. The firm includes each of the accepted projects in the capital budget and appropriates funds. Periodically, control is exercised over the expenditures made for the project. If the appropriated funds are insufficient, a budgetary review can be initiated to examine and approve the estimated overrun. The control step can be extended to include a continuous evaluation process to incorporate current information and check the validity of the original predictions.

The fifth capital budgeting step is the postaudit. This involves a comparison of the actual cash flow of a capital investment with those planned and included in the capital budget.

Estimating cash flow

One of the most important capital budgeting tasks for the evaluation of the project capital investments is the estimation of the *relevant cash flows* for each project, which refers to the incremental cash flow arising from each project. Because companies rely on accrual accounting rather than cash accounting, adjustments are necessary to derive the cash flow from the conventional financial accounting records.

Cash and Accrual Accounting

Capital budgeting determines a project's potential incremental cash inflows and outflows compared with the flows if the project were not initiated. The receipt and payment of cash is the significant event in recording the cash inflows and outflows and determining the cash income of a project. This cash income, however, differs in the following ways from the accounting income owing to the timing differences arising from the use of accrual accounting for external reporting:

1. The first differences arises from the capitalization of the cost of a capital asset at the time of purchase and the recognition of depreciation expenses over the asset's economic life. In a capital budgeting context, the cost of a capital asset is a cash outflow when paid.
2. Accrual accounting rests on the application of the matching of revenues and expenses, which leads to the recognition of revenues when earned and costs when incurred, even if no cash has been received or paid. This leads to the recognition of accounting receivable, accounts payable, and various asset balances as the result of the timing differences between accounting income and cash income.

To determine the cash income, adjustments in the accounting income are necessary to correct for these timing differences. Some Adjustments are illustrated in Exhibit 2.1.

Identifying the Project Cash Flows

Project cash flows are incremental cash flows arising from a project and are equal to the difference between the cash inflows and the cash outflows. The cash inflows include (1) after-tax net cash revenues, (2) savings in operating expenses, and (3) the salvage value of equipment from each project. The cash outflows include the cost of investment in each of the projects.

Effect of Charges on Cash Flows

Various charges affect the computation of cash flows. *Depreciation* and *amortization charges* are noncash expenses. However, they have an indirect influence on cash flow. Because depreciation is tax deductible, it provides a tax shield by protecting from taxation an amount of income equal to the depreciation deduction. The after-tax proceeds of a project are increased by the allowable depreciation times the tax rate. As shown by the following relationships:

Exhibit 2.1
Reconciliation of Cash Flow and Accounting Income

1. Accounting Income (Traditional Income Statement)
Assume that the purchase of a new machine costing $10,000
and having a ten-year life and disposal value is expected to earn the following for
the first year:

Sales	$10,000

Less: Operating Expenses, Excluding Depreciation	$5,000
Depreciation (Straight-line)	1,000

Total Expenses	$6,000

Operating Income before Income Taxes	$4,000
Less: Income Taxes at 40 Percent	1,600

Net Income after Taxes	$2,400

Other Accrual Information:
a. Sales are 40 percent cash.
b. The expenses, excluding depreciation, are 60 percent on credit.

2. Cash Flow (Cash Effects of Operations)

a. *Cash Inflow from Operations*	
Total Sales	$10,000
Less: Credit Sales: 60 Percent of $10,000 (Increase in Accounts Receivable)	6,000

Cash Collections from Sales	$4,000
	------------
b. *Cash Outflow from Operating Expenses*	
Total Expenses	$5,000
Less: Credit Expenditures: 60 Percent of $5,000 (Increase in Accounts Payable)	$3,000

Cash Payments for Operating Expenses	$2,000
	------------
c. *Net Cash Inflow: $4,000 - $2,000*	$2,000
d. *Income Tax Outflow*	$1,600
e. *After-Tax Net Cash Inflow*	$ 400
f. *Effect of Depreciation*	
Depreciation Expense	$1,000
Tax at 50%	500

Tax Shield	$ 500
	------------
g. *Total Cash Flow* (After-Tax Net Cash Inflow + Tax Shield)	$ 900

After- tax   Expenses
      cash   =   other than   -   Income tax.   (1)
   proceeds   depreciation

The income tax can be determined as follows:

    Income tax = Tax rate × Taxable income   (2)

or

                                       Expenses
   Income tax = Tax rate × (Revenues – other than   –   Depreciation).   (3)
                                  Depreciation

Therefore, the higher the depreciation, the lower the income tax.
      By substituting equation 3 into equation 1, the after-tax process can be expressed as follows:

After-tax   Expenses
            cash   = (1 – Tax rate) (Revenues – other than)   +   (Tax rate x Depreciation).
proceeds   depreciation

Financing charges are excluded from the cash flow computation used in capital budgeting. First, the interest factor would be counted twice by the use of present value methods of evaluation (to be presented in the next section). Second, the evaluation of a capital project is separate from the independent of the financing aspects.

Opportunity costs of scarce diverted from other uses because of the capital project should be charged against the investment project. They can be measured by estimating how much the resource (personnel time or facility space) would earn if the investment project were not undertaken.

Ranking Capital Projects

The project evaluation phase consists of evaluating the attractiveness of the investment proposals. Managers first choose the project evaluation methods best suited to the capital budgeting decision. The most common are the *discounted cash flow (DCF) methods (internal rate of return [IRR] method, net present value [NPV] method, and profitability index [PI]), the payback method,* and the *accounting rate of return (ARR) method.* Each of these methods will be examined in the following sections.

Discounted Cash Flow Methods

The discounted cash flow methods consider the *time value of money* in the evaluation of capital budgeting proposals. A dollar received now is worth more than a dollar received in the future; a dollar in the hand today can be invested to earn a return. Hence, to understand the discounted cash flow methods, it is necessary to grasp the time value concepts.

The discounted cash flow methods focus on cash flows generated over the life of a project rather than the accounting income. These methods involve discounting the cash flow of a project to its *present value* using an appropriate discount rate. There are two basic discounted cash flow methods: (1) the internal rate of return (or time-adjusted rate of return) method and (2) the net present value method.

Internal Rate of Return Method

The IRR is the interest rate that equated the present value of an investment's cash flows and the cost of the investment. The IRR equation follows:

$$\sum_{t=0}^{n} \frac{C_t}{(1+r)^t} = 0$$

where

C_t = Cash flow for period t, whether it be a net inflow or a net outflow, including the initial investment at $t = 0$.

n = Investment life, that is, the last period in which a cash flow is expected.

r = IRR as the discount rate that equates the present value of cash flow C_t to zero.

If the initial cash outlay or cost occurs at a time 0, the IRR equation becomes

$$\sum_{t=0}^{n} \frac{C_t}{(1+r)^t} = C_0 = 0.$$

Solving the r is on a trial-and-error basis; the procedures differ depending on whether the cash flows are uniform or nonuniform.

Uniform Cash Flows

To illustrate, assume a project considered by the Camelli Corporation requires a cash outlay of $39,100 and has an expected after-tax annual net cash savings of $10,000 for six years and no salvage value. Find the interest rate (r) that equates the present value of future annual cash flows of $10,000 and the initial outlay of $39,100 at time 0. Experimenting with two discount rates, 12 and 14 percent, you find

Discount Rate	Discount Factor	Cash Flow	Percent Value of Stream
12%	4.1110	$10,000	$41,110
14%	3.8890	$10,000	$38,890

Thus, the IRR that equates the present value of the stream of annual savings and $39,100 is between 12 and 14 percent. This rate can be found by interpolating between 12 and 14 percent:

12%	$41,110 (Too large)
14%	38,890 (Too small)
2%	$ 2,220

$$\frac{\$41,110 - \$39,100}{\$2,220} = 0.905.$$

$$\text{IRR} = 12\% + (0.905 \times 2\%) = 13.81\%$$

A trial-and-error process determines that 13.81 percent is the IRR that equates the present value of the stream of savings and the cost of the investment. This indicates that they investment will yield a return of 13.81 percent

Exhibit 2.2
Amortization Schedule: Proof for the Internal Rate of Return

Year	Unrecorded Investment at Beginning of Year	Annual Cash Savings or	13.81% Return Interest [a]	Cost Recovery [b]	Unrecorded Investment at End of Year[c]
1	$39,100.00	$10,000	$5,399.71	$4,600.29	$34,499.71
2	34,499.71	10,000	4764.41	5235.59	29,264.12
3	29,264.12	10,000	4041.38	5958.62	23,305.50
4	23,305.50	10,000	3218.49	6781.51	16,523.99
5	16,523.99	10,000	2281.96	7718.04	8,805.95
6	8,805.95	10,000	1216.10	8783.90	22.05[d]

[a]Return = Unrecorded investment × 13.81%.

[b]Cost recovery = Annual cash savings – Return

[c]Unrecovered investment at the end of the year = Unrecorded investments at the beginning of the year – Cost Recovery.

[d]Rounding error.

per year in addition to recovering the original cost of $39,100. Exhibit 2.2 depicts the amortization schedule of the investment: The six-year cash savings of $10,000 recovers the original investment plus an annual return of 13.81 percent on the investment.

The computation of the IRR does not determine if the project is to be accepted or rejected. To do so, the IRR generally is compared with a required rate of return. For example, if the IRR exceeds the required rate of return, the project is acceptable. The required rate of return, also known as a *cutoff rate* or *hurdle rate,* is the firm's cost of capital (the cost of acquiring funds). Passing this test does not mean the project will be funded, as funds may be rationed.

Nonuniform Cash Flows

The following example illustrates a project yielding cash flows that are not equal for all the periods of the project's life. We assume the machine considered by the Camelli Corporation costs $39,100 and yields the following cash savings:

Year	Cash Savings
1	$20,000
2	14,000
3	10,000
4	6,000
5	5,000
6	4,000

Solving for the IRR that equated the present value of these savings and the cost of the investment also requires trial and error. First, experimenting with an interest rate of 16 percent, we find

Year	Discount Factor	×	Cash Savings	=	Present Value Cash Savings
1	0.862		$20,000		$17,240
2	0.743		14,000		10,402
3	0.641		10,000		6,410
4	0.552		6,000		3,312

Year	Discount Factor	×	Cash Savings	=	Present Value Cash Savings
5	0.476		5,000		2,380
6	0.410		4,000		1,640
Present Value of Cash Savings					$41,384
Present Value of Cash Outflow (Cost of the Machine)					39,100
Difference					$2,284

Given that the percent value of cash savings is $2,284 higher than the present value of the cash outflow, the IRR must be higher than 16 percent.

Second, experimenting with an interest rate of 20 percent, we find

Year	Discount Factor	×	Cash Savings	=	Present Value Cash Savings
1	0.833		$20,000		$16,660
2	0.694		14,000		9,716
3	0.579		10,000		5,716
4	0.482		6,000		2,892
5	0.402		5,000		2,010
6	0.335		4,000		1,340
Present Value of Cash Savings					$38,408
Present Value of Cash Outflow (Cost of the Machine)					39,100
Difference (NPV)					$(692)

Given that the present value of cash savings is $692 lower than the present value of the cash outflow, the IRR must be *between* 16 and 20 percent, and closer to 20 percent.

Third, experimenting with 19 percent we obtain

Year	Discount Factor	×	Cash Savings	=	Present Value Cash Savings
1	0.840		$20,000		$16,800
2	0.706		14,000		9,884
3	0.593		10,000		5,930
4	0.499		6,000		2,994
5	0.419		5,000		2,095
6	0.352		4,000		1,408
Present Value of Cash Savings					$39,111
Present Value of Cash Outflow (Cost of the Machine)					39,100
Difference (NPV)					$11

Given that the present value of cash savings is only $11 higher than the cost of the machine, the IRR is approximately 19 percent.

Net Present Value Method
The NPV method compares the cost of an investment with the present value of the future cash of the investment as a selected rate of return, or hurdle rate. The NPV of an investment is

$$NPV = \sum_{t=1}^{n} \frac{C_t}{(1+r)^t} - C_0,$$

where

C_t = Project cash flows.
r = Selected hurdle rate.
N = Project life.
C_0 = Cost of the investment.

If the NVP is greater than or equal to zero, the project is deemed acceptable, but it may not be funded if there is rationing. The required rate of return, or hurdle rate, is usually the cost of capital. The NVP procedure differs depending upon whether the cash flows are uniform or nonuniform.

Uniform Cash Flow

To illustrate the NVP method, let us return to the camellia Corporation example in which a new machine costing $39,100 would yield an annual cash savings of $10,000 for the six years of its life. Assuming a cost of capital of 10 percent, the NPV of the project can be stated as follows:

$$NPV = \sum_{t=1}^{6} \frac{\$10,000}{(1 + 0.10)^6} - \$39,100,$$

The appropriate discount factor for the Camelli Corporation is 4.355. Thus, the NPV is computed as follows:

$$NPV = (\$10,000 \times 4.355) - \$39,100 = \$4,450$$

Given that the NPV is greater than zero, the Camelli Corporation should accept the new machine proposal. The positive NPV indicates that the Camelli Corporation will earn a higher rate of return on its investment than its cost of capital.

Different NPVs result from different hurdle rates. For example,

NPV at an 8% required rate = ($10,000 × 4.623) − $39,100 = $7,130.
NPV at an 14% required rate = ($10,000 × 3.889) − $39,100 = $(210).

Thus, given a stream of uniform cash flows, the higher the hurdle rate, the less attractive any investment proposal becomes.

The NPV method rests on two assumptions: (1) The cash flows are *certain* (this applies also to the IRR), and (2) the original investment can be viewed as either borrowed or loaned by the Camelli Corporation at the hurdle rate.

Thus, if the Camelli Corporation borrows $39,100 from the bank at 10 percent and uses the cash flows generated to repay the loan, it will obtain the same return as if it had invested $4,450 at the same rate. (See Exhibit 2.3.)

Exhibit 2.3
Amortization Schedule Underlying the Net Present Value

Option 1: Borrow and Invest in the Project

Year	Loan Balance at Beginning of Year	Interest at 10% per Year	Loan and Interest at End of Year	Cash Flow To Repay the Loan	Loan Balance at End of Year
1	$39,100.00	$3,910.00	$43,010.00	$10,000	$33,010.00
2	33,010.00	3,301.00	36,311.00	10,000	26,311.00
3	26,311.00	2,631.10	28,942.10	10,000	18,942.10
4	18,942.10	1,894.21	20,836.31	10,000	10,836.31
5	10,836.31	1,083.63	11,919.94	10,000	1,919.94
6	1,919.94	191.99	2,111.93	10,000	(7,888.06)

Option 2: Invest $4,450 at 10 Percent Rate of Returns

Year	Investment Balance Beginning of Year	Interest at 10% per Year	Investment And Interest at End of Year
1	$4,450.00	$445.00	$4,895.00
2	4,895.00	489.50	5,385.50
3	5,384.50	538.45	5,922.95
4	5,922.95	592.30	6,515.95
5	6,515.25	651.53	7,166.78
6	7,166.78	716.68	7883.46[a]

[a] The $4.60 difference between $7,888.06 and $7,883.46 is a rounding error.

Nonuniform Cash Flows

The following example illustrates a project yielding cash flows that are not equal for all periods of the project's life. Assume again that the machine considered by the Camelli Corporation yields annual cash savings of $20,000, $14,000, $10,000, $6,000, $5,000, and $4,000 for the six years, respectively, and the cost of capital is 10 percent. The computation of the NPV follows:

Year	Discount Factor	×	Cash Savings	=	Present Value Cash Savings
1	0.909		$20,000		$18,180
2	0.826		14,000		11,564
3	0.753		10,000		7,530
4	0.683		6,000		4,098
5	0.621		5,000		3,105
6	0.564		4,000		2,256

Present Value of Cash Savings $46,733
Present Value of Cash Outflow
(Cost of the Machine)   39,100
Difference (NPV) $7,633

The NVP method is easier to apply than the IRR method with nonuniform cash flows, because it does not require iterative numerical methods.

Profitability Index
The PI, or benefit cost ratio, is another form of the NPV method. It is generally expressed as

$$PI = \frac{\text{Present value of cash inflows}}{\text{Presnt value of cash outflows}}$$

For the Camelli Corporation example with uniform cash flows, the PI would be

$$PI = \frac{\$43,550}{\$39,100} = 1.114,$$

For the Camelli Corporation example with nonuniform cash flows, the PI would be

$$PI = \frac{\$46,733}{\$39,100} = 1.195.$$

The decision rule when evaluating different projects is to choose the project with the highest PI.
The NVP and the PI result in the same acceptance or rejection decision for any given project. However, the NPV and the PI can give different rankings for mutually exclusive projects. In such a case, the NPV method is the

Exhibit 2.4
Relationship between Net Present Value (NPV) and Internal Rate of Return (IRR)

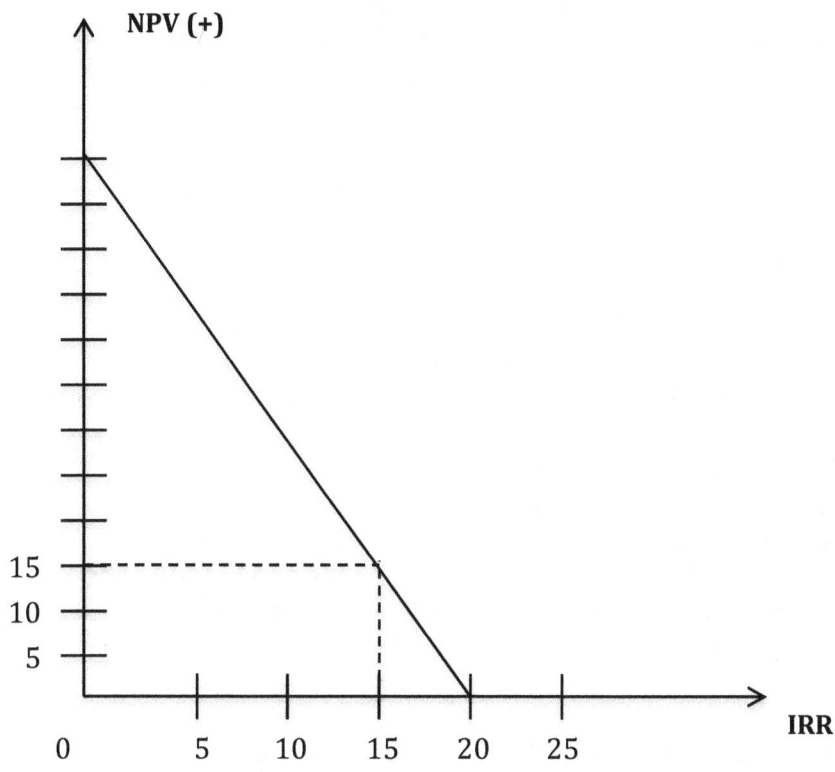

preferred method; it expresses the absolute profitability of a project, whereas the PI expresses the relative profitability.

Comparison between Net Present Value and Internal Rate of Return
Acceptance or Rejection Decision

The IRR and NPV methods lead to the same acceptance or rejection decisions for independent projects with one or more periods of outlays followed *only* by periods of net cash inflows. Exhibit 2.4 illustrates both the NPV and IRR applied to a capital project. At the zero discount rate, the NPV is equal to the sum of the total cash inflows less the total cash outflows. As the discount rate increases, the NPV decreases. Where the NPV reaches zero, the discount rate corresponds to the IRR, which is 20 percent in the fictional example. The following situations are possible:

1. If the requires rate of return used as a discount rate is less than the IRR, the project is acceptable under both methods. For example, if the required rate of return is 15 percent, the project is acceptable under both methods, given that at the rate Exhibit 2.4 shows an NPV superior to zero and a required rate inferior to the 20 percent IRR.
2. If the required rate of return is equal to the IRR, the Project is acceptable under both methods. In such a case the NPV is equal to zero, and the required rate of return is equal to the IRR.
3. If the required rate of return is higher than the IRR, the project is not acceptable under either method.

Conflicts between Net Present Value and Internal Rate of Return
The NPV and the IRR methods may lead to conflicting rankings. Which method provides the best result? To answer this question, the main conflicts between NPV and IRR must be examined, along with the problems associated with each of the methods.

The conflicts arise mainly in comparing mutually exclusive projects (projects capable of performing the same function). The evaluation of mutually exclusive projects by the NPV and the IRR methods can lead to at least three problems:

1. The problem when the mutually exclusive projects have different initial outlays is called the *scale effects problem.*
2. The problem when the mutually exclusive projects have a different timing of cash flows is called the *timing effects problem.*
3. The problem when the mutually exclusive projects have different lives is called the *live effects problem.*

Other problems arise from possible *multiple rates of return* when using the IRR method.
Both the conflicts and problems identified will be examined before we judge which method provides the best ranking.

Scale Effects
The NPV and the IRR methods yield conflicting rankings when mutually exclusive projects having different initial outlays are compared. Consider the example in Exhibit 2.5, where project X is ranked better with the IRR method, and project Y is ranked better with the NPV method.

Given this conflicting result, which project should be chosen? Project X and Y are incorrectly ranked by the IRR method because of the large difference in the cost of the projects. The incremental cost of $8,616 for project Y can be seen as an additional project W, which yields a positive NPV of $79.70 and an IRR of 15.10 percent, which

Exhibit 2.5
Mutually Exclusive Investments: Scale Effects

Project	Initial Outlay	Cash Inflow (End of Year 1)	NPV At 15%	IRR
X	$8,333	$10,000	$362.70	20%
Y	$16,949	$20,000	$442.40	18%
Z	$8,616	$10,000	$79.70	15.10%

Exhibit 2.6
Mutually Exclusive Investments: Timing Effects

Project	Initial Outlay	Cash Inflow (End of Year 1)	Cash Inflow (End of Year 2)	NPV At 10%	IRR
X	$2,310	$1,000	$2,000	$251.99	14%
Y	$2,310	$2,000	$ 788	$159.24	16%
Z	$ 0	$1,000	$1,212	$101.82	21.19%

is greater than the required rate of return of 15 percent. The incremental cost is acceptable under both the IRR and the NPV methods: thus, project Y should be selected. Since the NPV method has selected project Y, the NPV method is preferable.

Timing Effects

The NPV and IRR methods also yield conflicting results when mutually exclusive projects o equal size but with different timing of cash flows are compared. Consider the example in Exhibit 2.6, where project Y is ranked better with the IRR method, and project X is ranked better with the NPV method.
Given this conflicting result, should project X or Y be chosen? Again, use the incremental approach:

Year 0: $0 cash outlays for both projects.
Year 1: $1,000 project Y cash flow exceeds that of project X.
Year 2: $1,212 project X cash flow exceeds that of project Y.

This situation also can be conceived as an investment of $1,000 in year 1 yielding $1,212 in year 2. Such a project W will yield a positive NPV of $101.81 and an IRR of 21.19 percent. Thus, project X should be selected. Since the NPV method selected project X, it can again be concluded that the NPV method is preferable.

Live Effects: The Reinvestment Rate Assumption

The NPV and the IRR methods may yield conflicting results when mutually exclusive projects of equal sizes with different lives are compared. For example, consider the example in Exhibit 2.7, where project X is ranked better with the IRR method, whereas project Y is ranked better with the NPV method. This ranking difference is due to the difference in the investment rate assumption. The IRR method assumes a reinvestment rate equal to the internal rate, whereas the NPV method assumes a reinvestment rate equal to the required rate of return used as a discount factor.
The two reinvestment assumptions can be illustrated by calculating the terminal values of project X under each of the two assumptions. The terminal value using 15 percent for two years is equal to $7,601.50. The terminal value using the required rate of return of 10 percent is equal to $6,957.50. If we compare these two terminal values to the $7,025 terminal value of project Y, we obtain two situations:
   1. Using the IRR method, the terminal value of project X, $7,601.50, is greater than the terminal value of project Y, $7,025. The IRR method favors project X.
   2. Using the NPV method, the terminal value of project X, $6,957.50, is lower than the terminal value of project Y, $7,025. The NPV method favors project Y.
 The assumption of reinvestment at the required rate of return implied in the NPV method is considered to be the better one, the cost of capital being the minimum return acceptable to the firm.

Multiple Internal Rates of Return

Another problem with the IRR method arises from the possibility of multiple IRRs for "abnormal" projects. A "normal" project has one or more outflows followed by a series of inflows. An abnormal project is one that has negative cash flows in periods after the first positive cash flow. With abnormal projects, there may be several different returns that fit the equation, one for each change of the sign of the cash flows.
For example, suppose a capital project requires the following cash flows:

Year	Cash Flow
0	$(1,600)
1	10,000
2	(10,000)

Solving for the IRR, we find two rates: 25 and 400 percent. Neither rate is correct because neither measures investment value. Instead, the NPV method will give the correct decision and avoid the problem of multiple rates of return associated with some abnormal projects.

PAYBACK METHOD

The payback method, also called the *payout method,* is simply the number of years before the initial cash outlay of a project is fully recovered by its future cash inflows. For example, assume a firm is considering purchasing as $15,000 a delivery truck expected to save $5,000 per year in shipping expenses for four years. The payback formula is

$$\text{Packback} = \frac{\text{Initial cost of the project}}{\text{Annual net cash flows}}$$
$$= \frac{\$15,000}{\$5,000}$$
$$= 3 \text{ years.}$$

In other words, the cost of the delivery truck will be recovered in three years. If the payback period calculated is less than an acceptable maximum payback period, the firm should accept the truck proposal. For projects with nonuniform cash flow the procedure is slightly different. For example, assume the yearly cash savings are $4,000 in year 1, $5,000 in year 2, $3,000 in year 3, $3,000 in year 4,and $6,000 in year 5. It takes up to year 4 to recover a cumulative cash savings equal to the initial cost of the truck. Therefore, the payback period is four years.

An extension of the payback method is the *bailout method,* which takes into account both the cash savings and the salvage value needed to recover the initial cost of a project. Going back to the first example of the $15,000 truck with an expected savings of $5,000 per year in shipping expenses, assume also that the salvage value is estimated to be $8,000 at the end of year 1 and $5,000 at the end of year 2. The cash savings and salvage value if the truck for the next two years, then, are as follows:

Year	Cash Savings	Salvage Value	Cumulative Cash Savings and Salvage Value
1	$5,000	$8,000	$13,000 = $5,000 + $8,000
2	$5,000	$5,000	$15,000 = $5,000 + $5,000 + $5,000

Thus, at the end of year 2, the total of the cumulative cash savings and the salvage value is equal to the initial cost of the truck. The bailout period is two years.

Businesses commonly use the payback method to provide a quick ranking of capital projects. Some of its features follow, including both advantages and disadvantages:

1. It is easy to calculate and provide a quick answer to the question: How many years will it take before the initial cash outlay is completely recovered?
2. The payback method does not take into account the time value of money. The annual cash flows are given the same weight from one year to another. While the first feature can be interpreted as one of the strengths of the method, this feature is definitely a weakness.
3. The payback method ignores both the cash flows occurring after the payback period and the project's total physical life plan.

Exhibit 2.7
Mutually Exclusive Investments: Different Lives

			Cash Inflow		NPV	
	Initial					
	Initial				NPV	
Project	Outlay	Year 1	Year 2	Year 3	at 10%	IRR
X	$5,000	$5,750	-	-	$227.26	15%
Y	$5,000	-	-	$7,025	$277.95	12%

4. The payback period can be used to compute the *payback reciprocal*, which is equal to the IRR of the project, provided the project's expected cash flows are constant and are anticipated to continue until infinity. Although projects rarely, if ever, have a perpetual life, a rule of thumb states that the payback reciprocal yields a reasonable approximation of the IRR. The formula for the payback reciprocal is

$$\text{Payback reciprocal} = \frac{r}{\text{Payback period}}$$

ACCOUTNING RATE OF RETURN

The ARR method is a capital budgeting evaluation technique that uses the ratio of the average annual profit after taxes to the investment of the project. The ARR formula based in initial investment is

$$\text{ARR} = \frac{\text{Annual revenue from the project} - \text{Annual expenses of the project}}{\text{Initial investment}}$$

The ARR formula based on average investment is

$$\text{ARR} = \frac{\text{Annual revenue from the project} - \text{Annual expenses of the project}}{\text{Average investment}}$$

These computed ARR values are compared with a cutoff rate before an acceptance or rejection decision is made. For example, assume the Saxon Company is contemplating the purchase of a new machine costing $20,000 and having a five-year useful life and no salvage value. The new machine is expected to generate annual operating revenues of $7,000 and annual expenses of $5,000. The ARR can be computer as follows:

$$\text{ARR based on initial investment:} \quad \frac{\$7,000 - \$5,000}{\$20,000} = 10\%.$$

$$\text{ARR based on initial investment:} \quad \frac{\$7,000 - \$5,000}{\frac{\$20,000 + 0}{2}} = 20\%.$$

The ARR, then, depends on the choice of an initial or average investment base. Using an average investment base leads to substantially higher rates of return. This can be corrected, however, by choosing a higher required cutoff ARR.

The principle strength of the ARR may be its simplicity. It can be computed easily from the accounting records. Since this same characteristic can be perceived as a weakness, the ARR relies on accounting income rather than cash flows. It fails to take into account the timing of cash flows and the time value of money.

METHODS OF CALCULATING DEPRECIATION

The three widely used depreciation methods are the straight-line (SL), sum-of-the-years'-digits (SYD), and double declining balance (DDB) methods. Depreciation charges under the straight-line method are constant over an asset's useful life. Depreciation charges under the latter two methods are higher in the early years of an asset's life and taper off rapidly in later years. The best method for tax depreciation maximizes the present value of the depreciation tax shield (that is, reduces income taxes resulting from depreciation expense). The Economic Recovery Act of 1981 introduced new tax lives and an accelerated depreciation methods labeled the *Accelerated Cost Recovery System (ACRS)*, which is most cases results in the higher tax shield.

To determine which of the three depreciation methods maximizes the present value of the tax shield, let us use the example of a machine costing $100,000 with a ten-year useful and no expected salvage value. The required rate of return (r) is 10 percent, and the marginal tax rate (T) is 40 percent.

Straight-Line Depreciation

The annual straight-line depreciation charges is the difference between the cost of the asset (C) and its future salvage value (S) divided by the asset's useful life (N), where t = year:

Annual SL depreciation charge = SL,

$$= \frac{C - S}{N}$$
$$= \frac{\$100,000}{10}$$
$$= \$10,000.$$

Annual SL depreciation rate = SLR_0

$$= \frac{SL_t}{C - S}$$
$$= \frac{\$10,000}{100,000} = 10\%.$$

Depreciation tax shield =

$$\sum_{t-1}^{N} \frac{SL_1 \times T}{(1 + r)^t}$$
$$= \sum_{t=1}^{N} \frac{\$100,000 \times 0.40}{(1 + 0.10)^t}$$
$$= 24,580.$$

Double Declining Balance Depreciation

Under the double declining balance method, twice the straight-line rate is applied to the book value of the asset each year until the salvage value is reached:

$$\text{Annual DDB rate} = DDB_t = \frac{2}{N}\left(C - \sum_{t=1}^{n} DDB_t\right).$$
$$\text{Annual DDB rate} = \frac{2}{N} = \frac{2}{10} = 20\%.$$
$$\text{Depreciation tax shield} = \sum_{t=1}^{n} \frac{DDB \times T}{(1 + r)^t}.$$

Applying these formulae yields the following results:

1 Year	2 Book Value before Depreciation	3 Depreciation	4 Tax Shield (Col. 3 × 40%)	5 Discount Factor at 10%	6 Present Value (Col. 4 × Col. 5)
1	$100,000	$20,000	$8,000	0.909	$7,272
2	80,000	16,000	6,400	0.826	5,286
3	64,000	12,800	5,120	0.751	3,845
4	51,200	10,240	4,096	0.683	2,798
5	40,960	8,192	3,277	0.621	2,035
6	32,768	6,554[1]	2,622	0.564	1,479
7	26,214	6,553	2,621	0.513	1,345
8	19,661	6,554	2,622	0.467	1,224
9	13,107	6,553	2,621	0.424	1,111
10	6,554	6,554	2,621	0.386	1,012
	Present Value Tax Shield				$27,407

Sum-of-the-Years'-Digits Depreciation

Under the sum-of-the-years'-digits method, a mathematical fraction is applied to the base. The numerator for a given year is the number of years remaining in the life of the project taken from the beginning of the year. The denominator is the sum of the series of numbers representing the years of useful life. The sum of the numbers 1 through 10 is equal to 55. N = useful life, t = year, S = salvage value, T = tax rate, and C = acquisition price.

$$\text{Annual SYD depreciation} = \text{SYD},$$

$$= (C - S)\frac{N - t}{\frac{N(N + 1)}{2}}$$

$$= (C - S)\frac{2(N - t)}{\frac{N(N + 1)}{2}}$$

$$\text{Annual SYD rate} = \frac{\text{SYD}_t}{C - S}$$

$$\text{Depreciation tax shield} = \sum_{t=1}^{N} \frac{\text{SYD}_t \times T}{(1 + r)^t}.$$

Applying these formulae yields the following results:

1 Year	2 Fraction	3 Depreciation	4 Tax Shield (Col. 3 × 40%)	5 Discount Factor at 10%	6 Present Value (Col. 4 × Col. 5)
1	10/55	$18,182	$7,273	0.909	$6,611
2	9/55	16,364	6,546	0.826	5,407
3	8/55	14,545	5,818	0.751	4,369
4	7/55	12,727	5,091	0.683	3,477
5	6/55	10,909	4,364	0.621	2,710
6	5/55	9,091	3,636	0.564	2,051
7	4/55	7,273	2,909	0.513	1,492
8	3/55	5,455	2,182	0.467	1,019
9	2/55	3,636	1,455	0.424	617
10	1/55	1,818	727	0.386	281
Present Value Tax Shield					$28,033

The present value of the tax shield under each depreciation method has been found to be

Straight-Line	$24,580
Double Declining Balance	27,580
Sum-of-the-Years'-Digits	28,033

Therefore, the present value of the tax shield is highest under the sum-of-the-years'-digits method for this example, and this method should be used for tax depreciation.

CAPITAL BUDGETING ILLUSTRATIONS
Problems

1. *Payback Method.* A project being planned will cost $30,000. The annual cash inflow net of income taxes for the next five years is as follows:

Period	Cash Flow
1	$8,000
2	4,000
3	12,000
4	14,000
5	6,000

Required: Compute the payback period of the project.

2. *Multiple Internal Rate of Return.* A project calls for the outlay of $20,000,000 to develop a strip mine. The mine will produce a cash flow of $90,000,000 at the end of year 1. At the end of year 2, $80,000,000 will be used to restore the land to its original condition. Compute the IRR of the project.

3. *Internal Rate of Return.* A project offers an initial cash outflow of #33,000, an annual expected cash inflow of $10,000 for five years, and no salvage value. Compute the IRR for this project.
4. *Mutually Exclusive Projects: Different Outlays.* The Baski Company is considering two mutually exclusive, one-year projects. A and B requires outlays of $1,000 and $1,5000, respectively. Project A will generate a return of $1,250 at the end of the first year, and project B will generate a return of $1,830 at the end of the second year. The cost of capital is 10 percent.
   Required:

   1. Utilizing the NPV method, which project would the Baksi Company accept?
   2. Utilizing the IRR method, which project would the company accept?
   3. Which ranking is better?

5. *Mutually Exclusive Projects: Differential Timing of Cash Flows.* The Beachemin Company is considering two mutually exclusive, two-year projects. Projects A and B require an outlay of $1,000 each. Project A promises a return of $200 at the end of ear 1 and $1,290 at the end of year 2. Project B promises a return of $1,100 at the end of year 1 and $245 at the end of year 2. The cost of capital is 10 percent.
   Required:

   1. Using the NPV method, which would the Beauchemin Company accept?
   2. Using the IRR method, which project would the Beauchemin Company accept?
   3. Which ranking is better?

6. *Mutually Exclusive Projects: Different Lives.* The Express Company is considering two mutually exclusive projects. Project A and B receive an outlay of $1,000 each. Project A promises a return of $1,200 at the end of year 1, and project B promises only a return of $1,520 at the end of year 3. The cost of capital is 10 percent.
   Required:

   1. Using the NPV method, which project would the Express Company accept?
   2. Using the IRR method, which project would the company accept?
   3. Which ranking is better?

7. *Accounting Treatment of Accelerated Depreciation.* The McIntosh Company is considering the purchase of a piece of equipment for $100,000. The Equipment will have a ten-year useful life and no salvage value, and the tax rate is 10 percent. The equipment is expected to generate an annual net income before taxes and depreciation of $50,000. The McIntosh Company expects to take advantage of double declining balance depreciation for tax purposes, and for reporting purposes it expects to issue financial statements based on straight-line depreciation. The two approaches are reconciled by setting up a deferred tax credit amount.
Required

   1. Determine the annual tax liability under straight-line depreciation.
   2. Determine the annual tax liability under double declining balance depreciation.
   3. Make the annual entries to recognize the tax expense and the tax payable.

8. *Cash Flow and Accrual Accounting.* The Slattery Corporation purchased a new machine, which is expected to earn an accounting profit of $2,000 in 19X1, computed as follows:

Sales	$18,000
- Operating Expenses (8,000) and Depreciation (6,000)	14,000

= Operating Income before Tax	$4,000
-Income Tax Expense (50%)	2,000
= Operating Income after Tax	$2,000

Related accrual information included the following:

Uncollected sales total $400 at year-end.
Unpaid wages amount to $800 at year-end.
The tax return depreciation is $12,000 for 19X1.

Required: Determine the cash flow for 19X1.

9. *NVP Technique.* The Stefanski Company is considering the initiation of a new project. This project has a three-year life and initial outflow, or project cost, of $60,000. Revenues and expenses for the first year are estimated to be $100,000 and $50,000 respectively. It is assumed that an inflation rate of 10 percent per year will cause similar increases in cash revenues and cash expenses. The tax rate is assumed to be 40 percent.

Required:
1. Compute the income statements of the new project for each of the three years. (Assume a straight-line depreciation and no salvage.)
2. Compute the after-tax cash inflow for each of the three years.
3. Assuming that the before-tax borrowing rate is 15 percent, determine the NPV of the project.

Solutions
1. *Payback.* Evaluation the project with unequal cash flow using payback, we find:

Year	Cash Flow	Cumulative Cash Flow
1	$8,000	$8,000
2	4,000	12,000
3	12,000	24,000
4	12,000	36,000
5	6,000	42,000

In year 3, the cumulative cash flow for the project is:

Year 1	Year 2		Year 3	
$8,000	$4,000	+	$12,000	= $24,000

Since the recovery of the investment falls between the third and fourth year, the payback period is 3 and a fraction years. To calculate the fraction divide the amount of funds needed to recover the investment in year 4 by the amount of cash flow in that year. Since the cumulative cash flow in year 3 is $24,000, we need $6,000 to recover the investment of $30,000. The annual cash flow in year 4 is $12,000. The payback fraction is then $\frac{\$6,000}{\$12,000}$, or .5. The payback for the project is 3.5 years.

2. *Multiple Internal Rate of Return.* We can find the rates that are the solutions to this problem by solving the following equation:

$$\$20,000,000 = \frac{\$90,000,000}{(1+r)^2} - \frac{\$80,000,000}{(1+r)^2}$$

Let (1+r) = X and divide both sides of the equation by 10,000,000. We then obtain:

$$2 = \frac{9}{x} - \frac{8}{x^2} \text{ or } 2x^2 - 9x + 8 = 0$$

This type of equation has two roots, which can be computed as follows:

$$x = \frac{-b \pm \sqrt{b^2 - 4ac}}{2a}$$

The solutions are:

$$x_1 = 3.285 \text{ and } x_2 = 1.215$$

Since x = (1+r), the multiple internal rates of return for this project are 21.5% and 228.5%.

3. *Internal Rate of Return.* Experimenting with three discount rates, 14 percent, 15 percent, and 16 percent, we find:

Discount Rate	Discount Factor	Cash Flow Each Year	Present Value of Stream
16%	3.274	$10,000	$32,740
15%	3.352	$10,000	$33,520
14%	3.4331	$10,000	$34,331

Thus, the internal rate necessary to discount the stream to $33,000 falls between 15 and 16 percent. To approximate the actual rate, we interpole between 1 and 16 percent:

15%	$33,520
16%	$32,520
1%	$780

$$\frac{520}{789} = .66$$

Then 15% + .66 = 15.66%

IRR = 15.66%

4. *Mutually Exclusive Projects: Different Outlays.* The relevant results for the three questions are in the following table:

Project	Initial Outlay	Cash Flow Year 1	NPV at 10%	IRR
A	$1,000	$1,250	$136	25%
B	$1,500	$1,830	$163	22%

1. The projects are ranked B with NPV.
2. The projects are ranked A B with IRR.
3. The two projects are ranked incorrectly by the IRR method because the size of the initial outlays is ignored. The incremental outlay of $500 for project B provides an incremental cash inflow of $580, which gives an IRR of 16 percent on the incremental investment. An IRR of 16 percent is obviously acceptable for a company with a cost of capital of 10 percent. Thus, the incremental approach with IRR gives the same result as NPV: project B should be selected over project A. (Adapted with permission from James A. Hendricks. "Capital Budgeting Decisions: NPV or IRR?" *Cost and Management,* March-April 1980, pp. 16-20.)

5. *Mutually Exclusive Projects: Differential Timing of Cash Flows.* The relevant results for the three questions are in the following table:

Project	Outlay	Year 1	Year 2	NPV at 10%	IRR
		Cash Flows			
A	$1,000	$200	$1,290	$247	24%
B	$1,000	1,100	245	202	29%

1. The projects are ranked AB with NPV.
2. The projects are ranked BA with IRR.
3. The incremental approach with IRR will be useful:

Year 0	$0	Cash outlays are the same.
Year 1	$900	Project B cash flow exceeds that of A
Year 2	$1,045	Project A cash flow exceeds that of B

In year 1, the cash flow project B exceeds that of project A by $900, while in year 2, the cash flow of project A exceeds that of project B by $1,045. This can be considered to be an investment of $900 that returns $1,045 after one year. The IRR on an investment of $900 that returns $1,045 after one year is 16.1 percent, which is advantageous if the cost of capital is 10 percent. Thus, the incremental approach with IRR confirms what NPV revealed immediately – project A should be selected over project B. (Adapted with permission from James A. Hendricks, "Capital Budgeting Decisions: NPV or IRR?" *Cost and Management,* March-April 1980, pp. 16-20.)

6. *Mutually Exclusive Projects: Different Lives.* Consider the following results:

				Cash Flows		
Project	Outlay	Year 1	Year 2	Year 3	NPV at 10%	IRR
A	$1,000	$1,200	-	-	$91	20%
B	$1,000	-	-	$1,520	$142	15%

1. The projects are ranked BA using NPV.
2. The projects are ranked AB using IRR.
3. The different rankings of projects A and B are caused by different assumptions about the reinvestment of the cash proceeds from project A at the end of year 1. The IRR proceeds from project A at the end of year 1. The IRR technique implicitly assumes that these funds can be reinvested at the calculated IRR, 20 percent, while the NPV technique implicitly assumes that these funds can be invested at 10 percent, the cost of capital. Which reinvestment assumption should be adopted? Ideally, both assumptions should be rejected and management should predict an explicit reinvestment rate for the time between the end of the short-lived projects and of the project of larger life.

7. *Accounting Treatment of Accelerated Depreciation.*
1. The tax liability under the straight line depreciation is as follows:

Year	Net Income Before Taxes & Depreciation	Depreciation	Taxable Income	Tax Liability
1	$50,000	$10,000	$40,000	$16,000

Entries are the same each year.

2. The tax liability under the double declining balance depreciation is as follows:

Year	Net Income Before Taxes & Depreciation	Depreciation	Taxable Income	Tax Liability
1	$50,000	$20,000	$30,000	$12,000
2	50,000	16,000	34,000	13,600
3	50,000	12,800	37,200	14,880
4	50,000	10,240	39,760	15,904
5	50,000	8,192	41,808	16,723.2

Year	Net Income Before Taxes & Depreciation	Depreciation	Taxable Income	Tax Liability
6*	50,000	6,554	43,446	17,378.4
7	50,000	6,554	43,446	17,378.4
8	50,000	6,554	43,446	17,378.4
9	50,000	6,554	43,446	17,378.4
10	50,000	6,554	43,446	17,378.4

*Switch to straight line

3. Entry Year One

Tax Expense	$16,000	
Tax Liability		$12,000
Deferred Tax Credit		4,000

and so on through year 4

Year 5

Tax Expense	$16,000	
Deferred Tax Credit	723.2	
Tax Payable		$16,723.2

Year 6 through Year 10

Tax Expense	$16,000	
Deferred Tax Credits	1,378.4	
Tax Payable		$17,378.4

8. *Cash Flow and Accrual Accounting.*
Cash Flow:

1. Cash Receipts from Sales

Sales	$18,000
Less Uncollected Sales	400
	$17,600

2. Cash Payments for Operating Expenses

	$8,000
Total Expenses	800
Less Unpaid Wages	7,200

3. Net Cash Inflow $10,400
4. Income Tax Expense   2,000
5. After-Tax Net Cash Inflow $8,400
6. Effect of Depreciation

Tax reduction due to excess of tax return depreciation ($12,000) over accounting depreciation ($6,000) as a 50% rate $3,000

$11,400

9. *Net Present Value Technique.*
1. Income Statement

	Year 1	Year 2	Year 3
Revenues	$100,000	$110,000	$121,000
Expenses	50,000	55,000	60,500
Depreciation	20,000	20,000	20,000
Taxable Income	30,000	35,000	40,500
Taxes at 40%	12,000	14,000	16,200
Net Income	$18,000	$21,000	$24,300

2. After-Tax Cash Inflow

	Year 1	Year 2	Year 3
Net Income	$18,000	$21,000	$24,300
Depreciation	20,000	20,000	20,000
Cash Inflow	$38,000	$41,000	$44,300

3. The Discount Rate Is 9% (15% X .6)
   Discounted Cash Inflow

	Year 1	Year 2	Year 3
Cash Inflow	$38,000	$41,000	$44,300
Present Value@9%	.917431	.841680	.772183
Present Value	$34,862	$34,509	$34,208
	Total: $103,579		

Net Present Value:

Total Discounted Cash Inflow	$103,579
Initial Cost of the Project	60,000
Net Present Value	$43,579

CONCLUSIONS

Capital budgeting involved the appraisal of the desirability of capital projects. The conventional techniques covered in this chapter include (a) the discounted cash flow methods, (b) the accounting rate of return method, and (c) the payback method. The next chapter will expand these techniques to cover more complex issues that can be faced when evaluating a capital project.

NOTE

1. Under the general guidelines provided in the tax code, firms are permitted to switch from double declining balance to straight-line depreciation when it is to their advantage to do so. They switch at the point that minimizes the tax bill. From the seventh year in this case, straight-line depreciation charges are higher than double declining balance charges. This is because we are applying a constant rate to a declining balance, which will not carry to the end of the useful life.

Chapter 3
Advanced Capital Budgeting

INTRODUCTION

This chapter expands the previous chapter, covering the principles of capital budgeting. It covers the advanced issues of replacement decisions, capital rationing, capital budgeting under uncertainty, and capital budgeting under inflation.

REPLACEMENT DECISIONS

The examples used to illustrate capital budgeting techniques were based on expansion projects. The analysis for replacement projects is slightly different. The following sections illustrate the replacement decision first where the lives of the projects are equal and, second, where the lives of the projects are unequal.

Replacement Decisions: Equal Lives

Assume that a machine purchased ten years ago by the Litton Company at a cost of $20,000 had an expected twenty-year useful life when purchased and zero salvage value. A straight-line depreciation charge of $2,000 makes the machine's present book value equal to $10,000. A new machine now being considered to replace the old one can be purchased for $30,000 and is expected to reduce operating costs from $10,000 to $4,000 for its ten-year useful life. The old machine can be sold for $4,000. The new machine is expected to have a $6,000 salvage value. Taxes are 48 percent, and an investment tax credit of 10 percent of the purchase price can be claimed on the purchase of the new machine. The cost of capital is 12 percent. Should the Litton Company replace the old machine?

The NVP of the replacement decisions, computed in Exhibit 3.1 is $3,237. The new machine should be purchased to replace the old machine, given that it increases the value of the firm by $3,237.

Replacement Decisions: Unequal Lives

The procedure generally used to choose between two mutually exclusive replacement proposals with unequal lives is to convert the number of years of analysis to a common termination year through a series of *replacement chains.* For example, to choose between a four-year project X and a six-year project Y, it is necessary to compare a three-chain cycle for project X and a two-chain cycle for project Y, bringing the common termination year to 12.

Assume that the Shields Company is considering replacing a fully depreciated machine with one of two replacement machines. Machine X has a cost of $15,000, a five-year useful life, and will generate after-tax cash flow of $5,000 per year for five years. Machine Y has a cost of $18,000, a ten-year useful life, and will generate after-tax cash flows of $4,000 per year for ten years. The company's cost of capital is 12 percent. To determine which machine should be chosen, the NPV of each machine can be computed:

$$NPV\ (X) = \$5,000(3.605) - \$15,000 = \$3,025$$
$$NPV\ (Y) = \$4,000(5.650) - \$18,000 = \$4,600$$

From these computations it appears that machine Y should be chosen. The analysis is incorrect, however, since a second investment can be made after five years if machine X is chosen, and the second investment may be profitable. A better analysis would be based on the common denominator of ten years. Therefore,

Exhibit 3.1
Replacement Decision Analysis

	Amount before tax	Effect, Net of Taxes	Time Even Occurs	PV Factor at 12%
1 Cost of New Machine	$30,000	$30,000	0	1.0
2 Salvage Value of Old Machine	-$4,000	-$4,000	0	1.0
3 Tax Effect of Sale of Old Machine (a)	-$6,000	-$2,880	0	1.0
4 Investment Tax Credit	-$3,000	-$3,000	0	1.0
5 Total Present Value of Outflows				
Net Inflows of the Life of the New Machine (t = 1 to 10)				
6 Decrease in Operating Costs (b)	$6,000	$3,120	1 to 10	5.650
	-------------	-------------	-----------	
7 Depreciation on New Machine	$2,400	--	-	--
	-------------	-------------	-----------	
8 Depreciation on Old Machine	$1,000	--	-	--
9 Net Changes in Tax Savings from Depreciation	$1,400	$672	1 to 10	5.650
10 Salvage Value of New Machine	$6,000	$6,000	1 to 10	0.322
11 Total Present Value of Inflows				
12 NPV = $23,357 - $20,120 = $3,237				

(a) The tax effect of sale of old machine: Loss X t = [($10,000 - $4,000) x 0.48] = $2,880
(b) Cost reduction: Decrease in cost X $(1 - t)$ = $4,000(1 - 0.48) = $2,080

Present value   Present value

NVP (X) = of first investment + of second investment

            of machine X   of machine Y

      = \$3,025 + \$3,025(0.567) = \$4,740.

NVP (Y)   = \$4,600.

The NVP of machine X is \$4,740, which is higher than the NPV of machine Y.

CAPITAL RATIONING

Capital rationing exists when a firm faces limited supplies of funds, which precludes the acceptance of potentially profitable projects. Among the causes cited for capital rationing are (1) limits imposed on new borrowing, (2) a debt limit imposed by an outside agreement (for example, bond covenants), (3) limits on capital spending imposed on divisional management, and (4) management's desire to maintain a given dividend policy or a specific earnings-per-share or price/earnings ratio.

      Conventional methods of evaluation with capital rationing consist of (1) ranking the projects under consideration from highest to lowest for whichever evaluation model is used, that is, IRR, NPV, or the profitability index (PI); and (2) selecting projects starting at the top of the ranking until funds are exhausted. Although these conventional methods based on either the IRR or the NPV techniques are simple, discontinuities or size disparities between projects prevent the choice of optimal projects. For example, a 20 percent return on \$1,000 is considered better than a 15 percent return on \$2,000, according to the conventional capital rationing method.

      To correct the limitations of the conventional capital rationing methods, mathematical programming can be used to select the optimal combination of projects. In 1955, James H. Lorie and Leonard J. Savage were the first to suggest mathematical programming- in the form of a heuristic programming approach to deal with capital rationing. This attempt was followed by a more comprehensive treatment of the problem by H. Martin Weingartner, whose basic model follows:

$$\sum_{j=1}^{m} b_j X_j,$$

Because of the use of the last two constraints, this mathematical programming model is knows as *integer programming.*

      To illustrate the integer programming approach to capital budgeting, let us use the data shown in Exhibit 3.2. The present values of the two budget constraints are \$90 in period 1 and \$30 in period 2. The model will look like the following:

      Maximize

$$20_{x1} + 20_{x2} + 40_{x3} + 50_{x4}$$

Subject to

$$10_{x1} + 20_{x2} + 30_{x3} + 40_{x4} \le 90.$$
$$5_{x1} + 10_{x2} + 10_{x3} + 30_{x4} \le 30.$$
$$0 \le X_j \le 1 \text{ for } j = 1,2,3, \text{ and } 4.$$

Exhibit 3.2
Capital Rationing Example

Investment Proposal	Present Value Of Outlay (Period 1)	Present Value Of Outlay (Period 2)	NPV
1	$10	$5	$20
2	$20	$10	$30
3	$30	$10	$40
4	$40	$30	$50

subject to

$$\sum_{j=1}^{m} C_{tj}X_j \le C_t \; for \; t = 1, \ldots, n.$$

$$0 \le X_j \le 1.$$

X_j is an integer,
where

b_j =Net present value of investment proposal j.
$X_j = 0$ if the project is accepted, and 1 if the project is rejected.
C_{tj} = Net cash need for proposal j in period t.
C_j = Total budget for period t.

X_j is an integer.

CAPITAL BUDGETING UNDER UNCERTAINTY
Nature of Risk

Because the cash flows of a project often may be estimated on the basis of incomplete information, the capital budgeting evaluation must be performed in a climate of uncertainty. Although *uncertainty* and *risk* are sometimes used synonymously, they are different in the strict mathematical sense. *Risk* refers to the possible outcomes of a project to which probabilities can be assigned, whereas *uncertainty* refers to outcomes to which it is difficult to assign probabilities. Thus, the real interest lies with risk, because it is measureable.

       Most decision makers are risk averse and perceive risk in different ways:
1. The *dollar price risk* is the risk associated with a decline in the number of dollars used to acquire a financial asset.
2. The *purchasing power risk* is the risk associated with a decline in the purchasing power of the monetary unit.
3. The *interest rate risk* is the risk associated with changes in the interest rate, which affect market values of many types of securities.
4. The *business risk* is the risk associated with the operational cash flows of a firm.
5. The *financial risk* is the risk associated with financial leverage.
6. The *systematic risk* or *market risk* is the risk associated with the common stocks of a particular industry.
7. The *unsystematic risk* is the risk associated with a particular company. Because the perception of risk by decision makers affects their decision, it should betaken into account in the decision-making process. Capital budgeting under uncertainty should incorporate risk in the evaluation process.

Risk-Adjusted Discount Rate Method

One of the techniques for incorporating risk in the evaluation process is the risk-adjusted discount rate, which consists of manipulating the discount rate applied to the cash flows to reflect the amount of risk inherent in a project. The higher the risk associated with a project, the higher the discount rate applied to the cash flows. If a given project us perceived to be twice as risky as most acceptable projects to the firm and the cost of capital is 12 percent, then the correct risk-adjusted discount rate is 24 percent. In spite of its simplicity, the risk-adjusted discount rate method is subject to the following limitations:

1. The determination of the exact risk-adjusted discount rate is subjective and, therefore, subject to error.
2. The method adjusts the discount rate rather than the future cash flows, which are subject to variability and risk.

Certainty Equivalent Method

       Another technique for incorporating risk in the avaluation process is the certainty equivalent method, which involves adjusting the future cash flows so a project can be evaluated on a riskless basis. The adjustment is formulated as follows:

$$NPV = \sum_{t=1}^{n} \left[\frac{\alpha_t CF_t}{1 + R_F} \right] - I_0,$$

where

α_t = Risk coefficient applied to the cash flow of period t(CF$_t$).
I_0 = Initial cost of the project.

R_F = Risk-free rate.

As this formula shows, the method proceeds by multiplying the future cash flows by certainty equivalents to obtain a riskless cash flow. Note also that the discount rate used is R_F, which is a risk-free rate of interest.

To illustrate the certainty equivalent method, assume an investment with the following characteristics:

I_0 = Initial cost = $30,000.
CF_1 = Cash flow, year 1 = $10,000.
CF_2 = Cash flow, year 2 = $20,000.
CF_3 = Cash flow, year 3 = $30,000.
α_1= Certainty equivalent, year 1 = 0.9.
α_2= Certainty equivalent, year 2 = 0.8.
α_3= Certainty equivalent, year 3 = 0.6.

The NPV of the investment using a risk-free discount rate of 6 percent is computed as follows:

Period	Cash Flow $(CF_t)(\alpha_t)$	Risk Coefficient	Certainty Equivalent	Risk-Free Rate (R_F)	Present Value
1	$10,000	0.9	$9,000	0.943	$8,487
2	$20,000	0.8	$16,000	0.890	$14,240
3	$30,000	0.6	$18,000	0.840	$15,120
Present Value of Cash Flows					$37,847
Initial Investment					$30,000
Net Present Value					$7,847

Since the NPV is positive, the investment should be considered acceptable. The main advantage of the certainty equivalent method is that it allows the assignment of a different risk factor to each cash flow, given that risk can concentrate in one or more periods.

The certainty equivalent method and the risk-adjusted discount rate method are comparable methods of evaluating risk. To produce similar ranking, the following equation must hold:

$$\frac{(\alpha_t CF_t)}{(1 + R_F)^t} = \frac{CF_t}{(1 + R_A)^{t'}}$$

where

α_t = Risk coefficient used in the certainty equivalent method.
R_F = Risk-free discount rate.
R_A = Risk-adjusted discount rate used in the risk-adjusted discount rate method.
CF_t = Future cash flow.

Solving for α_t yields

$$\alpha_t = \frac{(1 + R_F)^t}{(1 + R_A)^{t'}}$$

Given that R_A and R_F are constant and $R_A > R_F$, then α_t, decreases over time, which means that risk increases over time. To illustrate, assume that in the previous example R_A = 15%. Then

$$\alpha_t = \frac{(1+R_F)^1}{(1+R_A)^1} = \frac{(1+0.06)^1}{(1+0.15)^1} = 0.921.$$

$$\alpha_t = \frac{(1+R_F)^2}{(1+R_A)^2} = \frac{(1+0.06)^2}{(1+0.15)^2} = 0.848.$$

$$\alpha_t = \frac{(1+R_F)^3}{(1+R_A)^3} = \frac{(1+0.06)^3}{(1+0.15)^3} = 0.783.$$

In many cases this assumption of increasing risk may not be realistic.

Probability Distribution

The probability distribution approach to the evaluation of risk assigns probabilities of each cash flow outcome. Various measures of risk can then be computed, giving information about the dispersion or tightness of the probability distribution. *Standard deviation* is a conventional measure of dispersion. For a single period, the standard deviation is computed as follows:

$$\theta_t = \sqrt{\sum_{t=1}^{n} [X_{it} - E_t(X)]^2 P(X_i)_t},$$

where

α_t = Standard deviation of period $t's$ cash flows.
X_{it} =Cash flow for the rth outcome in period t.
$E_t(X)$ = Expected value of cash flows in period t.
$P(X_i)_t$ =Probability of occurrence of cash flow X, in period t.

The expected cash flow $E_t(X)$ is computed as follows:

$$E_t(X) = \sum_{t=1}^{n} X_{it}P(X_i),$$

All things being equal, the higher the standard deviation, the greater the risk associated with the expected value.

Another measure of relative dispersion is the *coefficient of variation* (CV), a measure that compares the expected value and risk of a probability distribution. The coefficient of variation is computed as follows:

$$CV = \frac{\alpha}{E(X)}.$$

All things being equal, the smaller the coefficient of variation, the better the project. To illustrate these risk concepts, assume that projects A and B have the following discrete probability distributions of expected cash flows in each of the next three years:

| Project A | | Project B | |
Probability	Cash Flow	Probability	Cash Flow
0.2	$1,000	0.3	$1,500
0.5	$2,000	0.3	$1,000
0.2	$3,000	0.2	$3,500
0.1	$4,000	0.2	$3,750

The expected value of cash flows of both projects can be computed as follows:

$$E(A) = 0.2(\$1,000) + 0.5(\$2,000) + 0.2(\$3,000) + 0.1(\$4,000) = \$2,200.$$
$$E(B) = 0.3(\$1,500) + 0.3(\$1,000) + 0.2(\$3,500) + 0.2(\$3,750) = \$2,200.$$

On the basis of the expected values as a measure of central tendency in the distribution, projects A and B are equivalent. To determine which project is riskier, the standard deviations for both projects can be computed as follows:

$$\alpha(A) = [0.2(\$1,000 - \$2,200)^2 + 0.5(\$2,000 - \$2,200)^2$$
$$+ 0.2(\$3,000 - \$2,200)^2 + 0.1(\$4,000 - \$2,200)^2]^{1/2} = \$871.77.$$
$$\alpha(B) = [0.3(\$1,500 - \$2,200)^2 + 0.3(\$1,000 - \$2,200)^2$$
$$+ 0.2(\$3,500 - \$2,200)^2 + 0.2(\$3,750 - \$2,200)^2]^{1/2} = \$1,182.15.$$

Thus, project B has a significantly higher standard deviation, indicating a greater dispersion of possible cash flows.

The standard deviation is an absolute measure of risk. For comparison, the project also should be evaluated on the basis of their coefficient of variation, which measures the relative dispersion within the distribution. The coefficient of variation for both projects can be computed now:

$$= CV(A)\frac{\theta_A}{E(A)} \times 100 = \frac{\$871.77}{\$2,200} = 39.6\%.$$
$$= CV(B)\frac{\theta_B}{E(B)} \times 100 = \frac{\$1,182.15}{\$2,200} = 53.7\%.$$

The coefficient of variation for project B is significantly higher than for project A, which indicates again that project B presents a degree of risk.

The coefficient of variation is an especially useful measure when the comparison between projects leads to the acceptance of a given project based on a comparison between means, or when the comparison leads to the acceptance of a different project based on a comparison between standard deviations.

Multiperiod Projects

The computation of the measure of risk becomes more complicated when several periods are involved. Some assumptions must be made regarding the relationships between the period cash flows, namely, whether the cash flows are independent or dependent.

To illustrate, let us return to project A and assume (1) that the applicable discount rate (R) is 10 percent and (2) that the project calls for a $5,000 investment.

Independent of the nature of the relationship between cash flows in the three periods, the NPV of project A can be computed as follows:

$$NPV = \sum_{t=1}^{3} [\frac{\$2,000}{(1 + 0.10)^t}] - \$5,000 = \$471.$$

The standard deviation of the project will be computed differently according to whether we assume that the cash flows are dependent, independent, or mixed.

Independent Cash Flow

If we assume serial independence of the cash flows between the periods, the standard deviation of the entire project is

$$\theta = \sqrt{\sum_{t=1}^{n} \theta_t^2/(1+r)^{2t}},$$

where

θ_t = standard deviation of the probabilty distribution of the cash flows in period t.

Hence the standard deviation of project A, assuming serial independence, is

$$\theta_A = \sqrt{\left(\frac{\$871^2}{(1+0.10)^2}\right) + \left(\frac{\$871^2}{(1+0.10)^4}\right) + (\$871^2/(1+0.10)^6)}$$

$$= \$358.04.$$

Dependent Cash Flows

In general, the cash flows of a given period are expected to influence the cash flows of subsequent periods. In the case of perfect correlation, the standard deviation of the entire project is

$$\theta = \sum_{i=1}^{n} \theta_t/(1+r)^t$$

Therefore, the standard deviation of project A, assuming perfect correlation between interperiod cash flows, is

$$\theta_A \sum_{t=1}^{3} \$871/(1+0.10)^i = \$2,166.17$$

Note that the standard deviation under the assumption of independence is $358.04, while under the assumption of perfect dependency it is considerably higher ($2,116.17). If the cash flows are perfectly correlated there is more risk inherent in the project than if the cash flows are independent.

Mixed Correlation

A project may include some independent and some dependent cash flows, Frederick's Hillier proposed a model to deal with a mixed situation:

$$\theta = \frac{\Sigma_{t=0}^{r} \theta_{Yt}^2}{(1+r)^{2t}} + \sum_{j=1}^{m}[\sum_{j=1}^{T} 6_{zjt}/(1+r)^t]^2$$

Y_t = The independent component of the net cash flow in period t.

Z_{jt} = The jth perfectly correlated component of the net cash flow in period t.

To illustrate the computation of the standard deviation of a project with mixed correlation. Hillier assumed the following project data for a new product addiction:

Year	Source	Expected Value of Net Cash Flows (In Thousands)	Standard Deviation
0	Initial Investment	($600)	$50
1	Production Cash Outflow	($250)	$20
2	Production Cash Outflow	($200)	$10
3	Production Cash Outflow	($200)	$10
4	Production Cash Outflow	($200)	$10
5	Production Outflow – Salvage Value	($100)	$10\sqrt{10}$
1	Marketing	$300	$50
2	Marketing	$600	$100
3	Marketing	$500	$100
4	Marketing	$400	$100
5	Marketing	$300	$100

Hiller also assumed that all the outflows were independent and that all marketing flow were perfectly correlated. If 10 percent is used as the risk-free rate, the expected value of the NPV for the proposal is

$$NPV = \sum_{t=1}^{S} [\bar{X}/(1 + 0.10)^t] - C_0$$

or

$$NPV = \frac{\$300 - 250}{(1.10)} + \frac{\$600 - \$200}{(1.10)^2} + \frac{\$500 - \$200}{(1.10)^3} + \frac{\$400 - \$200}{(1.10)^4}$$
$$+ \frac{\$400 - \$200}{(1.10)^5} - 600 = \$262.$$

The standard deviation is

$$\theta = \sqrt{50^2 + (20^2/(1.10)^2) + (10\sqrt{10^2/(1.10)^{10}} + [\frac{50}{1.10} + \cdots}$$
$$+ \frac{100}{(1.10)_5]^2} = \$339.$$

Moderate Correlation

In most cases, cash flows cannot be easily classified as either independent or perfectly correlated, and a decision tree approach can be used. In a capital budgeting context, this approach involves the multiplication of the conditional probabilities of correlated periods to obtain the joint probabilities that will specify the probabilities of multiple events. Exhibit 3.3 illustrates the decision tree approach to compute the joint probabilities and the expected value of a project.

Simulation

The preceding methods of dealing with uncertainty apply only when two probability distributions are considered. In most realistic capital budgeting situations, more than two variables are significant, and more than two variables are subject to uncertainty. The simulation technique takes into account the interacting variables and their corresponding probability distributions. David B. Hertz proposed a simulation model to obtain the dispersion about the expected rate of return for an investment proposal. He established nine separate probability distributions to determine the probability distribution of the average rate of return for the entire project. The following nine variables were considered.

Market Analysis
1. Market size.
2. Selling price.
3. Market growth rate.
4. Share of market.

Investment Cost Analysis
5. Investment required.
6. Residual value of investment.

Operating and Fixed Costs
7. Operating costs.
8. Fixed costs.
9. Useful life of facilities.

The computer simulates trial values of each of the nine variables and then computes the return on investment based on the simulated values obtained. These trials are repeated often enough to obtain a frequency distribution for the return on investment. This approach can also be used to determine the NPV or the IRR of a project

Exhibit 3.3
Decision Tree Approach to Capital Budgeting

Period 1 Net Cash Flows A	Period 1 Initial Probability p(1)	Period 2 Net Cash Flows A	Period 2 Conditional Probability p(2/1)	Number of Cases	Joint Probability p	Total Net Cash Flows A	Expected Value of Total Net Cash Flows
	0.6	$20	0.3	1	0.18	$50	$9.00
$30	0.6	$30	0.4	2	0.24	$60	$14.40
	0.6	$40	0.3	3	0.18	$70	$12.60
	0.4	$30	0.2	4	0.08	$70	$5.60
$40	0.4	$40	0.5	5	0.02	$80	$16.00
	0.4	$50	0.3	6	0.12	$90	$10.80
Mean Value							$68.40

CAPITAL BUDGETING UNDER INFLATION

Beginning with seminal work by Irving Fisher, economists have shown fairly conclusively that market rates of interest include an adjustment of expected inflation rates- the nonexistent "homogeneous expectation." This consensus forecast, therefore, is built into the discount rate used in capital budgeting. When rates of inflation were relatively low (say 2 to 3 percent) this did not lead to serious distortions in the IRR or NPV models, because any error in the rate estimation was immaterial in most cases. With the higher rates of inflation we are now experiencing, it is desirable to explicitly consider the rate of inflation in developing cash flow forecasts. The correct analysis can be done in either of two ways: (1) using a money discount rate to discount money cash flows, or (2) using a real discount rate to discount real cash flows.

Before illustrating either approach, let us explore the differences between money cash flows and real cash flows, and between real discount rate and money discount rate. Money cash flows are cash flows measured in dollars from various periods having different purchasing power. Real cash flows are cash flows measured in dollars having the same purchasing power. The real cash flow for a given year, expressed in terms of dollars of $year_0$ (the base year) is equal to the money cash flow for that year, multiplied by the following ratio:

$$\frac{\text{Price level index in } year_0}{\text{Price level index in } year_1}$$

For example, if an investment promises a money return of $100 for three years and the price index for years 0 through 3 is 100, 110, 121, and 133.1, respectively, then the real cash flows are as follows:

$$\text{Year 1: } \$100 \times \frac{100}{110} = 90.90.$$
$$\text{Year 2: } \$100 \times \frac{100}{121} = 82.64.$$
$$\text{Year 3: } \$100 \times \frac{100}{133.1} = 75.13.$$

The money discount rate, r, can also be computed. Assuming that f is the annual rate of inflation, I is the real discount rate, and the decision maker is in the zero tax bracket, then

$$r = (I + f)(1 + I) - 1,$$

or

$$r = I + f + if.$$

For example, if the real return before taxes is 3 percent, and the rate of inflation is 10 percent, then the nominal discount rate is

$$0.03 + 0.10 + 0.003 = 0.133.$$

To illustrate the correct analysis under inflation, assume the same data as in the previous example. The correct analysis can be either of two, as follows.
1. The first analysis discounts the money cash flows using a money discount rate. The present value of the investment will be computed as follows:

Nominal Present

Period	Money Cash Flow	Value Factor At 13.3%	Present Value
1	100	0.8826	88.26
2	100	0.7792	77.92
3	100	0.6874	68.74
			234.92

2. The second analysis discounts the real cash flows using a real discount rate. The present value of the investment will give the same present value, as follows:

Period	Real Cash Flow	Real Present Value at 3%	Present Value
1	90.9	0.9709	88.254
2	82.64	0.9426	77.896
3	75.13	0.9151	68.751
			234.901

Assuming a marginal tax rate t on nominal income, the nominal discount rate will be computed as follows:

$$1 + (1 - t)r = (1 + f) + 1 + I(1 - t).$$

or

$$r = I + If + f(1 - t.)$$

Assuming the tax rate to be 30 percent, the nominal rate is then computed as follows:

$$r = 0.03 + (0.03 \times 0.10) + 0.10(1 - 0.30)$$
$$= 0.1758.$$

In other words, a nominal rate of 17.58 percent is needed for an investor in a 30 percent tax bracket and facing an inflation of 10 percent to earn a real discount rate of 3 percent.

CAPITAL BUDGETING ILLUSTRATIONS

Problems

1. *Certainty Equivalent Method.* A project offers an initial cash outlay of $40,000, a annual expected cash inflow of $20,000 for three years, and no salvage value. The risk coefficients for the three periods are estimated to be 0.90, 0.80, and 0.75, respectively. The risk-free rate of interest is estimated to be 6 percent. Compute the NPV of the project.
2. *Probability Distribution and Capital Budgeting.* The Santini Company can invest in one of two mutually exclusive projects. The probability distribution of the two projects' NPVs is shown here:

Project A		Project B	
Net Present Value	**Probability**	**Net Present Value**	**Probability**
0.3	$2,000	0.4	$3,000
0.6	$4,000	0.4	$2,000
0.1	$6,000	0.2	$7,000

Required

1. Compute the expected value, the standard deviation, and the coefficient of variation of each project.
2. Which of these two mutually exclusive projects should the Santini Company choose? Why?
3. *Capital Budgeting under Uncertainty.* Mr. Oliver is evaluating whether to invest $3,000,000 in a research project. If the research project is successful, the revenues net of operating costs (excluding the $3,000,000 outlay for the research and an initial investment in equipment) are estimated to be as follows:

Anticipated Net Revenue	**Probability**
$10,000,000	0.10
$20,000,000	0.25
$25,000,000	0.35
$30,000,000	0.20
$35,000,000	0.10

However, Oliver knows there is a 60 percent chance that the project will be unsuccessful.
Required: Assuming Oliver wishes to maximize the expected value of net cash flows, should the investment be made in the research project? Show all calculations.

4. *Capital Rationing.* The Francis Company is considering eight projects. The cost of capital is 12 percent, and the capital constraint is $500. Each project has a one-year life. The initial outlay and the cash flow at the end of year 1 for each project are as follows:

Project	Initial Outlay	Cash Inflow, End of Year 1
A	$100	$122
B	$100	$118
C	$100	$115
D	$200	$238
E	$200	$234
F	$300	$348
G	$400	$468

Required

1. Compute the NPV and the IRR for each project.
2. Assuming the eight projects are not mutually exclusive, which combination of projects should the Francis Company choose? (Use NPV.)
3. Assuming projects A, B, E, and G are mutually exclusive, which combination of projects should the company choose? (Use NPV.)

5. Mathematical Programming and Capital Budgeting. The Pen-aids Company is considering the following investment proposals:
Projects 1 and 3 are mutually exclusive. The company has a budget constraint of $40,000 in year 1 and $30,000 in year 2.

Required:

1. Set up the selection process as a mathematical programming problem to maximize the NPV available from investment subject to the two budget constraints.
2. Set up the dual program assuming projects 1 and 3 are no longer mutually exclusive.
3. Explain the meaning of the dual values.

6. Multiperiod Projects. The Dickenson Company has determined the following discrete probability distributions for net cash flows generated by a contemplated project:

Period 1		Period 2	
Probability	**Cash Flow**	**Probability**	**Cash Flow**
0.10	$5,000	0.10	$6,000
0.20	$4,500	0.10	$2,000
0.10	$3,000	0.25	$5,000
0.20	$3,500	0.25	$3,000
0.40	$4,000	0.30	$4,000

The after-tax risk-free rate is 10 percent, and the project requires an initial outlay of $6,000.
   Required:

1. Determine the expected value of the NVP.
2. Determine the standard deviation of the NVP, assuming that the probability distributions of cash flows for future periods are independent.
3. Determine the standard distribution of the NVP, assuming that the probability distributions of cash flows for future periods are dependent.

7. Replacement Decisions: Unequal Lives. The Hass Company is considering replacing a fully depreciated lathe for trimming molded plastic with a new machine. Two replacement machines are available. Lathe X has a cost of $50,000, will last five years, and will produce after-tax cask flows of $15,000 per year for five years. Lathe Y has a cost of $60,000, will last ten years, and will produce net cash flows of $12,000 per year for ten years. The company's cost of capital is 10 percent. Should lathe X or Y be selected to replace the old machine?
8. Replacement Decisions: Equal Lives. The Davidson Company purchased a computer ten years ago with a cost of $20,000, a useful life of twenty years, and a zero salvage value at the end of its useful life. Straight-line depreciation is used. A new manager suggested that a new computer costing $30,000 be purchased. The new computer has a ten-year life and could reduce operating costs from $10,000 to $5,000. The old Computer can be sold now at an estimated $4,000 and the new computer can be sold at the end of the ten years for $5,000. Taxes are at 48 percent rate, and the company's cost of capital is 10 percent. An investment tax credit of 10 percent of purchase price can be used if the new machine is acquired. Should the Davidson Company buy a new computer?
9. Real and Money Discount Rates. Dr. Eric Magnum is considering a $900 investment that is expected to yield a return of $133 for the first two years and $1,133 in the third year. A rate of inflation of 10 percent and a

real rate of 3 percent are expected. Magnum is in the zero tax bracket. Determine the net present value of the investment using: (1) a nominal discount rate, and (2) a real discount rate.

Solutions
1. *Certainty Equivalent method.*

Period	Cash Flow	Risk Coefficient	Certainty Equivalent	Risk Free Rate	Present Value
1	$20,000	0.9	$18,000	0.943	$16,974
2	$20,000	0.8	$16,000	0.890	$14,240
3	$20,000	0.75	$15,000	0.840	$12,600
					$43,814
					$40,000
					$3,814

Investment
NVP

2. *Probability Distribution and Capital Budgeting.*

1. a. The expected value as follows:
E(x) = $2,000(0.3) + 4,000(0.6) + 6,000(0.1) = $3,600
E(y) = $3,000(0.4) + 2,000(0.4) + 7,000(0.2) = $3,400
b. The standard deviations of both projects may be computer as follows:
$\propto (x) = [0.3(2,000 - 3,600)^2 + 0.6(4,000 - 3,600)^2 + 0.1(6,000 - 3,600)^2]^{1/2}$
= $1,200.
$\propto (y) = [0.4(3,000 - 3,400)^2 + 0.4(2,000 - 3,400)^2 + 0.2(7,000 - 3,400)^2]^{1/2}$
= $1,854.72
c. The coefficients of variation of both projects may be computed as follows:
CV(x) = $1,200/3,600 = 33.33%
CV(y) = $1,854.72/3,400 = $54.557.
2. Project A should be chosen. It has a higher NPV and both a lower standard deviation and coefficient of variation.

3. *Capital Budgeting under Uncertainty.* Generally, the students did well on this question. Many of my students failed to deduct the $3,000,000 cash outlay when computing the expected net cash flow if successful.

Anticipated Net

Revenues	Probability	Expected Value of Net Revenues
$10 million	0.10	$1,000,000
$20 million	0.25	$5,000,000
$25 million	0.35	$8,750,000
$30 million	0.20	$6,000,000
$35 million	0.10	$3,500,000
		$24,250,000

Payoff Table

Action		State Success Prob. = .4	Unsuccessful Prod = .6
	Invest	$21,250,000	-$3,000,000
	Don't Invest	$0	$0

$$E(invest) = P(Success) \times \left(\frac{payoff}{success}\right) + P(successful) \times (payoff/unsuccessful)$$
$$= .4(21,250,000) + .6(-3,000,000)$$
$$= 8,500,000 - 1,800,000$$
$$= 6,700,000$$

The decision is then to invest.

4. *Capital Rationing*

1. NPV and IRR Results.

Projects	Outlays	Cash Inflows	PV of Cash Inflow at 12%	NPV	IRR
A	$100	$122	$108.95	$8.95	92%
B	$100	$118	$105.37	$5.37	18%
C	$100	$115	$102.70	$2.70	15%
D	$200	$238	$212.53	$12.53	19%
E	$200	$234	$208.96	$8.96	17%
F	$300	$348	$310.76	$10.76	16%
G	$400	$468	$417.92	$17.92	17%

3. With NPV, we compute the NPVs for all combinations of projects whose outlays total $500.

A,B,C,D	$29.55	A,D,E	$30.44
A,B,C,E	$25.98	B,D,E	$26.86
A,B,F	$25.08	C,D,E	$24.19
A,C,F	$22.41	A,G	$26.87
B,C,F	$18,83	B,G	$23.29
D,F	$23.29	C,G	$20.62
E,F	$19.72		

The combination of projects with the highest NPV is A,D,E with $30.44. The cost of the firm's shareholders of capital rationing is equal to the total NPV of all the projects, $67.19, minus the NPV of the chosen combinations, $30.44, which is equal to $36.75.

3. The acceptable combinations are:

A,C,F	$22.41	C,G	$20.62
B,C,F	$18.83	D,F	$23.29
C,D,E	$24.19	E,F	$19.72

The combination of projects with the highest NPV is C,D,E. (Adapted with permission from James A. Hendricks, "Capital Budgeting, Decisions: NPV or IRR?" *Cost and Management,* March-April 1980, pp.16-20.)

5. *Mathematical Programming and Capital Budgeting.*

1. Primal Problem
    Max 30,000x1 + 50,000x2 + 24,000x3 + 55,000x4
    Subject to
    $$17,000x_1 + 22,000x_2 + 15,000x_3 + 25,000x_4 \leq 40,000$$
    $$14,000x_1 + 26,000x_2 + 15,000x_3 + 16,000x_4 \leq 30,000$$
    $$x_1 + x_3 \quad \leq 1$$
    $$x_1, x_2, x_3, x_4 \leq 0$$

    All x's are integers.
2. Dual Problem
    Min 40,000y1 + 30,000y2
    Subject to
    $$17,000_{y1} + 14,000_{y2} \geq 30,000$$
    $$22,000_{y1} + 26,000_{y2} \geq 50,000$$
    $$15,000_{y1} + 15,000_{y2} \geq 24,000$$
    $$25,000_{y1} + 16,000_{y2} \geq 55,000$$
    $$y_1, y_2 \geq 0$$
3. The dual values provide the shadow costs or opportunity costs of the resources, which are the rationed in years 1 and 2, respectively, so that the solution to the dual in this case will be the impact interest rates, or maximum opportunity costs of money in years 1 and 2 to make the projects worthwhile. In other words, the solutions y1y2 yield the effective "prices" of money in periods 1 and 2, respectively, expressed in terms of year 0.

6. *Multiperiod Projects*

1. Expected value of the NPV
    a. The expected value of cash flows for period 1 and 2 are:
        EV(1) = 0.10(5,000) + 0.20(4,500) + 0.10(3,000) + 0.20(3,500) +

0.40(4,000) = $4,000

EV(2) = 0.10(6,000) + 0.10(2,000) + 0.25(5,000) + 0.25(3,000) + 0.30(4,000) = $4,000

b. The expected Value of NPV is:

$$NPV = \sum_{i=1}^{2} (\frac{\$4,000}{1 + 0.10)^2} - \$6,000 = \$942.$$

2. Standard deviation: independent cash flows
   a. The standard deviation of cash flows for periods 1 and 2 are:

   $\theta(1) = \{0.10(5,000 - 4,000)^2 + 0.2(4,500 - 4,000)^2 + 0.10(3,000 - 4,000)^2 + 0.20(3,500 - 4,000)^2 + 0.40(4,000 - 4,000)^2\}^{\frac{1}{2}} = \$548$

   $\theta(2) = \{0.10(6,000 - 4,000)^2 + 0.10(2,000 - 4,000)^2 + 0.25(5,000 - 4,000)^2 + 0.25(3,000 - 4,000)^2 + 0.30(4,000 - 4,000)^2\}^2 = \$1,140$

   b. The standard deviation of the project assuming serial dependence of the cash flows between the various periods:

   $$\theta = \sqrt{\frac{((548)^2}{(1+0.10)^2} + \left(\frac{(1,140)^2}{(1+0.10)^4}\right)} = \$580.26$$

   c. Dependent cash flows

   $$\theta = \frac{((548)^2}{(1 + 0.10)^t} + \left(\frac{(1,140)^2}{(1 + 0.10)^4}\right) = \$1,440.33$$

7. *Replacement Decisions: Unequal Lives.*

   NPV(x) = Present value of first investment in x + present value of second investment in x.
   = {15,000(3.7980) -50,000} + {8882(0.8209)} = $11.123
   NPV(y) = {12,000(6.1446)- 60,000} = $13.735

Lathe Y should be chosen.

8. *Replacement Decisions: Equal Lives*

Worksheet for Replacement Analysis
Net Outflow at the Time the Investment Is Made t=0

	Amount Before Tax	Amount After Tax (net effect)	Year Event Occurs	PV at 10%	PV
1. Cost of the New Equipment	$30,000	$30,000	0	1.0	$30,000
2. Salvage Value of Old Equipment	($4,000)	($4,000)	0	1.0	($4,000)
3. Tax Effect of Sal of Old Equipment	($6,000)	($4,000)	0	1.0	($2,880)
4. Investment Tax Credit	($3,000)	($3,000)	0	1.0	($3,000)
5. Present value of costs					$20,120

9. Real and Money Discount Rates

1. At the nominal discount rate of 13.3 percent, the present value is computed as follows:

Period	Money Cash Flow	Nominal Present Value Factor	Present Value
1	$133	0.8826	$117.39
2	$133	0.7790	$103.61
3	$1,133	0.6876	$779.00
			$1,000.00

Net Present Value = $1,000 - $900 = 100

2. At the real discount rate, the present value is computed as follows:

Period	Money Cash Flow (1)	Price Level Relative (2)	Real Cash Flow (1)/(2)	Real Present Value Factor At 3%	Present Value
1	$113	1.100[A]	$120.91	0.9709	$117.39
2	$113	1.210[B]	$109.82	0.9426	$103.61
3	$1,113	1.331[C]	$851.24	0.9151	$779.00
					$1,000.00

Net present Value = $1,000 - $900 = $100
A = $1.00 × (1 + 0.10) = $1.10
B = $1.10 × (1 + 0.10) = $1.21
C = $1.21 × (1 + 0.10) = $1.33

CONCLUSION

Many capital budgeting techniques exist in the literature and in practice. The discounted cash flow methods take the time value of money into account to evaluate capital budgeting proposals. The two basic discounted cash flow methods are the internal rate of return and the net present value methods. Management should consider some of the conflicts between these two methods when choosing between them. Other problems in using capital budgeting techniques include problems with replacement decisions, problems with capital rationing, and problems with capital budgeting under certainty.

GLOSSARY

Accounting Rate of Return (ARR) Method. An evaluation process that used the ratio of the average annual profit after taxes to the investment of a project.

Annuity. An arrangement for a series of cash flows payable at fixed intervals as the result of an invest.

Capital Budgeting. Long-term planning for proposed capital outlays and their financing.

Capital Rationing. The process of placing constraints upon the acquisition or use of capital resources in: capital budgeting decision.

Cash Flow. The amount of cash receipts and disbursements over a specific period of time for a given segment of a firm.

Discounted Cash Flow (DCF) Method. An evaluation process that uses present value concepts to measure the profitability of a project.

Internal Rate of Return (IRR) Method. An evaluation process that computes the interest rate equating the present value of an investment's cash flows and the cost of the investment.

Net Present Value (NPV) Method. An evaluation process that computes the cost of an investment with the present value of the future cash flows of the investment at a selected rate of return, or hurdle rate.

Payback Method. An evaluation process that computes the number of years before the initial cash outlay of a project is fully recovered by its future cash inflows.

Present Value. The amount that should be paid for the right to receive a payment (or a series of payments in the future [at an assumed interest rate] if the payment is to be received after a specific period of time).

Risk. A measure of the probability that unforeseen occurrences will cause estimates to vary from projections.

Time value of Money. The ability of money to earn more money in the future.

SELECTED READINGS

Bailes, Jack C.; James F. Nielsen; and Steve Wendell. "Capital Budgeting in the Forest Products Industry." *Management Accounting* (July 1979), pp. 46-51, 57.

Bavishi, Vinod B. "Capital Budgeting Proactices at Multinationals." *Management Accounting* (August 1981), pp.32-35.

Bergeon, Pierre G. "The Other Dimensions of the Payback Period." *Cost and Management* (May 1978), pp. 35-39.

Doenges, R. Conrad. "The Reinvestment Problem in a Practical Perspective." *Financial Management* (Spring 1972), pp. 85-91.

Elliot, Grover S. "Analyzing the Cost of Capital." *Management Accounting* (December 1980), pp. 13-18.

Fremgen, James M. "Capital Budgeting Practices: A Survey." *Management Accounting* (May 1973), pp. 19-25.

Gaertner, James F., and Ken Milani. "The TRR Yardstick for Hospital Capital Expenditure Decisions." *Management Accounting* (December 1980), pp.25-33.

Glahn, Gerald L.; Kent T. Fields; and Jerry E. Trapnell. "How to Evaluate Mixed Rate Capital Projects." *Management Accounting* (December 1980), pp. 34-38.

Hendricks, James A. "capital Budgeting Decisions: NPV or IRR?" *Cost and Management* (March-April 1980), pp.16-20.

Hertz, David B. "Investment Policies that Pay Off." *Harvard Business Review* (January- February 1968), pp. 96-108.

Hertz, David B. "Risk Analysis in capital Investment." *Harvard Business Review* (January- February 1964), pp. 95-106.

Hillier, Fredrick. "The Deviation of Probabilistic Information for the Evaluation of Risky Investments." *Management Science* (April 1963), pp.443-457.

Hing-Ling, Amy, and Hong-Shiang Lau. "Improving Present value Analysis with a Programmable Calculator." *Management Accounting* (November 1979), pp. 52-57.

Johnson, Robert W. *Capital Budgeting* (Belmont, Calif.: Wadsworth Publishing, 1970).

Kim, Suk H., and Edward J., Parragher. "Current Capital Budgeting Practices." *Management Accounting* (June 1981), pp. 26-31.

Kim, Suk H. "Making the Long-Term Investment Decision." *Management Accounting* (March 1979), pp. 41-49.

Lemer, Eugene M., and Alfred Rappaport. "Limit DCF in Capital Budgeting." *Harvard Business review* (September-October 1968), pp. 133-139.

Norgaard, Corine T. "The Post-Completion Audit of Capital Projects." *Cost and Management* (January-February 1979), pp. 19-25.

Osteryoung, Jerome S. *Capital Budgeting: Long-term Asset Selection* (Columbus. Ohio: Grid, 1974).

Osteryoung, Jerome S.; Eiton Scott; and Gordon S. Roberts. "Selecting Capital Projects with the Coefficient of variation." *Financing management* (Summer 1977), pp. 65-70.

Pettway, Richard H. "Integer Programming in Capital Budgeting: A Note on Computational Experiemce." *Journal of Financial and Quantitative Analysis* (September 1973), pp.665-672.

Pugisi, D.J., and L. W. Chadwick. "Capital Budgeting with Realized Terminal Values." *Cost and Management* (May-June 1977), pp. 13-17.

Raiborn, D.D., and Thomas A. Rattcliffe. "Are You Accounting For Inflation in Your Capital Budgeting Process?" *Management Accounting* (September 1979), pp. 19-22.

Roemmich, Roger A.; Gordon L. Duke; and William H. Gates. "Maximizing the Present Value of Tax Savings from Depreciation." *Management Accounting* (September 1978), pp. 55-57, 63.

Sangeladji, Mohammad A. "True Rate of Return for Evaluating Capital Investments." *Management Accounting* (February 1979), pp. 24-27.

Suver, James D., and Bruce R. Neumann. "Capital Budgeting for Hospitals." *Management Accounting* (December 1978), pp. 48-50, 53.

Truitt, Jack F. "A Solution to Capital Budgeting Problems Concerning Investments with Different Lives." *Cost and Management* (November-December 1978), pp. 44-45.

Uhl, Franklin S. "Automated Capital Investment Decisions." *Management Accounting* (April 1980), pp. 41-46.

Weingartner, H. Martin. "Capital Budgeting of Interrelated Projects: Surveys and Synthesis." *Management Science* (March 1966), pp. 485-516.

William, H. Jean, "On Multiple Rates of Return." *Journal of Finance* (March 1968), pp. 187-191.

Chapter 4
Capital Budgeting For Multinational Firms

INTRODUCTION

Multinational companies rely on capital budgeting techniques for the evaluation of their direct foreign investment projects. The use of capital budgeting techniques is a direct consequence of their adoption of the stockholders' wealth maximization model as objective function.[1] Maximization of owners' wealth dictates the application of capital budgeting techniques in both the domestic and international contexts. There are specific problems, however, that may complicate capital budgeting for the multinational corporation. Accordingly this chapter examines the specific uses of capital budgeting techniques by multinational corporations in analyzing the financial benefits and costs of a potential investment. It also examines the problems associated with the management of political risks that can be faced when investing internationally.

FOREIGN DIRECT INVESTMENT

Multinational capital budgeting is a direct consequence of a foreign direct investment decision. Motives for direct foreign investment includes: (1) strategic motives, (2) behavioral motives, (3)economic motives.[2]

Strategic Motives

Strategic motives for foreign investment include the five following categories. [3]

1. *Market seekers,* who produce in foreign markets either to satisfy local demand or to export to markets other than local market.
2. *Raw material seekers,* who extract raw material whatever they can be formed, either for export or for further processing and sale in the host country.
3. *Production efficiency seekers,* who produce in countries where one or more of the factors of production are underpriced relative to their productivity.
4. *Knowledge seekers,* who invest in foreign countries to gain access to technology or managerial expertise.
5. *Political safety seekers,* who invest in countries that are considered unlikely to expropriate or interfere with their businesses. [4]

Behavior Motives

Behavioral motives are those arising from estimates and some auxiliary motives.[5] The four arising are:

1. An outside proposal provided it comes from a source that can not be easily ignored. The most frequent sources of such proposals are foreign governments, the distributors of the company's products, and its clients.
2. Fear of losing a market.
3. The "bandwagon" effect: very successful activities abroad of a competing firm in the same line business, or a general belief that investment in some area is "a must."
4. Strong competition from abroad in the home market.[6]

The four motives are:
1. Creation of a market for component and other products.
2. Utilization of old machinery.

3. Capitalization of know-how; spreading of research and development and other fixed costs.
4. Indirect return to a lost market through investment in a country that has commercial agreements with these lost territories.[7]

Economic Motives

Economic motives for direct foreign investment are generally based on the theory of imperfection of individual natural markets for products, factors of production, and financial assets. As argued by Eiteman et al.:[8]

1. Product and factor market imperfections provide an opportunity for multinational firms to outcompete local firms, particularly in industries characterized by worldwide oligopolistic competition, because the multinational firms have superiority in economies of scale, managerial expertise, technology, differentiated products, and financial strength.
2. Oligopolistic competition also motivates firms to make defensive investments abroad to save both export and home markets from foreign competition.
3. The product theory suggests that new products are first developed in the most advanced countries by large firms that have the ability to undertake research and development. The new products are introduced into the home market and later exported. As the product matures and the production process becomes standardized, foreign competition reduces profits and threatens the home market. Part of the production process is then defensively relocated abroad to take advantage of lower unit costs of labor or other factors of production.
4. Defensive direct foreign investment may also motivated by "follow-the-leader" behavior; a desire to establish credibility with local customers; a "grow-to-survive" philosophy; a desire to gain knowledge by acquiring firms with valuable expertise; and a need to follow the customer in the case of service firms.
5. The theory of internationalization holds that firms having a competitive advantage because of their ability to generate valuable propriety information can only capture the full benefits of innovation through direct foreign investment.

RISK ANALYSIS

Direct capital investment is not without specific risks that can affect the value and the feasibility of the project. The following list includes some of the risks that can be faced in the global economy.

1. A distortion of the value of the project may arise with the failure of distinguish between project and parent cash flows. A decision has to be made whether to analyze the capital budgeting decision from a project or a parent perspective.
2. Fluctuating exchange rates can also distort the value of the cash flows and the desirability of the project. Accurate forecasting of the exchange rates over the life of the project may be necessary for an accurate and reliable analysis of the capital budgeting decision.
3. Changes in the general price or specific price levels in the foreign country can also create a distortion in the capital budgeting decision if they are not accounted for. The inflation factor has to be incorporated in the analysis.
4. Various obstacles may be created by the foreign country to hinder the remittance of earnings to the parent firm. Examples of obstacles include fund blockages, exchange control appropriation, and various forms of foreign currency controls.
5. Other factors that can affect the remittance of funds to the parent company include tax laws and institutional factors as well as political factors.

Each of these risks needs to be accounted for in the analysis of a capital budgeting decision by multinational firms. The following questions need to be addressed:

- What level of confidence is present in the various elements of the cash flow forecast?
- For the elements involving the greatest degree of uncertainty, what will be the result of a large forecasting error?
- How sensitive is the value of the investment to the foreseeable risks?[9]

PROJECT VERSUS PARENT CASH FLOWS: THE ISSUES

Project cash flows and parent cash flows differ as a result of the various tax requirements and exchange controls that can affect the final amounts remitted to the parent company. Two schools of thought are instrumental in the choice of cash flows. One school of thought that discounts the effect of restriction on repatriation favors the use of the project cash flows in the capital budgeting analysis. Following this precept, the list of elements of projected return from an overseas industrial investment includes the following:

1. All income, operating and nonoperating, from the overseas operating unit, based in its demonstrated capacity to supply existing markets with its present management and excluding any impact of the merger of resources with those of the investing company.
2. Additional operating income of the overseas unit resulting from the merger of its own capabilities with those of the investing corporation.
3. Additional income from increased export sales resulting from the proposed investment action, including (a) additional export income at each U.S. operating the manufactures products related to those that will be produced overseas and (b) additional earnings from new export activity at the overseas operating unit resulting from it increased capabilities to sell beyond the boundaries of its traditional national markets.
4. Additional income from increased licensing opportunities shown both in the books of the affected U.S. units and the books of the overseas unit.
5. Additional income from importing technology, product design, or hardware from the overseas operating unit to U.S. operating units.
6. Income presently accruing from the investment but seriously and genuinely threatened by economic, political, or social change in an overseas region.[10]

A second position, derived from economic theory, is that the value of a project is determined by the net present value of future cash flows back to the investor. Therefore, the project cash flows that are or can be repatriated are included, since only accessible funds can be used to pay dividends and interest, amortize the firm's debt, and be reinvested.[11] in spite of the strong theoretical argument in favor of analyzing foreign projects from the viewpoint of the parent company, empirical evidence from survey of multinationals shows that firms are using project flows and rates of return as well as parent flows and rates of return. [12] In fact, a more recent survey showed that multinationals were almost evenly split among those that looked at cash flow solely from the parents' perspective, solely from the subsidiaries' perspective, and from both perspectives.[13] Those who viewed cash flow from the point of view of the subsidiary felt that the subsidiaries were separate businesses and should be viewed as such. Those who took the parent company's view argued that the investment was ultimately made from the parent company's stockholders. Finally, those who adopted both perspectives considered this the safest approach, providing two ways of making a final decision. One of the respondent treasures pit it as follows:

The project must first be evaluated on its chances of success locally. It must be profitable from the subsidiary's point of view. Then you step back and look at it from the parents' point of view. What cash flows are available to be reminded or otherwise used in another country? What's going to come back to the parent is the real issue. The project has to meet both tests to be acceptable.[14]

What appears from the above discussion is that the use of the parent company's view is compatible with the traditional view of net present value in capital budgeting, whereas the use of the project's view leads to a closer approximation of the effect on consolidated earnings per share.[15]

An operational differentiation between project cash flows and percent cash flow is as follows:

1. Cash flows generated by subsidiary
2. Corporate taxed paid to host government
3. After-tax cash flows to subsidiary
4. Retained earnings by subsidiary
5. Cash flows remitted by subsidiary
6. Withholding tax paid to host government
7. After-tax cash flows remitted by subsidiary
8. Exchange rate
9. Cash flows received by parent
10. Corporate taxes paid to local government
11. Cash flows receivable to parent

PROJECT VERSUS PARENT CASH FLOWS: AN EXAMPLE

To illustrate the differences the subsidiary perspective and the parent company perspective in multinational budgeting, consider the example of a Jordanian subsidiary and a U.S.-based multinational corporation considering the decision to invest in new equipment on the basis of the following information:

- The cost of investment is JD 39,100. The exchange rate is $2/JD.
- The cash flows for an estimated useful life of six years are respectively, JD 20,000, JD 14,000, JD 10,000, JD 6,000, JD 5,000, and JD 4,000.
- The required rate of return is 10 percent.
- The Jordanian government does not tax the earnings of the subsidiary, but requires a withholding tax of 10 percent on funds remitted to the parent company.
- The U.S. tax rate on foreign earnings of the subsidiary is 25 percent.
- The exchange rate of the Jordanian dinar is estimated to be $2.00 at the end of years 1 and 2, $1.80 at the end of years 3 and 4, and $1.50 at the end of years 5 and 6.

The capital budgeting from the project of subsidiary perspective is shown in Exhibit 4.1. The cumulative net present value (NPV) is JD 7,633; therefore, the project is acceptable from the subsidiary's point of view. The

Exhibit 4.1
Subsidiary Views of Foreign Direct Investment

	Year 1	Year 2	Year 3	Year 4	Year 5	Year 6
Cost of Investment JD 39,1000						
Cash Flows	JD 20,000	JD 14,000	JD 10,000	JD 6,000	JD 5,000	JD 4,000
Discount Factor 10%	0.909	0.826	0.753	0.683	0.621	0.564
PV of Cash Flows	JD 18,180	JD 11,564	JD 7,530	JD 4,098	JD 3,105	JD 2,256
Cumulative NPV	-JD 20,920	- JD 9,356	- JD 1,826	- JD 2,272	- JD 5,377	- JD 7,633

Exhibit 4.2
Capital Budgeting: Parent Company's Perspective

	Year 1	Year 2	Year 3	Year 4	Year 5	Year 6
Cost of Investment	$78,200					
Cash Flows	JD 20,000	JD 14,000	JD 10,000	JD 6,000	JD 5,000	JD 4,000
Withholding Tax (10%)	JD 2,000	JD 1,400	JD 1,000	JD 600	JD 500	JD 400
Funds Remitted	JD 18,000	JD 12,600	JD 9,000	JD 5,400	JD 4,500	JD 3,600
Exchange Rate	$2	$2	$1.80	$1.80	$1.50	$1.50
Funds to be Received	$36,000	$25,200	$16,200	$9,720	$6,750	$5,400
US Taxes Paid (25%)	$9,000	$6,300	$4,050	$2,430	$1,687.50	$1,350
After Tax Funds	$27,000	$18,900	$12,150	$7,290	$5,062.50	$4,050
Discounting Factor	0.909	0.826	0.753	0.683	0.621	0.564
PV of Cash Flows	$24,543	$15,611.40	$9,148.95	$4,979.07	$3,143.81	$2,284.20
	-	-	-	-	-	-
Cumulative NPV	-$53,657	$38,045.60	$28,896.65	$23,917.58	$20,773.77	$18,489.57

K = weighted average cost of capital
K_d = cost of debt
K_e = test of equity
T = tax rate
D = value of the firm's debt
E = value of the firm's equity
$V = D + E$ = total value of the firm.

capital budgeting from the parent's perspective is shown in Exhibit 4.2. The project appears profitable from the subsidiary's perspective, and unprofitable from the parent's perspective.

COST OF CAPITAL FOR THE MULTINATIONAL FIRM

In both the international rate-of-return method and the net present value method, a cost of "capital," or a "hurdle rate," is needed. The two rules of thumb are as follows:

1. The internal rate of return must be superior to the hurdle rate to be acceptable.
2. The present value, obtained by discounting cash flows at the hurdle rate, must be positive for a project to be acceptable.

For a multinational corporation, the overall cost of capital is the sum of the costs of each financing source, weighted by the proportion of that financing source in the firm's total capital structure. The weighted average cost of capital is therefore:

$$K = \frac{E}{V} \times K_e + \frac{D}{V} K_d (1 - t)$$

The cost of capital of a multinational corporation is assumed to be affected by a host of factors, including size of the firm, access to international capital markets, international diversification, tax concession, exchange risk, and country risk.[16] The larger the firm, the greater the access to international capital markets; the greater its international diversification, the more it capitalizes on tax concessions; the lower its exchange rate exposure, the lower the country risk and the lower the cost of capital to the multinational corporation (MNC).

A MULTINATIONAL CAPITAL BUDGETING EXAMPLE

Theoretically the capital budgeting process for a MNC involves the following phases:

1. The identification of cash flows generated by the proposed project.
2. The identification of cash flows available for repatriation to the MNC.
3. The concession of cash flows by means of exchange rates.
4. The adjustments to compensate for financial risks, including sensitivity analysis.
5. The selection of a minimum rate of return.
6. The calculation of investment profitability, including sensitivity analysis.
7. The acceptance or rejection of the proposed investment.[17]

The input of multinational capital budgeting decisions are:

a. Initial investment
b. Consumer demand
c. Price
d. Variable cost
e. Fixed cost
f. Project lifetime
g. Salvage (liquidation) value
h. Fund-transfer restriction
i. Exchange rates
j. Required rate of return[18]

The net present value (NPV) method, is used, based on line on the following formulas:

$$NPV = -IC + \sum_{t=1}^{n} \frac{CF_t}{(1+K)^t} + \frac{SV_n}{(1+K)^n}$$

where

IC = Initial cost of the investment
CF_t = Cash low in period t
SV_n = Salvage value
K   = Required rate of return on the project
N   = Lifetime rate of return on the project

If the internal rate of return is used, the equation would be:

$$0 = -IC + \sum_{t=1}^{n} \frac{CF_t}{(1+r)^t} + \frac{SV_n}{(1+r)^n}$$

where

r = internal rate of return

An illustration concerns the case of Computer Inc., a U.S.-based manufacturer that is considering exporting its PCs to Denmark. The decision was made to create a Danish subsidiary that will manufacture and sell the PCs in Europe.

1. *Revenue information:* The forecast price and sales of the PCs were as follows:

Year	Price per PC	Sales in Denmark and Europe
1	Krone 600	5,000,000 units
2	Krone 700	6,000,000 units
3	Krone 000	0,000,000 units

2. *Initial investment:* The parent company intends to invest a total of $200,000,000.
3. *Variable costs per unit* are estimated as follows:

Year	Variable Cost per Unit
1	Krone 100
2	Krone 120
3	Krone 150

4. Fixed expenses are estimated to be KR 1,100,000,000 per year for he first three years.
5. Noncash expenses including depreciation expenses are estimated to be KR 200,000,000 per year.
6. Most government taxes include a 20 percent tax on earning and a 10 percent tax on remittances to parent. The subsidiary intends to remit 50 percent of net cash flow to the parent company.
7. Exchange rates are estimated to be as follows:

Year	Exchange Rates of Krone
1	$0.15
2	$0.17
3	$0.20

8. Requires rate of return for the project is 10 percent.

The capital budgeting analysis is shown in Exhibit 4.3. This shows that for the first three years considered, the project has a cumulative positive cash flow in year 3 of $219,010,514 The decision should be to accept the project.

CAPITAL BUDGETING ISSUES FOR MULTINATIONALS

Capital Budgeting under Inflation

Changes in the general price level can create a distortion in the capital budgeting analysis of multinationals. A specific consideration of the impact of inflation on the analysis is warranted. The correct approach includes either using a money discount rate to discount money cash flows, or using a real discount rate to discount reach cash flows. Money cash flows are cash flows measured in dollars from various periods having different purchasing power. Real cash flows are cash flows measured in dollars having the same purchasing power. The real cash flow for a given year t expressed in terms of dollars of 0 (the base year) is equal to the money cash flow for that year t multiplied by the wing ratio:

$$\frac{\text{Price level index in year 0}}{\text{Price level index for year 1}}$$

For example, if an investment promised a money return of $100 for the three years and the price index for years 0 through 3 is 100.0, 110.0, 121.0, and 133.1, respectively, the real cash flows are as follows:

$$\text{Year 1:} \$100 \times 100/110 = 90.90$$
$$\text{Year 2:} \$100 \times 100/121 = 82.64$$
$$\text{Year 3:} \$100 \times 100/133.1 = 75.13$$

The money discount rate r can also be computed. Assuming that f is the annual rate of inflation, I is the real discount rate, and the decision maker is in the zero bracket, then

$$r = (1+f)(1+i) - 1$$
$$\text{or}$$
$$r = i + f + if$$

For example, if the real return before taxes is 3 percent, the rate of inflation is 10 percent, and the nominal

Exhibit 4.3
Capital Budgeting Analysis: Computer Inc.

	Year 0	Year 1	Year 2	Year 3
1. Sales in Units		5,000,000	6,000,000	8,000,000
2. Price per Unit		KR600	KR700	KR800
3. Total Sale = (1) x (2)		KR3,000,000,000	KR4,200,000,000	KR6,400,000
4. Variable Cost		KR100	KR120	KR150
5. Total Variable Cost Per Unit		KR500,000,000	KR720,000,000	KR1,200,000,000
6. Fixed Cost		KR1,100,000,000	KR1,100,000,000	KR1,100,000,000
7. Noncash Expense		KR200,000,000		KR200,000,000
8. Total Expense = (5) + (6) + (7),		KR1,800,000,000	KR2,020,000,000	KR2,500,000,000
9. Before Tax Subsidiary Earnings = (3) - (8)		KR1,200,000,000	KR2,180,000,000	KR3,900,000,000
10. Danish Government Tax(20%)		KR240,000,000	KR436,000,000	KR780,000,000
11. After Tax Subsidiary Earnings		KR960,000,000	KR1,744,000,000	KR3,120,000,000
12. Net Cash Flow to Subsidiary (11) + (7)		KR1,160,000,000	KR1,944,000,000	KR3,320,000,000
13. Remittance by Subsidiary		KR580,000,000	KR972,000,000	KR1,660,000,000
14. Withholding Tax (10%)		KR58,000,000		KR166,000,000
15. Net Remittance by Subsidiary		KR522,000,000	KR874,800,000	KR1,494,000,000
16. Exchange Rate of Danish Krone		$0.15	$0.17	$0
17. Cash Flow to Parent		$78,300,000.00	$147,716,000.00	$298,800,000.00
18. PV of Parent Cash Flows at (1090)		$71,174,700.00	$122,839,416.00	$224,996,400
19. Initial Investment	$200,000,000.00		-	
20. Cumulative NPV of Cash Flows		$128,825,300.00	-$5,985,884.00	$219,010,516.00

discount rate is 10 percent, the nominal discount rate is:

$$0.03 + 0.10 + 0.003 = 0.133$$

To illustrate the correct analysis under inflation, assume the same data as in the previous example. The correct analysis can be either of two procedures. The first analysis discounts money cash flows using a money discount rate. The present value of the investment will be computed as follows:

Period	Money Cash Flow	Nominal Present Factor at 13.3%	Present Value
1	100	0.8826	88.26
2	100	0.7792	77.92
3	100	0.6874	68.74
			234.92

The second analysis discounts the real cash flows using a real discount rate. The present value of the investment will give the same present value as follows:

Period	Money Cash Flow	Nominal Present Factor at 13.3%	Present Value
1	90.9	0.9709	88.254
2	82.64	39426	77.896
3	75.13	0.9151	68.751
			234.901

Assuming a marginal tax rate t on nominal income, the nominal discount rate will be computed as follows:

$$1 + (1 - t)r = (1 + f) + 1 + i(1 - t)$$
$$\text{or}$$
$$r = i + if + f/(1 - t)$$

Assuming the tax rate to be 30 percent, the nominal rate is then computed as follows:

$$r = 0.03 + (0.03 \times 0.10) + 0.10/(1 - 0.30) = 0.1758$$

In other words, a nominal rate of 17.58 percent is needed for an investor in a 30 percent tax bracket and facing an inflation rate of 10 percent to earn a real discount rate of 3 percent.

Impact of Exchange Rate Changes

Capital budgeting for multinational corporations can lead to different results depending on the nature of the expectation of the levels of exchange rates. In general, three scenarios are possible: (1) a stable exchange rate, (2) a strong exchange rate characterized by increasing values over the life of the project, and (3) a weak exchange rate by decreasing values over the life of the project. Exhibit 4.4 to 4.6 illustrate the impact of each of these three scenarios on the cumulative NPV of cash flows of a capital project by the Jordanian subsidiary of an American multinational corporation. The NPVs of the project are $43,610 under a strong rate scenario, $24,210 under a stable rate scenario, and $14,400 under a weak rate scenario. The large differences between these scenarios points to the importance of exchange rate fluctuations in multinational capital budgeting and also the importance of accurate exchange rate forecasting.

Foreign Tax Regulations

The tax regulations in the country where the project is planned are extremely important to the capital budgeting analysis. The first reason concerns the requirements of using tax cash flows for the capital budgeting decisions as well as a tax-adjusted project cost of capital. The second reason is that countries levy different income tax rates on the earnings of subsidiaries as well as remittance taxes when they are finally remitted to the parent company. The percentage of the profit that can be remitted can also be the subject of regulations that attempt to limit the amount of funds leaving the country, especially in case of the developing countries. Some countries, in fact, may require that a certain percentage of the profit be reinvested in specific areas of importance to the economic and social growth of the country.

Political and Economic Risk

Multinational companies face the risks created by political, exchange, and economic changes. Tis chapter covers some of the techniques used to manage political and economic risks. In a capital budgeting context, various ways may be used to account for political risks. One is to adjust each year's cash flows by the cost of an exchange risk adjustment. Other ways include shortening the minimum payback period, raising the discount rate or required rate of return without adjusting cash flows, and adjusting cash flows and raising the discount rate. A consensus seems to suggest that multinationals should use either the risk-adjusted discount rate or the certainty-equivalent approach to adjust proper estimates for political risk.[19]

Risk-Adjusted Discount Rate Method

One of the techniques for incorporating risk in the evaluation process is the risk-adjusted discount rate, which involves manipulating the discount rate applied to the cash flows to reflect the amount of risk inherent in a project. The higher the risk associated with a project, the higher the discount rate applied to cash flows. If a given project is perceived to be twice as risky as most projects acceptable to the firm and the cost of capital is 12 percent, the correct adjusted discount rate is 24 percent.

Certainty-Equivalent Method

Another technique for incorporating risk in the evaluation process is the certainty-equivalent method, which involved adjusting the future cash flows so that a project can be evaluated on a riskless basis. The adjustment is formulated as follows:

$$NPV = \sum_{t=0}^{n} \frac{\alpha_t CF_t}{(1 + R_F)^t} - I_0$$

where

α = Risk coefficient applied to the cash flow of period t (CF_t)

Exhibit 4.4
Capital Budgeting Analysis under a Strong Rate Scenario*

	Year 1	Year 2	Year 3	Year 4	Year 5	Year 6
Funds Remitted After Withholding Taxes	JD 20,000	JD 20,000	JD 20,000	JD 20,000	JD 20,000	JD 20,000
Exchange Rate	$2.00	$2.10	$2.20	$2.30	$2.40	$2.50
Cash Flow to the Parent	$40,000	$42,000	$44,000	$46,000	$48,000	$50,000
Discount Rate	0.909	0.826	0.753	0.683	0.621	0.564
PV of Cash Flows	$36,360	$34,692	$33,132	$31,418	$29,808	$28,200
Cumulative NPV of Cash Flows	-$113,640	-$78,948	-$45,816	-$14,398	$15,410	$43,610

*Initial investment by the parent: $150,000.

82

Capital Budgeting Analysis under a Stable Rate Scenario*

	Year 1	Year 2	Year 3	Year 4	Year 5	Year 6
Funds Remitted After Withholding Taxes	JD 20,000	JD 20,000	JD 20,000	JD 20,000	JD 20,000	JD 20,000
Exchange Rate	$2.00	$2.00	$2.00	$2.00	$2.00	$2.00
Cash Flow to the Parent	$40,000	$40,000	$40,000	$40,000	$40,000	$40,000
Discount Rate	0.909	0.826	0.753	0.683	0.621	0.564
PV of Cash Flows	$36,360	$33,040	$30,120	$27,320	$24,540	$22,560
Cumulative NPV of Cash Flows	-$113,640	-$80,600	-$50,480	-$23,160	$1,680	$24,240

*Initial investment by the parent: $150,000.

Exhibit 4.6
Capital Budgeting Analysis under a Weak Rate Scenario*

	Year 1	Year 2	Year 3	Year 4	Year 5	Year 6
Funds Remitted After Withholding Taxes	JD 20,000	JD 20,000	JD 20,000	JD 20,000	JD 20,000	JD 20,000
Exchange Rate	$2.00	$1.80	$1.60	$1.40	$1.20	$1.00
Cash Flow to the Parent	$40,000	$36,000	$32,000	$28,000	$24,000	$20,000
Discount Rate	0.909	0.826	0.753	0.683	0.621	0.564
PV of Cash Flows	$36,360	$29,736	$24,096	$19,124	$14,904	$11,280
Cumulative NPV of Cash Flows	-$113,640	-$83,904	-$59,808	-$40,684	-$95,780	-$14,500

*Initial investment by the parent: $150,000.

I_0 = Initial cost of the project
R_F = Risk-free rate

As the formula shows, the method multiplies the future cash flows by certainty equivalents to obtain a riskless cash flow. Note also that the discount rate used is R_F is a risk-free of interest.
To illustrate the certainty:

I_0 = Initial cost = $30,000
CF_1 = cash flow, year 1 = $10,000
CF_2 = cash flow, year 2 = $20,000
CF_3 = cash flow, year 3 = $30,000

α_1 = certainty equivalent, year 1 = 0.9
α_2 = certainty equivalent, year 2 = 0.8
α_3 = certainty equivalent, year 3 = 0.6

The NPV of the investment using a risk-free discount rate of 6 percent is computed as in Exhibit 4.7.
Since the NPV is positive, the investment should be considered acceptable. The main advantage of the certainty-equivalent method is that it allows the assignment for a different risk factor of each cash flow, given that risk can be concentrated in one or more periods.
The certainty-equivalent method and the risk-adjusted discount rate method are comparable methods of evaluating risk. To produce similar ranking, the following equation most hold:

$$\frac{\alpha_t CF_t}{(1+R_F)^t} = \frac{CF_t}{(1+R_A)^t}$$

where

α_t = Risk coefficient used in the certainty-equivalent method
R_F = Risk-free discount rate
R_A = Discount rate used in the risk adjusted discount rate method
CF_t = Future cash flow.

Solving for t yields:

$$\alpha = \frac{(1+R_F)^t}{(1+R_A)^t}$$

Given that R_A and R_F are constant and $R_A < R_F$ then αt decreases over time, which means that risk increases over time. To illustrate, assume that in the previous example R_A= 15 percent. Then

$$\alpha_1 = \frac{(1+R_F)^1}{(1+R_A)^1} + \frac{(1+0.006)^1}{(1+0.15)^1} = 0.921$$
$$\alpha_2 = \frac{(1+R_F)^2}{(1+R_A)^2} + \frac{(1+0.006)^2}{(1+0.15)^2} = 0.848$$
$$\alpha_3 = \frac{(1+R_F)^3}{(1+R_A)^3} + \frac{(1+0.006)^3}{(1+0.15)^3} = 0.783$$

In many cases this assumption of increasing risk may not be realistic.

Expropriation

Multinational companies sometimes face the extreme outcome of political risk expropriation. One way to account for expropriation is to charge a premium for political risk insurance to each year's cash flow, whether or not such insurance is actually purchased. Another way, suggested by Shapiro, is to examine the impact of expropriation on the project's present value to the parent company. As a result, the old and new present values will be

$$\text{Old present value} = -C_0 + \sum_{t=1}^{n} \frac{X_t}{(1+k)^t}$$

$$\text{New present value} = -C_0 + \sum_{t=1}^{n} \frac{X_t}{(1+k)^t} + \frac{G_h}{(1+k)^t}$$

where

C_0 = initial investment outlay
X_t = Parent's expected after-tax cash flow from the project in year t
n = Life of the project
k = Project cost of capital
h = Year in which expropriation takes place
G_h = Expected value of the net compensation provided.

The compensation (G_h) is supposed to come from one of the following sources:

1. Direct compensation paid to the firm by the local government.
2. Indirect compensation, such as other business contracts to the firm expropriated (an example would be the management contracts received by oil companies after the Venezuelan government nationalized their properties).
3. Payment received from political insurance.
4. Tax deductions received after the parent declares the expropriation as an extraordinary loss.
5. A reduction in the amount of capital that must be repaid by the project equal to the unamortized portion of any local borrowing.

Blocked Funds

Multinationals sometimes face the situation in which funds are blocked for various reasons, including forms of exchange control. Again, Shapiro suggested raising the present value expression to include the impact of blocked funds on the project's cash flows. As a result, the old and new present values will be

$$\text{Old present value} = -C_0 + \sum_{t=1}^{n} \frac{X_t}{(1+k)^t}$$

Exhibit 4.7
Using a Risk-Free
Discount Rate

Period	Cash Flow (CF1)	Risk Coefficient	Certainty Equivalent	Risk Free Rate (RF)	Present Value
1	$10,000	0.9	$9,000	0.943	$8,487
2	$20,000	0.8	$16,000	0.89	$14,420
3	$30,000	0.6	$18,000	0.84	$15,120
Present Value Cash Flows					$37,847
Initial Investment					$30,000
Net Present Value					$7,847

New present value

$$= -C_0 + \sum_{t=1}^{n} \frac{X_t}{(1+k)^t} + \sum_{t=j}^{n} \frac{Y_t}{(1+k)^t}$$

$$+ (1-\alpha_j) \sum_{t=j}^{n} \frac{(X-Y_t)}{(1+k)^t} + \alpha_j \sum_{t=j}^{n} \frac{(X-Y_t)}{(1+r)^{n-1}}$$

where the symbols C_0, X_t, n, and k are as in the formulas used for expropriation. The new symbols are

j = Year in which funds become blocked
n = Year in which exchange controls are removed
α_j = Probability of exchange controls in year 1 and 0 in other years
Y_t = Units of currency that can be repatriated when exchange costs do exist.

Uncertain Salvage Value

When the salvage value may be uncertain, Madura suggested the estimation of a break-even salvage value or break-even terminal value, the salvage value for which NPV = 0. The break-even salvage value is estimated by setting the net present value equal to zero as follows:

$$\text{NPV} = -\text{OI} + \sum_{t=1}^{n} \frac{CF_t}{(1+r)^t} + \frac{SV_n}{(1+z)^n}$$

$$0 = -\text{OI} + \sum_{t=1}^{n} \frac{CF_t}{(1+r)^t} + \frac{SV_n}{(1+z)^n}$$

$$SV_n = \left[OI - \sum_{t=1}^{n} \frac{CF_t}{(1+r)^t} \right] (1+z)^n$$

where

NPV = Net present value
0 = Zero
SV_n = Salvage value
OI = Original investment
CF_t = Cash flow at time t
r = Desired rate of return.[20]

EVALUATION OF INTERNATIONAL ACQUISITIONS

Foreign mergers and acquisitions are on the increase, particularly in the United States, owing to the resulting wealth effects. The reasons for foreign investment in the United States including the following.[21]

1. Dollar devaluation effect expressed as a documented inverse relation between the exchange rate of the U.S. dollar and the level of foreign investment in the United States.[22]
2. Favorable tax treatment for foreign buyers because overseas firms that acquire American companies may have the ability to deduct interest on acquisition debt both in the United States and in their home countries, through, for example, the creation of a third-country subsidiary to finance the deal when this tax treatment of such units is favorable.[23] A description of a typical plan follows:

A typical plan would have the foreign acquired borrow 100 percent of the acquisition cost and establish two subsidiaries, a US acquisition subsidiary and a finance subsidiary in a third country. The foreign acquirer injects a fraction of the borrowed funds as equity into its third country finance subsidiary. The third-country finance subsidiary then would loan all of its funds to its brother/sister company, the US acquisition subsidiary. The foreign acquirer deducts interest expense on acquisition debt and receives an income tax benefit on its own operation from its home country. Meanwhile, the bulk of the borrowed funds are loaned by the third-country finance subsidiary, which deducts the interest expense on the debt against the income of the acquired operations and receives a US tax benefit. If the interest income that the third-country finance subsidiary receives from the US acquisition subsidiary does not trigger significant taxation in the form of US with-holding tax, income taxation by the host country of the finance subsidiary or income taxation for the foreign parent, an extra tax benefit for the acquisition interest expense has been achieved.[24]

3. Goodwill accounting treatment because foreign companies create acquired goodwill through their choice of acquisition accounting:

In deciding how high to bid, foreign companies do not have to worry about penalizing future profits. They can write off goodwill immediately against their balance sheet reserves; this shrinks the balance sheet but profits are unaffected. If acquired goodwill is left on the balance sheet as is done in United States (and Canada), companies must then amortize it from profit over forty years; reported profits are reduced by the amortization charge each year for as many years as it takes to eliminate the acquired goodwill from the balance sheet altogether. [25]

The evaluation of international acquisition is similar to a capital budgeting problem. The decision is to determine if the net present value of a company from the acquiring firm's perspective (NPV$_a$) is positive. It may be computed as follows:

$$NPV_a = -(IO_f)SP_{-t} + \sum_{t=1}^{n} \frac{(CF_{f,t})(SP_t)}{(1+r)^t} + \frac{SV_f SP_n}{(1+r)^n}$$

where

NPV$_n$ = Net present value of a foreign takeover prospect
IO$_f$ = Acquisition price in foreign currency
SP   = Spot rate of the foreign currency
CF$_{f,t}$ = Foreign currency cash flows per period to be remitted
r = Required rate of return on the acquisition of the company
SV$_f$ = Salvage value in foreign-currency units
n = Time at which the company will be sold.[26]

MANAGING POLITICAL RISK

Capital budgeting decisions as well as other operating, financing, and distribution decisions taken by multinational forms need to take into account the impact of political risk on the potential outcomes of these decisions: There is objective need for a definition of the nature of political risk, methods for forecasting it, and a role for management accounting in the management of this political risk.

Nature of Political Risk

Political risk is a phenomenon that characterizes an unfriendly human climate in both developed and developing countries. A high crime rate, or an upsurge of violent unrest, even in highly developed countries qualifies such countries for the dubious title of "political risk." Political risk essentially refers to the potential economic losses arising as a result of governmental measures or special situations that may either limit or prohibit the multinational activities of a firm. Examples of these situations include those (1) when discontinuities occur in the business environment, (2) when they are difficult to anticipate, and (3) when they result from political change.

Political risk can affect all foreign firms; in such a case it is *macropolitical risk.* It may, however, affect only selected foreign firms or industries, or foreign firms with specific characteristics. In such a case it is *micropolitical risk.* In both cases the risk refers to "that uncertainty stemming from unanticipated and unexpected acts of governments or other organizations which may cause a loss to the business firm."[27] It is manifest through a climate of uncertainty dominated by a probable loss to the business enterprise. It may arise from different sources. Root noted that a wide spectrum of political risks may be generated "by the attitudes, policies and overt behavior of those governments and other local power renters such as rival political, parties, labor unions, and nationalistic groups."[28] A study prepared for the Financial Executives research Foundation identified the following twelve political risk factors:

- radical change in government composition or policy;
- expropriation;
- nationalization;
- attitude of opposition groups;
- probability of opposition-group takeover,
- attitude toward foreign investment;
- quality of government management;
- ownership requirements;
- anti-private-sector influence;
- labor instability
- relationship with the company's home government;
- relationship with neighboring countries.[29]

Political risk may lead to various outcomes, namely expropriation/nationalization, compulsory local equity participation, operational restrictions, discrimination, price controls, blockage of remittances, and breach of government contracts. Given the negative impacts of the outcomes of political risk on foreign operations, especially in the extreme case in which a government takes over a business activity through confiscation and expropriation, there is a strong need to be able to forecast political risk.

How to forecast Political Risk

It would not be surprising to learn that various proposals have been made about how to forecast political risks; Robock and Simmonds suggested an evaluation of the vulnerability of a company to political risk by an analysis of its operations, with the following questions in mind:

- Are periodic external inputs of new technology required?
- Will the project be competing strongly with local nationals who are in, or trying to enter, the same field?
- Is the operation dependent on natural resources, particularly minerals or oil?
- Does the investment put pressure on the country's balance of payments?
- Does the enterprise have a strong monopoly position in the local market?
- Is the product socially essential and acceptable?[30]

Robert Stobaugh noticed that a number of U.S.-based multinational enterprises had developed scales with which to rate countries on the basis of their investment climates.[31] An *Argus Capital Market Report* offered for country risk analysis a laundry of economic indicators to "educate the decision-maker and force him to think in term of the relevant economic fundamental."[32] These indicators are monetary base, domestic base, foreign reserves, purchasing power parity index, currency/deposit ratio, consumer prices as a percentage change, balance of payments, goods and services as a percentage of foreign reserves, percentage change exports/percentage change imports, exports as a percentage of the GNP, imports as a percentage of the GNP, foreign factor income payments as a percentage of the GNP, average tax rate, government deficit as a percentage of the GNP, government expenditures, real GNP as a percentage change, and real per capita GNP as a percentage change.

Shapiro offered the following common characteristics of country risk:

1. A large government deficit relative to GDP.
2. A high rate if money expansion if it is combined with a relatively fixed exchange rate.
3. High leverage combined with highly variable terms of trade.
4. Substantial government expenditures yielding low rates of return.
5. Price controls, interest rate ceilings, trade restriction, and other government-imposed barriers to the smooth adjustment of the economy to changing relative price.
6. A citizenry that demands, and a political system that accepts, government responsibility for maintaining and expanding the nation's standard of living through public sector spending. The less stable the political system, the more important this factor is likely to be. [33]

More recently, Rummel and Heenan provided a four-way classification of attempts to forecast political interference: "grand tours," "old hands," Delphi techniques, and quantitative method.[34] A "grand tour" involves a visit of the potential host country by an executive or a team of people for an inspection tour and later to the home office. Superficiality and overdose of selective information have marred the grand tour technique.

The "old hands" technique involves acquiring area expertise from seasoned educators, diplomats, journalists, or businesspeople. Evidently, too much implicit faith is put in the judgment of these so-called experts.

The Delphi techniques may be used to survey a knowledgeable group. First, selective elements influencing the political climate are chosen. Next, experts are asked to rank these factors toward the development of an overall measure or index of political risk. Finally, countries are ranked on the basis of the index. As stated by Rummel and Heenan, the "strength of the Delphi technique rests on the posing of relevant questions. When they are defective, the entire structure crumbles. "[35]

The quantitative methods technique involves developing elaborate models using multivariate analysis to either explain and describe underlying relationships affecting a station-state, or to predict future political events. Two such political risk models using this technique may be identified and are examined next.

The Knudsen "Ecological" Approach

Harold Knudsen's model involves gathering socioeconomic data depicting the "ecological structures" or investment climate of a particular foreign environment to be used to predict political behavior in general and the national propensity to expropriate in particular.[36] (The model is shown in Exhibit 4.8.) The model maintains that national propensity expropriate may be explained by "a national frustration" factor and "scapegoat of foreign investment." Basically, if the level of national frustration is high and at the time the level of foreign investment presence is also high, these foreign investments become a scapegoat, leading to a high propensity to expropriate. The level of frustration is envisaged as the difference between the level of aspirations and the level of welfare expectations. The scapegoat of foreign investment is determined by the perceived general and special role of foreign investment.

The variables are measured as follows. First, national aspirations may be measured by six proxy variables, namely degree of urbanization, literacy rate, number of newspapers, number of radios, degree of labor unionization, and the national endowment of national resources. Second, the welfare of people may be measured by proxy variables, namely infant survival rate, caloric consumption, number of doctors per population size, number of hospital beds per population size, percentage of housing with piped water supply, and per capita gross national product. Third, national expectations may be measured by the percentage change in per capita gross national product and the percentage of gross national product being invested. These are surrogate measures of the underlying factors in Knudsen's model. The model's reliability may be improved by a search for more relevant measures by subjecting a bigger selection of these surrogate measures to factors analysis. Such an analysis used in a confirmatory way may reduce their number to only the salient measure. But more research, especially in the management accounting field, may be needed to improve and test Knudsen's model or similar "components-based" models of predicting political risk.

The Haendel-West-Meadow "Political System Stability Index"

Another components approach to the forecasting of political risk was provided by Haendel, West, and Meadow in an empirical, indicator-based measure of political system stability, the Political System Stability Index (PSSI), in sixty-five developing countries.[37] It is composed of three equally weighted indices: the socioeconomic index, the governmental process index, and the societal conflict index, which is itself derived from three subindices on public unrest, internal violence, and coercion potential. All of these indices are derived from fifteen indirect measures of the political system: stability and adaptability. Basically, the higher the PSSI score, the greater the stability of the political system. The index was based on data from the 1961-66 period. There is a need to test the validity of the index with more recent data before using it as a forecasting tool. In any case, the model demonstrates again the feasibility of the components approach to the study of political risk. As stated by Haendel, the Political System Stability Index derives its importance from the role the political system plays in establishing power relationships and norms for resolving conflicts in society. It assumes that the degree of political stability in a country may indicate the society's capacity to cope with a new demands.[38]

The Belkaoui and Belkaoui's Determinants of Political Risk Model

Exhibit 4.8
The National Propensity to Expropriate Model

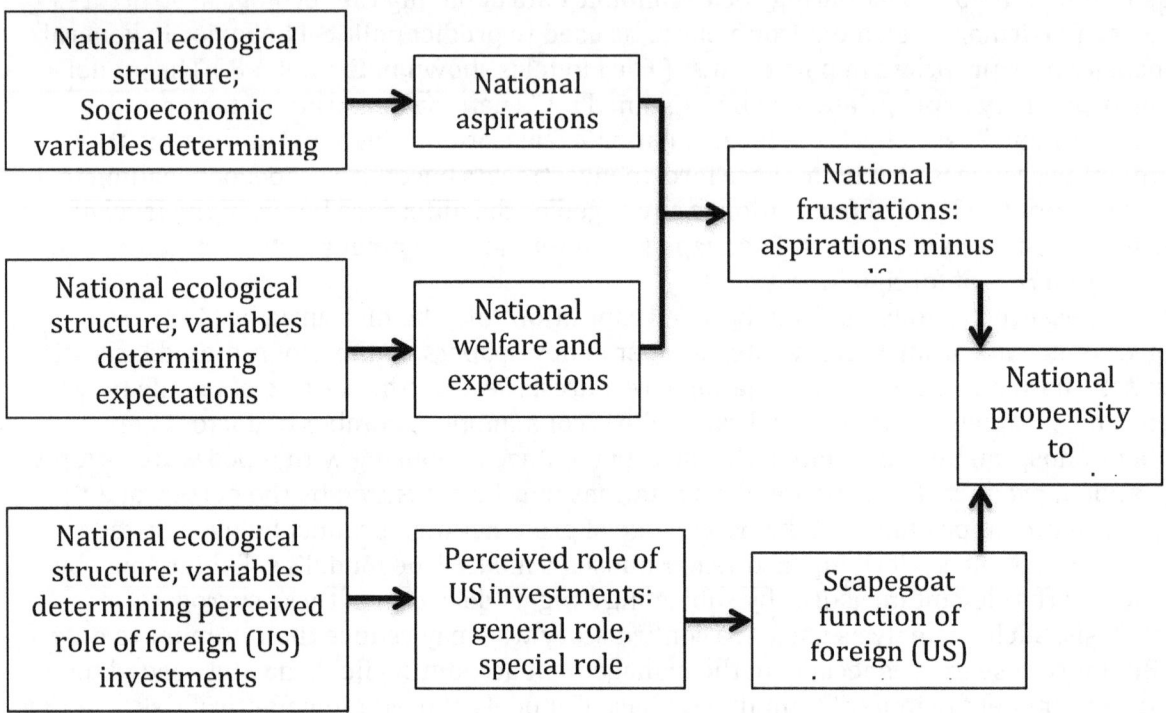

Belkaoui and Belkaoui developed a model for the specification and prediction of political risk (PR).[39] The dependent variable used is the political risk component of the ICRG (International Country Risk Guide). The independent variables are:

1. The United Nations Human Development Index (HDI).
2. The gross domestic saving as a percentage of gross domestic product.
3. The labor force as a percentage of total population (LFTP).
4. The terms of trade (TOT).
5. The total expenditures in educational and health as a percentage of gross domestic product (TEEHG).
6. The military expenditures as a percentage of gross national product (MEG).

The model is as follows:
PR = -10.281 + 63.103 HDI + 0.561 GDSP + 0.435 LETP
    -0.154 TOT + 1.105 TEEHG – 1.120 MEG

Basically, the higher the political risk, the lower the human development index, the lower the labor force as a percentage of the total population, the lower the gross domestic saving as a percentage of gross domestic product, and the lower the total expenditures in educational and health as a percentage of gross domestic product. Similarly, the higher the political risk, the higher the terms of trade, and the higher the military expenditures as a percentage of gross national product. This model is better explicated in the next chapter.

Coping with Political Risk

Forecasting political risk is not enough; the problem is how to cope and live with it and how to minimize it. Various techniques have been proposed for minimizing it. Eiteman and Stonehill suggested the following three categories of techniques for dealing with political risk:

1. Negotiating the environment before investment by concluding concession agreements, adaptation to host country goals, planned investment, and investment guarantees.
2. Implementing specific operating strategies after the investment decision in production, logistics, marketing, finance, organization, and personnel. For example, local zoning, a safe location of facilities, and control of transportation and of patents and processes are examples of operating strategies in production and logistics that may reduce the likelihood of political interference or expropriation.
3. Restoring to specific compensation strategies after expropriation, including rational negotiation, application of power tactics to bargaining legal remedies, use of the International Center for Settlement of Investment Disputes, and surrenders in the interest of seeking salvage.[40]

Another way of coping with political risk is to negotiate a tight investment agreement that spells out the specific rights and responsibilities of both the foreign firm and the host government. Eiteman and Stonehill suggested that the investment agreement spell out, among other things, the following policies on financial and managerial issues:

- The basis of which fund flows, such as dividends, management fees, and loan repayments, may be remitted.
- The basis for setting any applicable transfer prices.
- The right to export to third-country markets.
- Obligations to build, or fund, social and economic overhead projects, such as schools, hospitals, and retirement systems.
- Methods of taxation, including the rate, the type of taxation, and how the rate base is determined.
- Access to host country capital markets, particularly for long-term borrowing.

- Permission for 100 percent foreign ownership versus required local ownership (joint venture) participation.
- Price controls, if any, applicable to sales in the host country markets.
- Requirements for local sourcing versus import of raw materials and components.
- Permission to use expatriate managerial and technical personnel.
- Provision for arbitration of disputes.[41]

Haendel classified, appropriately, the traditional tools of risk management into five general categories:

1. Avoidance, whereby the risk manager may recommend not investing or diversifying or else impose a ceiling on the exposure a firm allows country.
2. Transfer, whereby the risk manager may recommend including local individuals as either investor or managers.
3. Diversification and loss prevention, whereby the risk manager may recommend diversifying to reduce the reliance on a production facility of natural resource supply in any one country.
4. Insurance, whereby the risk manager may recommend that the firm secures insurance against political risk as a way of shielding the firm's assets from unexpected losses. This may even include self-insurance in the form of a separate fund.
5. Retention, whereby the risk manager may recommend that not all political risks can be avoided, transferred, diversified, or insured against. In such a case the firm should include political risk analysis in its decision-making process.[42]

The question remains to know what the multinationals actually do to cope with political risk. A study prepared for the Financial Executives Research Foundation found a number of techniques that could be used both before the investment and when operating overseas.[43] The techniques found to be most useful by participant firms in their preinvestment negotiations with local business, once investment had been made and the firms were committed, were maximizing the use of local debt and local funding, adapting to changing governmental priorities, sourcing locally to stimulate the economy and to reduce dependence on imports, and increasing exports. Besides using those techniques, the respondent firms admitted to insuring against the losses that might be caused by expropriation/confiscation, nationalization, foreign exchange inconvertibility, war, revolution or insurrection damages, kidnapping and ransom, long-term currency losses, and even inflation. The insurance was provided by the Overseas Private Investment Corporation (OPIC), a credit insurance program administered by the Export/Import Bank of the United States (Eximbank) jointly with Foreign Credit Insurance Association (FCIA), and private political risk insurance organizations like the American International Group (AIG) and Lloyd's of London.

Accounting for Political Risk

Accounting for political risk calls for a systematic approach to the assignment of a risk premium to a ROI budget. One approach consists of adjusting the corporate ROI by a numerical risk index developed for each country of operation. For example, assume that the Mantis company owns three affiliates in countries A, B, and C. For the first year, the actual divisional income and investment of each affiliate are as follows:

Division	Total Investment	Divisional Income
A	$1,000,000	$200,000
B	$5,000,000	$1,550,000
C	$2,200,000	$550,000

The Mantis Company requires an 8 percent return on its investments locally. In evaluating its foreign affiliates, the Mantis company relied on a political risk instrument containing forty risk attributes. The scores for countries A, B, and C are as follows:

Country	Political Risk Index
A	$20
B	$10
C	$10

Other things being equal, the best performance is obtained by the affiliate in country B.

COUNCLUSIONS

Capital budgeting for multinationals relies on the same evaluation techniques as for domestic operations. There are, however, many adjustments to be made to account for: project cash flows, the impact of inflation, the impact of changes in the exchange rate, foreign tax regulations, political and economic risk, expropriation, blocked funds, and uncertain salvage value. These issues and their corresponding solutions have been examined in this chapter. Political risk needs to be accounted for and managed when investing abroad.

NOTES

1. Ahmed Riahi-Belkaoui, *Accounting Theory* (London: International Thomson, 2000).

2. Thomas G. Evans, Martin E. Taylor, and Oscar J. Holzmann, *International Accounting and Reporting* (Cincinnati, Ohio: South-Western Publishing Co., 1994), pp. 322.

3. David K.Eiteman, Arthur I. Stonehill, and Micheal H. Moffett, *Multinational Business Finance* (Reading, Mass., 1992).

4. Ibid.

5. Yani Abaromi, *The Foreign Investment Decision Process* (Boston: Harvard Braduate School of Business Administration, Division of research, 1966).

6. Ibid., pp. 54-55.

7. Ibid., pp. 70-71.

8. Eiteman, Stonehill, and Moffett, *Multinational Process Finance*, pp. 32-33.

9. Michael R. Czinkota, Rieta Rivoli, and Illslea A. Ronkainen, *Internal Business* (Chicago: Dryden press, 1989), p. 529.

10. Paul O. Graddis, "Analyzing Overseas Investments," *Harvard Business Review* (May-June 1966), p. 119.

11. A.C. Sharpio, "Capital Budgeting and Long-Term Financing," *Financing Management* (Spring 1978), p. 8.

12. V.B. Bavishi, "Capital Budgeting Practices of Multinationals," *Management Accounting* (August 1981), pp. 32-35.

13. Charles M. Newman II and I. James Czechowica, *International Risk Management* (Morristown, NJ: Finacing Executives Research Foundation [FERF], 1983), p. 88.

14. Ibid., p. 89.

15. The weighted cost of capital concept can be extended to include debt denominated in foreign currencies, debt issued by foreign subsidiaries, and retained earnings of foreign subsidiaries.

16. Arthur Stonehill and Lessard Nathanson, "Capital Budgeting Techniques and the Multinational Corporation," *Journal of International Business Studies* (Spring 1975), p. 67.

17. John J. Clark, Thomas J. Hindlelang, and Robert E. Pritchard, *Capital Budgeting: Planning and Control of Capital Expenditures,* 2nd ed. (Englewood Cliffs, N.J.: Prentice-Hall, 1984), pp. 419-426.

18. Jeff Madura, *International Financial Management* (St. Paul, Minn.: West, 1995), pp. 504.

19. Alan C. Shapiro, "Capital Budgeting for the Multinational Corporation," *Financial Management* (Spring 1978), p. 11.

20. Madura, *International Financial Management,* p. 457.

21. Nusret Calkici, Chris Hessel, and Kishore Tandon, "Foreign Acquisitions in the United States and the Effect on Shareholder's Wealth," *Journal of International Financial Management and Accounting* (March 1, 1991), pp. 38-60.

22. R. Caves, "Corporate Mergers in International Economic Integration," Working Paper (Center for Economic Policy Research, Harvard University, 1990).

23. R. Haas and J. Karls, "How Foreign Buyers Can Get Double Tax Deductions," *MergersAcquisitions* (July/August, 1989).

24. Ibid., p. 20.

25. Calkici, Hessel, and Tandon, "Foreign Acquisitions in the United States," p. 46.

26. Jeff Madura, *International Financial Management,* 3rd ed. (St. Paul, Minn.: West, 1992), pp. 518.

27. Fred Greene, "management of Political Risk," *Best's Review* (July 1974), p. 15.

28. Ibid., p. 73.

29. Newman and Czechowicz, *International Risk Management,* pp. 15-16.

30. S. H. Robock, and K. Simmonds, *International Business and Multinational Enterprises* (Howard, Ill.: Irwin, 1973), pp. 371.

31. Robert Stobaugh, Jr., "How to Analyze Foreign Investment Climates," *Harvard Business Review* (September-October 1969), pp. 101-102.

32. "A Primer on Country Risk," *Argus Capital Market Report* (June 4, 1975), pp. 15-25.

33. Alan C. Shapiro, "Currency Risk and country Risk in International Banking," *Journal of Finance* (July 1985), p. 891.

34. R.J. Rummel and David A. Heenan, "How Multinationals Analyze Political Risk," *Harvard Business Review* (January-February 1978), pp. 67-76.

35. Ibid., p. 70.

36. Harald Knudsen, "Explaining the National Propensity to Expropriate: An Ecological Approach," *Journal of International Business Studies* (Spring 1974), pp. 51-71.

37. Dan Haendel and Gerald T. West, with Robert G. Meadow, *Overseas Investment and Political Risk,* Monograph Series, no. 21 (Philadelphia: Foreign Policy Research Institute, 1957).

38. Dan Haendel *Foreign Investments and the Management of Political Risk* (Boulder, Colo.: Westview Press, 1979), pp. 106-107.

39. Janice Monti-Belkaoui and Ahmed Riahi-Belkaoui, *The Nature, Estimation, and Management of Political Risk* (Westport, Conn.: Greenwood Publishing, 1999).

40. D. K. Eiteman and A. I. Stonehill, *Multinational Business Finance* (Reading, mass.: Addison-Wesley, 1989), pp. 203-223.

41. Ibid., p. 503.

42. Haendel, *Foreign Investments,* pp. 139-146.

43. Newman and Czechowicz, *International Risk Management,* p. 81.

SELECTED READINGS

Booth, Laurence D. "Capital Budgeting Frameworks for the Multinational Corporation." *Journal of International business Studies* (Fall 1982), pp. 114-123.

Collins, J. Markham, and William S. Sekely. "The Relationship of Headquarters Country and Industry Classification to Financial Structure." *Financial Management* (Autumn 1983), pp. 45-51.

Doukas, John, and Nickolas G. Travlos. "The Effect of Corporate Multinationality on Shareholders' Wealth: Evidence from International Acquisitions." *Journal of Finance* (December 1988), pp. 1162-1175.

Kester, W carl. "Capital and Ownership Structure: A Comparison of United States and Japanese Manufacturing Corporations." *Financial Management* (Spring 1956), pp. 5-16.

Kim, Suk H., Edward J. Farragher, and Trevor Crick. "Foreign Capital Budgeting Practices Used by the U.S. and Non-U.S. Multinational Companies." *The Engineering Economist* (Spring 1984), pp. 207-215.

Monti-Belkaoui, Janice, and Ahmed Riahi-Belkaoui. *The Nature and Estimation and management of Political Risk* (Westport, Conn.: Greenwood Publishing, 1999).

Oblak, David J., and Roy J. Helm, Jr. "Survey and Analysis of Capital Budgeting Methods Used by Multinationals." *Financial Management* (Winter 1981), pp. 34-41.

Riahi-Belkaoui, Ahmed. *Handbook of Cost Accounting: Theory and Techniques* (Westport, Conn.: Greenwood Publishing, 1991).

---------. *The New Foundations of Management Accounting* (Westport, Conn.:Greenwood Publishing, 1991).

Shapiro, A.C. "Capital Budgeting and Long term Financing." *Financial Management* (Spring 1978), pp. 5-25.

Srinivasan, Venkat, and Yong H. Kim. "Integrating Corporate Strategy and Multinational capital Budgeting: An Analytical Framework." *Recent Developments in International Banking and Finance* (1988), pp. 381-397.

Stanley, Margorie T. "capital Structure and Cost of Capital for the Multinational Firm." *Journal of International Business Studies* (Spring-Summer 1981), pp. 103-120.

Stanley, Marjorie T., and Stanley B. Block. "A Survey of Multinational Capital Budgeting." *Financial Review* (March 1984), pp. 36-54.

--------, "An Empirical Study of Management and Financial Variables Influencing Capital Budgeting Decisions for Multinational Companies in the 1980s." *Management International Review* (November 1983), pp. 61-71.

Chapter 7
Capital Budgeting for Social Projects

INTRODUCTION

Capital budgeting for social projects requires a consideration and measurement of environmental effects of the evolution and implications of the social projects. One way of contributing to a solution is to suggest ways of conceptualizing microsocial accounting and ways of measuring and evaluating the environmental effects of organizational behavior. The conceptualizing of microsocial accounting will provide a conceptual framework to justify and rationalize the new field and guide future developments. The techniques of measurement and evaluation will provide management with tools to incorporate consideration of the social consequences of its actions explicitly into a decision-making process and action and to provide both a corporation's particular constituencies and the general public with valid, pertinent data other than profit-and-loss statement information on which to base their evaluation of management's performance.[1] Accordingly, this chapter will present an "emerging" conceptual framework for microsocial accounting and ways of measuring and evaluating the environmental effects of organizational behavior.

TOWARD A CONCEPTUAL FRAMEWORK OF MICROSOCIAL ACCOUNTING

A conceptual framework for microsocial accounting is equivalent to constitution; it should be a coherent system of interrelated and fundamentals that can lead to consistent standards and that prescribes the nature, function, and limits of microsical accounting. Such a framework would be useful for the development of a coherent set of standards and techniques, for the resolution of new and emerging practical problems, for increasing users' understanding of confidence in social reporting, and for enhancing comparability among companies' social reports.

A conceptual framework for microsocial accounting does not exist for the moment in either the professional or academic literature. However, various attempts have been made in the accounting literature to outline some of the elements of the framework contributing to an "emerging" conceptual framework for microsocial accounting. These elements are the objectives, fundamental concepts, and operational guidelines.

Proposed Objectives

The objectives for microsocial economics are the first and essential steps to the formulation of a microsocial accounting framework. Then the socioeconomic accounting concepts will be true because they will be based on accepted objectives. In spite of the importance of these objectives, there has never been a formal attempt by the profession to accomplish such a task.

Several notable exceptions, which may serve as de facto objectives for microsocial accounting, were provided in an article by K. V. Ramanathan.[2] Three objectives are (1) to identify and measure the periodic net social contribution of an individual firm, including not only the costs and benefits internalized to the firms but also those arising from externalities affecting different social segments; (2) to help determine whether an individuals firm's strategies and practices that directly affects the relative resource and power status of individuals, communities, social segments, and generations are consistent with widely shared social priorities on the one hand and individuals' legitimate aspirations on the other; (3) to make available in an optimal manner to all social constituents relevant information on a firms goals, policies, programs, performance, and contributions to social goals.[3]

The first two objectives are presented as measurement objectives of social accounting, while the third objective is a reporting objective. The first objective calls for the measurement of a firm's periodic net social contribution, which includes both private and social costs and benefits. The second objective calls for the measurement of the firm's contribution to social goals. The third objective calls for a reporting of the results of the first two objectives.

Proposed Concepts

Concepts based on the objectives of microsocial accounting would constitute the basic foundation for a microsocial accounting theory. In the article cited earlier, K. V. Ramanathan proposed six concepts of social accounting.[4]

1. A *social transaction* represents a firm's utilization or delivery of a socioenvironment resource that affects the absolute or relative interests of a firm's various social constituents and that is not proposed through the marketplace.
2. *Social overheads (returns)* represent the sacrifice (benefit) to society from those resources consumed (added) by a firm as a result of its social transactions.
3. *Social income* represents the periodic net social contribution of a firm. It is computed as the algebraic sum of the firm's traditionally measured net income, its aggregate social overheads, and its aggregate social returns.
4. *Social constituents* are the different distinct social group (implied in the second objective and expressed in the third objective of social accounting) with whom a firm is presumed to have a social contract.
5. *Social equity* is a measure of he aggregate changes in the claims that each social constituent is presumed to have in the firm.
6. *Net social asset* of a firm is a measure of its aggregate nonmarket contribution to the society's well-being less its nonmarket depletion of the society's resources during the life of the firm.[5]

The first concept, the social transaction, calls for recognition of all the "transactions" between the firm and society that are not handled presently through the marketplace. These nonmarket transactions are basically positive or negative externalities. The second concept is that of social overhead and social return. The nonmarket transactions resulting from the social transaction generate either a social overhead, which is a social cost imposed on society, or a social return, which is a social benefit. The third concept, social income, is a measure of the overall performance of the firm to include the traditional net income, the social overheads, and the social returns. The fourth concept is that of social constituents. To measure adequately, the social overheads, social returns, and the resulting social income, the different social groups likely to be affected by the firm's operational and other activities need to be identified. These groups are the social constituents of the firm, with whom the firm has an explicit or implicit social contract. The fifth concept is that of social equity, that is, the claims that each social constituent has in the firm. The sixth concept, social assets, constitutes the firm's nonmarket contribution to society, which are increased by positive externalities and decreased by negative externalities.

Proposed Qualitative Characteristics

To be useful, a microsocial accounting report must meet certain qualitative criteria. These criteria are intended to guide the social accountant to produce the "best," or most useful, information for managers. The Financial Accounting Standards Board, a standard-setting body for microsocial accounting, has proposed certain criteria for selecting and evaluating financial accounting and reporting policies.[6] These criteria, which also apply to microsocial accounting, include decision usefulness, benefits over costs, relevance, reliability, neutrality, verifiability, representational faithfulness, comparability, timeliness, understandability, completeness, and consistency. These criteria may be organized as a hierarchy of informational qualities.

Most microsocial accounting is concerned to some degree with decision making; thus, *decision usefulness* becomes the overriding criterion for choosing among microsocial accounting alternatives. The type of information chosen is the one that, subject to any cost considerations, appears the most useful for decision making.

Microsocial accounting information, like any other commodity, will be sought if the benefits to be derived from the information exceed its costs. Thus, before preparing and disseminating the cost accounting information, the benefits and costs of providing the information must be compared.

Relevance has been appropriately defines as follows: "For information to meet the standard of relevance, it must bear upon or be usefully associated with the action it is designed to facilitate or the result it is desired to produce. This requires that either the information or the act of communicating it exert influence ... on the designated actions."[7] Relevance, therefore, refers to the information's ability to influence managers' decisions by changing or confirming their expectations about the results or consequences of actions or events. There can be degrees of relevance. The relevance of particular information will vary among users and will depends on their needs and the particular contexts in which the decisions are made.

Reliability refers to the "quality which permits users of data to depend upon it with confidence as representative of what it proposed to represent."[8] Thus, the reliability of information depends on its degree of faithfulness in the representation of an event. Reliability will differ among users depending on the extent of their knowledge of the rules used to prepare the information. Similarly, different users may seek information with different degrees of reliability.

The absence of bias in the presentation of accounting reports or information is neutrality. Thus, neutral information is free from bias toward attaining some desired result or inducing a particular mode of behavior. This is not to imply that the preparers of information do not have a purpose in mind when preparing the reports; it only means that the purpose should not influence a predetermined result. Notice that neutrality is in conflict with one of the concepts of social accounting, namely, the feedback concept. It may be argued that social accounting reports are intended to report on managerial performance and influence behavior and hence cannot be neutral.

Verifiability is "that attribute ... which allots qualified individuals working independently of one another to develop essentially similar measures or conclusions from an examination of the same evidence, data, or records."[9] It implies consensus and absence to measurer bias. Verifiable information can be substantially reproduced by independent measures using the same measurement methods. Notice that verifiability refers only to the correctness of the resulting information, not to the appropriateness of the measurement method used.

Representational faithfulness and completeness refer to the correspondence between the accounting data and the events those data are supposed to represent. If the measure portrays what it is supposed to represent, it is considered free of measurement and measurer bias.

Comparability describes the use of the same methods by different firms, and consistency describes the use of the same method over time by a given firm. Both qualitative characteristics are more important for financial accounting information than for social accounting information.

Timelessness refers to the availability of data when they are needed or soon standability. The preparer's level of understanding is generally different from the user's. Thus, efforts should be made by the preparer to increase the understandability of accounting information, in both form and content, to increase its usefulness to the user.

Proposed Conceptual Framework

A conceptual framework is a constitution, a coherent set of interrelated *objectives* and *fundamentals* that can lead to consistent standards and that prescribes the nature, function, and limits of financial accounting and financial statements. The objectives identify the goals and purposed of accounting. The *fundamentals* are the underlying concepts of accounting, concepts that guide the selection of events to be accounted for, the measurement of those events, and the means of summarizing and communicating them to interested parties. Concepts of that type are fundamental in the sense that other concepts flow from them and repeated reference to them will be necessary in establishing, interpreting, and applying accounting and reporting standards.[10]

Applied to microsocioeconomic accounting, the conceptual framework is intended to act as a constitution for the process of choosing techniques of measurement, evaluation, and communication of social information. The constitution specifies both objectives and fundamentals. The discussion in the previous sections centered on proposed objectives and fundamentals applicable to socioeconomic accounting. Therefore, an "emerging" conceptual framework for microsocial accounting seems to exist. Exhibit 7.1 provides an overview of the conceptual framework for microsocial accounting. At the first level, the proposed objectives identify the goals and purposes of microsocial accounting. At the second level are the proposed concepts and qualitative characteristics of microsocial accounting. Finally, at the third level, the operational guidelines specifies the techniques of measurement and evaluation for microsocial accounting. Examples of techniques of measurement and evaluation will be presented in the rest of the chapter. The conceptual framework for microsocial accounting presented in Exhibit 7.1 is only tentative, awaiting formalization by the accounting profession and other concerned groups.

MEASUREMENT AND EVALUATION IN MICROSOCIAL ACCOUNTING
The Concept of Environmental Damage

The environment is a resource that affects the ways things live and develop. It is above all a nonreproducible capital offering vital services to man. The most valuable of these services involves "the *dispersing, storing,* or *assimilating of residuals* which are generated as a byproduct of economic activity."[11] This service is generally portrayed in the materials balance model and its corollary, the principle of materials balance, which "portrays the flow of raw materials into consumer goods, then into wastes from production and residuals from consumption."[12] The other services provided by the environment involve a support of human life, amenity services, and a source of material inputs. Given these services the environmental quality is affected when the level and composition of these services are altered. The alteration or damage is generally caused by the wastes and residuals that the environment may fail to absorb or assimilate:

In economic terms, this damage is equal to the reduction in the value of environmental quality caused by the disposal of residuals. Hence, whenever residuals disposal impairs life, reduces the value of property, or constrains the quality of natural recreation sites, the quality and quantity of nonresidual environment services is reduced and environmental damage exist. These damages are measured by the value of the non-waste-receptor environmental services forgone because the disposal or residuals. As such, environmental damage conforms to the classic economic notion of opportunity costs.[13]

Environmental damage is first a consequence of the overuse and abuse of what is in fact a free commodity. Second, it is aggravated by the widely held belief that the use of the residual absorptive services of the

Exhibit 7.1
A Conceptual Framework for Microsocial Accounting

Objectives			First Level:
1. Measurement			Objectives
2. Reporting			

Qualitative Characteristics		Concepts	Second Level
			Fundamental
1. Decision usefulness		1. Social transaction	concept
2. Benefits over costs		2. Social overhead	
3. Relevance		3. Social income	
4. Reliability		4. Social constituents	
5. Neutrality		5. Social equity	
6. Timeliness			
7. Understanding			
8. Verifiability			
9. Representational faithfulness			
10. Comparability			
11. Consistency			
12. Completeness			

Techniques Measurement	Techniques of Evaluation	Techniques of Reporting	Third Level: Operational guidelines

environment is limitless and costless. In fact, the damage itself results in reduction in the other environment services in addition to a reduction in the residual absorption services.

Optimal Level of Environmental Quality

The above discussion implies that environmental quality can be achieved by a reduction in environmental damage. There are two types of costs of damage associated with the use of the waste-absorptive services of the environment: the total damage costs created by the reduction in the nonresidual absorptive services of the environment due to residual discharges and the cost of abatement needed to reduce the residuals released to the environment. The optimal level of environmental quality will be the level that minimizes the sum of these two costs: damage costs and abatement costs. This strategy may be applied to any type of residual.

There are several studies attempting to estimate environmental damage in economic terms. These studies have attempted to measure *direct* damage in monetary terms and disamenities such as recreational and aesthetic losses. They are examined next.

Air Pollution

National estimates of air pollution damage exist for the United States, Canada, and Great Britain.[14] The damage caused by air pollution has also been examined in terms of its impact on human health, materials, vegetation, and property values.

With respect to human health, various studies have tried to assign economic values to the health effects of air pollution.[15] For example, Ridker defines four types of costs: those due to premature death, those associated with mobility, treatment costs, prevention or avoidance costs. The costs of premature death due to disease are calculated as the sum of an individual's expected earnings discounted for each additional productive year of life had he not died prematurely. The following formula was used:

$$V_a = \sum_{n=a}^{\infty} \frac{Pa_1^n * Pa_2^n * Pa_3^n * Yn}{(1+R)^{n-a}}$$

where

V_a = present value of the future earnings of an individual at age n;
Pa_1^n = probability that an individual at age a will live to age n;
Pa_2^n = probability that an individual at age a will live to age n;
Pa_3^n = probability that an individual at age a living at age n will be in the labor force at age n;
Yn = earnings at age n;
R = rate of interest.

Similarly, the burial costs associated with premature death are calculated as the difference between the present cost of burial and the present value of the future expected cost of burial. The following formula was used:

$$C_a = C_0[1 - \sum_{n=a}^{\infty} (Pa_1^n)/(1+R)^{n-a}]$$

where

C_0 = cost of burial;
C_a = present value of the next expected gain from delaying burial at age a;
Pa_1^n and R as above.

Ridker computed the costs associated with various diseases and assume that 20 percent of the costs may be attributed to air pollution. In fact, most other studies adopted the same approach, which is to estimate the costs of specific diseases and attribute a percentage of these costs to air pollution.

With respect to materials, the negative effects of air pollution include corrosion of metals, deterioration of paint, and soiling. Various studies have tried to assign economic values to those consequences.[16] For example, the Midwest Research Institute (MRI) presents the results of a systematic study of all the physical and chemical interactions between materials, pollutants, and environmental parameters needed to assess the economic damage to materials from air pollution. The MRI study computes the economic value of the material and then applies the rate of deterioration of this value to estimate the economic loss from deterioration. The economic value of material exposed to air pollution Q is calculated as follows:

$$Q = P \times N \times F \times R$$

where

P = product of the annual dollar production volume;
N = economic life of the material based on usage;
F = weighted average factor for the percentage of material exposed to air pollution;
R = labor factor reflecting the in-place or as-used value of the material.

The rate of deterioration of interaction V is then calculated by estimating the difference between the deterioration rates in polluted and unpolluted environments divided by the average thickness of the material. The MRI study also computes the costs due to soiling by assigning an economic value to aesthetic loss suffered by a material through soiling.[17] The formula used is

$$L = Q \times V$$

where

Q = value of the exposed material as defined earlier
V = soiling interaction value per year
$V_{fibers} = 0.10 \ \Delta f / RW$
$V_{nonfibers} = 0.10 \ \Delta f / RW$ pt

where

W = material price per pound;
R = labor force;
p = density;
t = average thickness;
Δf = increasaed frquency of cleaning due to pollution.

With respect to vegetation, several studies attempted to estimate damage to vegetation from air pollution.[18] These studies were, however, criticized for the limitations of their methodologies.[19]

With respect to property values, several studies attempted to estimate the effects of air pollution on residential property values. The estimates were based on linear regression models using either a cross-sectional or a time series approach. The units show negative, although not significant, effects of pollution on property value, rent, and land use intensity.

Noise

The effects of noise are generally assembled through its effects on property values, with property values as dependent variables and noise parameters as one of the independent variables.[20] Other studies relied on a survey in which people were asked how much less a certain house in a noise-defined environment would have to be than an ordinary house before one could consider buying it. [21] These studies are far from being conclusive in the damage produced by noise. To that effect Wyzga states:

Theoretically from surveys, litigation, etc., it appears as if these is damage involved, which includes a decrease in property value, but the studies to date have been largely unsuccessful in uncovering any relationship between noise levels and property values. It could be that most of these studies have not properly adjusted for housing supply or the fact that some individuals are more sensitive to noise than others. These and other potential influences need to be investigated, and more realistic models need to be developed if we are to obtain reasonable estimates of the relationship between noise and property values.[22]

Water Pollution

Various studies investigating the damages caused by water pollution focused on the disamenities due to pollution. Most studies concerned themselves with measuring the recreational benefits arising from the use of unpolluted water. Various measurement methods used for estimating recreational benefits are given by Clawson and Knetsch.[23] These are as follows:

1. *Maximum price method:* estimates the total benefit of a recreational resource to be the sum of the maximum process that various used would pay for the employment of the resource.
2. *Gross expenditure method:* estimates the total amount spent on recreation by the user as a surrogate measure of recreational benefits.
3. *Market value of fish method:* estimates the market value of fish caught by the user as a surrogate measure of recreational benefits.
4. *Cost method:* equates the benefits to the costs used to generate them.
5. *Market value method:* uses the prices charged at privately owned recreational areas as a surrogate measure of recreational benefits.
6. *Direct interview method:* assesses directly how much the users are willing to pay for using the resource.

Estimating Social Costs

Having identified the nature of the environmental damage and the resulting environmental damage functions, the next step is the economic measurement of the environmental damage. The idea is to attach a monetary value to each type of damage. In general, two types of damages are considered: financial losses and amenity losses.[24] Financial losses may be defined as the change in the level of outlays following a change in environmental quality. Examples of financial losses include productivity losses resulting from the environmental damage and increased costs of health care. Amenity losses may be defined as the psychic costs resulting from the suffering, bereavement, and limitation imposed on individuals, families, and society.

The estimation of financial losses generally relies on direct determination of the monetary value of changes in the demand for marketable goods and services due to the environmental changes. Four problems may be identified with this approach:

1. the specification of effects, or the problem of identifying the marketable goods and services that are affected by a change in the environment;
2. the relating of effects to a specific level of environmental deterioration;

3. the problem of finding the proper prices, including the interest rate, that should be used in a monetary evaluation;
4. the problem of interpreting the calculated financial values and relating them to the monetary damage in the context of the problem under study.[25]

The estimation of amenity losses differs because of their intangible nature. The methods used tend to be indirect. One method may be to use questionnaires in which the effected individuals are asked to specify the amount of money necessary to compensate them for environmental deterioration. A second method is to use the relationship between the loss of a specific amenity and the demand for private goods to estimate the amenity loss. A third method is to use the market reactions in terms of changes in prices. A comparison of land values, for example, may indicate a loss of amenity. Finally, litigation results may be used to estimate amenity losses.

Estimating Social Benefits

Social benefits are the gains associated with a reduction of the externality or nuisance. In the case of pollution, for example, the benefits are measured by a comparison of the existing level of pollution and "acceptable" level of pollution. Thus, benefits result from a "willingness to pay" to reduce the nuisance. It implies the existence of a demand curve for the effects of improvement of environmental quality Benefit estimation is then reduced to a determination of the demand curve for environmental quality.[26] Three techniques have been used to estimate the demand in connection with air and water pollution: measuring benefits from market data; measuring benefits from nonmarket data; and measuring benefits on the basis of property values.

Measuring benefits from market data uses the relationships between private marketed goods and public goods to draw inferences on the demand of public goods. The demand for the public good is inferred from market transactions on the related private good. The level of environmental quality as a public good, however, enters the individual utility functions in the broad categories. First, it is an input in the production of market goods and services. Its demand can be estimated by examining changes in factor incomes such as land units, costs saving in production, and changes in consumer associated with the private good savings in production, and changes in consumer associated with the private good outputs.[27] Second, if it enters directly in the utility functions as a consumption good, its demand can be estimated in terms of shifts in the demand curve for a private complementary good, or in terms of the demand for a perfect substitute.

Measuring benefits from nonmarket data relies on nonmarket means such as surveys, questionnaires, bidding games, and voting. The idea is to induce people to reveal directly or indirectly their preferences for the provision of public goods. Basically, three approaches may be used. The first approach is to ask people about their willingness to pay to obtain a given level of public goods. [28] The second approach is to ask individuals how much of the public good they would demand at a given price or under given conditions of taxation.[29] The third approach uses a voting mechanism in which two parties or candidates compete for votes after adopting different positions on the provision of a public good.[30]

Ronals Ridker was the first to use property values as a basis for benefit estimation. He argues as follows:

If the land market were to work perfectly, the price of a plot of land would equal the sum of the present discounted streams of benefits and costs derivable from it. If some of its costs (e.g., if additional maintenance and cleaning costs are required), or if some of its benefits fall (e.g., if one cannot see the mountains from the terrace) the property will be discounted in the market to reflect people's evaluation of these changes. Since air pollution is specific to locations and the supply of locations is fixed, there is less likelihood that the negative effects of air pollution can be significantly shifted on to other markets. We would therefore expect to find the majority of effects reflected in this market, and we can measure them by observing associated changes in property values.[31]

Following Ridker's example, the approach adopted was to derive benefit measures from property value differences at a point in time.

Various social programs may be necessary to connect some of the social ills imposed by the environmental effects of organizational behavior. A choice has to be made for the program most suitable and most feasible given the state of the technology and the funds available. This section of the chapter presents two widely accepted techniques for the evaluation programs: cost-benefit analysis and cost-effectiveness analysis.

Cost-Benefit Analysis

Cost-benefit analysis is a method used to assess the desirability of projects when it is necessary to take both a long and a wide view of the impact of the proposed project on the general welfare of a society.[32] It calls for an enumeration and evaluation of all the relevant costs and benefits the project may generate and for choosing the alternatives that maximize the present value of all benefits less costs, subject to specified constraints and given specified objectives. Cost-benefit analysis is very useful when all the economic impacts of a project, indirect as well as direct effects, have to be considered. It is a favorite method of analysis by governmental agencies for assessing the desirability of particular program expenditures and/or policy changes. In fact, it has been formally adopted into U.S. federal government budgetary procedures under the Planning- Programming-Budgeting System (PPBS).[33] It acts as a structure for a general theory of government resource allocation. Above all, it is a decision technique whose aims are first to take all effects into consideration and second to maximize the present value of all benefits less that of all costs, subject to specified constraints. This brings into focus the major considerations of cost-benefit analysis:

1. What are the objectives and constraints to be considered?
2. Which costs and benefits are to be included?
3. How are the costs and benefits to be valued?
4. What are the investment criteria to be used?
5. Which discount rate should be used?

Objectives and Relevant Constraints

The main objective of cost-benefit analysis is to determine whether or not a particular expenditure is economically and socially justifiable. The basic criteria used in cost-benefit analysis is an efficiency criterion. One such efficiency criterion is Pareto optimally. A program is said to be Pareto efficient if at least one person is made better off and no one is made worse off. This criterion is too strong and too impractical for cost-benefit analysis, however, given that few programs are likely to leave some individuals better off and no one worse off. A weaker notion of efficiency, known as the Kaldor-Hides criterion, is generally used for cost-benefit analysis. Under this criterion, also known as the potential Pareto improvement criterion, a program is acceptable if it is Pareto optimal or if it could redistribute the net benefits to everyone in the community so that everyone is at least as well off as they were before the initiation of the program.[34] Basically, a program is efficient and should be undertaken if its total discounted societal benefits exceed the total discounted costs.

Besides the objectives of cost-benefit analysis, which are basically intended to maximize society's wealth, it is important to recognize some of the constraints. Eckstein provided a helpful classification of constraints.[35] These include:

1. *Physical constraints:* The program alternatives considered may be constrained by the state of technology and more generally by the production function, which relates the physical inputs and outputs of a project.

2. *Legal constraints:* The program alternatives considered must be done within the framework of the law. Examples of legal constraints property rights, time needed for public inquires, regulated pricing, the right of eminent domain, and limits to the activities of public agencies.

3. *Administrative constraints:* Each of the alternative programs requires the availability and the hiring of individuals with the right administrative skills.

4. *Distributional constraints:* Any program is bound to generate gainers and losers. The unfavorable effects on income distribution may be alleviated by expressing the objective of cost-benefit analysis as either maximizing the excess of total benefits over total costs subject to constraints on the benefits less costs of particular groups or maximizing the net gain (or minimizing the net loss) to a particular group subject to a constraint relating to total benefits and costs.

5. *Political constraints:* Political considerations may act as constraints, shifting the decision from what is *best* to what is *possible.* Regional differences and presence of various competing interest groups are examples of actors bound to create political constraints on the choice of the best program.

6. *Budgetary constraints:* Capital rationing and evaluating may act as constraints, shifting the objective function from maximizing to suboptimizing of net benefit given a target budget.

7. *Social and religious constraints:* Social and religious taboos are bound to act as constraints, shifting the decision from what is *best* to what is *acceptable.*

Enumeration of Costs and Benefits

Enumeration of costs and benefits is important in determining which of the costs and benefits of a particular project should be included in a cost-benefit analysis.

Benefits of a project are either direct or indirect. Primarily or direct benefits of a project "are those benefits which accrue directly to the users of the service provided by the project." They consist of "the value of goods or services that result from conditions with the project as compared to conditions without the project."[36] Indirect or secondary benefits of a project are those benefits accruing to others that the users of the service provided by the project. They are of two types: real or technological benefits or pecuniary benefits.[37] Real or technological benefits are those benefits resulting from changes in total production possibilities and consumption opportunities. For example, if a dam creates a reduction in flooding and more pleasant scenery, these benefits are real benefits. Pecuniary benefits are those benefits that alter the distribution of total income without changing its volume. They generally take the form of lower input costs, increased volumes of business, or changes in the land values. *Only direct real benefits should be included; pecuniary benefits should be excluded in the enumeration of the benefits of a project.* Other benefits that are of an intangible nature and difficult to identify should be considered also. Costs of a project are also either direct or indirect. Direct or primary costs of a project are costs incurred directly by the users of the service provided by the project. They include the capital costs, operating and maintenance costs, and personnel expenses required by the project. Indirect and secondary costs are incurred by others than the users of the service provided by the project. They may also be of two types: real or technological and pecuniary costs. *Again, only the real secondary cost should be counted in a cost-benefit analysis.*

Briefly, in enumerating the costs and benefits of a project, the analyst must be careful to distinguish their allocative effects from their pecuniary or distributional effects. In fact, the confusion of pecuniary and allocative effects constitutes a primary defect in many analyses of the efficiency of public projects. The only effects that should be taken into account in enumerating the costs and benefits of a public project are the real or technological externalities, that is, those that affect total opportunities for production and consumption, as opposed to pecuniary externalities, which do not affect total production or consumption.

Valuation of Costs and Benefits

In general, benefits should measure the value of the additional goods or services produced or the value of cost savings in the production of goods or services, while costs should measure the value of real resources displaced from other uses.

Assuming a competitive economy, benefits and costs will be valued on the basis of the observable market prices of the outputs and inputs of the program. More precisely, the benefits will be valued in either the market price of the output of the program or on the amounts users are willing to pay if charged (i.e., the consumers' surplus, which is the difference between the aggregate willingness to pay and the costs of the projects).

Where market prices do not accurately reflect the value of the market transactions to society as a result of externalities, the shadow prices, as adjusted or input prices, may be used. The general principle for estimating shadow prices for the output of public projects is to simulate what users would be willing to pay if they were charged as if the goods were sold in perfectly competitive markets.

Investment Criteria

Cost-benefit analysis is a method used to evaluate long-term projects. As such, the benefits and costs of each project have to be discounted to be comparable at time 0 when evaluation and decision on the projects have to be made. There is a need to rely on some form of discounting in the choice of investment criteria. There are exactly three possible investment or decision criteria: net present value; benefit-cost ratio; and internal rate of return.

Under the net present value, the present value of a project is obtained by discounting the net excess of benefits (B_t) over costs (C_t) for each year during the life of the project back to the present time using a social discount rate. More explicitly,

$$V = \sum_{t=1}^{\infty}(B_t - C_t)/(1+r)^t$$

where

V = value of the project;
B_t = benefit in year t;
C_t = cost of year it;
r = Social discount rate;
∞ = life of the project.

Basically a project is found acceptable if the present value V is positive. If there are binding constraints on a project (for example, budget appropriation, foreign exchange, private investment opportunity forgone), then the following model proposed by Steiner[38] would be more appropriate:

$$V = \sum_{t=1}^{\infty}(B_t - C_t)/(1+r)^t - \sum_{j=1}^{n}p_jk_j,$$

where

p_j = shadow price of a binding constraint;
k_j = number of units of a constrained resource.

Under benefit-cost ratio, the decision criterion is expressed in terms of the ratio of the present value of benefits to the present value of costs (both discounted at the social discount rate). More explicitly, the benefit-cost ratio is:

$$\frac{\sum_{t=1}^{\infty} b_t/(1+r)^t}{\sum_{t=1}^{\infty} c_t(1+r)^t}$$

Basically all projects that are not mutually exclusive with a benefit-cost ratio in excess of 1 are acceptable.

Under internal rate or return, the decision criterion is expressed in terms of the internal rate of return; that is to say, the discount rate will equate the net benefits over the life of the project with the original cost. In other words, 2 is the rate of interest for which

$$\sum_{t=1}^{\propto} b_t/(1+r)^t - \sum_{t=1}^{\propto} c_t(1+r)^t = 0$$

Basically all projects where the internal rate of return exceeds the closer social discount rate are deemed acceptable.

Choice of a Discount Rate

The choice of a discount rate is important for at least two reasons. A high rate will lead the firm or the government away from the undertaking of the project, while a low rate may make the project more acceptable from a return point of view. Furthermore, a low discount rate tends to favor projects yielding net benefits further into the future relative to projects yielding more current net benefits. Choosing the appropriate interest rate therefore becomes an important policy question. There are several possible alternative rates.

Given that the discount rate allows the allocation of resources between the public and private sectors, it should be chosen so that it indicates when resources should be transferred from one sector to another. This means that the discount rate should represent the opportunity cost of funds withdrawn from the private sector to be used in the public sector. As Baumol states, "the correct discount rate for the evaluation of a government project is the percentage rate of return that the resources utilized would otherwise provide in the private sector."[39]

These considerations enter in the choice of the *marginal productivity of capital as a discount rate in private investment*: "(1) an effort to minimize governmental activity; (2) a concern for efficiency; and (3) a belief that the source of funds for government investment in the private sector or that government investment will displace private investment that would otherwise by made."[40]

Social time preference expresses a concern for further generations in the sense that the welfare of the future generations will be increased if investments are made now. It follows that the discount rate should be the *social rate of time preference*, that is to say, the compensation required to induce consumers to refrain from consumption and save. One study committee argued that the federal government should use the "administration's social rate of time discount" to be established by the president in consultation with his advisors, such as the Council of Economic Advisors.[41] The strongest argument for the social rate of time preference was made by Pigou, who suggested that individuals were short-sighted about the future ("defective telescopic faculty") and the welfare of future generations would require governmental invention.[42]

Advantages and Limitations

There are thousands of cost-benefit analyses of government projects. The popularity of the method is a witness to some of its advantages. There are also some limitations well recognized in the literature. Let's examine some of the advantages and limitations of both. Among the advantages of cost-benefit analysis we may cite the following:

1. It is most effective in dealing with cases of intermediate social goods.[43]
2. It establishes a framework for a reasonably consistent evaluation of alternative projects, especially where the choice set is narrow in the sense that the projects are not only similar but generate the same volume of externalities.

3. It allows one to ascertain the decisions most advantageous in terms of the objectives accepted.

Among its limitations we may cite the following:
1. There are limits within which social objectives can be measured in money terms. An example of nonefficiency objectives that are not measureable in dollar terms is an equitable distribution of income.
2. Cost-benefit analysis falls under what is known as particular equilibrium analysis. It is useful in evaluating only projects that have negligible impact outside the immediately affected areas of the economy.
3. There are obvious problems of enumeration an evaluation of the costs and benefits of particular projects.[44] A committee of the House of Representatives, pointing to the difficulty inherent in estimating the direct effects of a policy and assigning dollar terms to them, argued that such estimates are seldom accurate.[45] Similarly, Baram argued that "monetization of environmental and health amenities constitutes an inappropriate treatment of factors that transcend economies."[46]

COST-EFFECTIVENESS ANALYSIS

The difference between cost-effectiveness analysis and cost-benefit analysis is merely a difference of degree and not in kind. While cost-benefit analysis is concerned with qualifying both benefits and costs in money terms and determining the most efficient way to conduct a given program, cost-effectiveness assumes that the outputs of a given program are useful and valuable without attempting to measure their values. Thus, cost-effectiveness analysis may be merely defined as " a technique for choosing among *given* alternative courses of action in terms of their cost and effectiveness in the attainment of *specified* objectives."[47] This definition assumes that the objectives are known and well specified and the only concern in with cost-effectiveness considerations. Consider, however, another definition where cost-effectiveness is "a technique for evaluating broad management and economic implications of alternative choices of action with the objective of assisting in the identification of the preferred choice."[48] This last definition implies less well-defined objectives, solutions, and criteria of effectiveness. In any case, the methodology will be the same under both approaches.

Methodology

Before introducing the methodology, we should keep in mine that cost-effectiveness analysis is used generally for projects where the aim is to minimize the costs associated with the attainment of any given objective or objectives. As such it may be outlines as a sequence of general steps:[49]

1. *Definition of objectives:* The basic requirement for cost-effectiveness analysis is that the objectives are *specifiable.*
2. *Identification of alternatives:* Devising various feasible options for accomplishing objectives.
3. *Selection of effectiveness measures:* This step is considered the most difficult in cost-effectiveness analysis since the desirability of a given program may change depending on the type of effectiveness measure used.[50]
4. *Cost estimates:* The estimation of costs for each alternative, precisely as in cost-benefit analysis.
5. *Selection of a decision criterion:* Two major types of criteria are used in cost-effectiveness analysis: a constant cost criterion, or a least-cost criterion. The constant cost criterion allows one to determine the output that may be achieved from a number of alternative systems, all of which require the same outlay of funds. In short, the constant criterion specifies what the analyst can get for his or her money and how to maximize effectiveness at a given cost. The least cost criterion allows one to identify the least expensive option for achieving a certain level of output. In other words, it attempts to minimize cost while attaining a given level of effectiveness. N. M. Singer illustrated adequately the differences between the constant cost and least-cost criteria: "The differences among the various types of systems

analysis can be seen by comparing the operations research problem, to collect refuse with a given fleet of trucks, to studies that would be made under the other methodologies. At least cost study would determine the collection system of minimum cost for the given pick-up location: that is, the capital and labor inputs would be permitted to vary. A constant cost study would examine the various outputs that could be produced for the cost of the garbage truck fleet: commuter transit if the money were spend on buses, highway safety if the money were spent on roadgrading equipment, education if the funds were spent on schools, and so forth. Finally, a benefit-cost study would estimate the value that consumers place on the garbage pick-up and would then recommend whether or not to undertake the program."[51]

6. *Creation of models:* The next step is to formulate analytical relationships among costs, effectiveness, and environmental factors. Given these relationships, the next step is to choose either the alternative that maximizes effectiveness with given cost or the alternative that minimizes costs given a desired level of effectiveness.

Limitations

Three limitations of cost-effectiveness analysis are generally considered.[52] First, judgment may be necessary to delineate factors and interrelationships and to interpret the results. Second, it may be difficult to select measures of effectiveness. Third, imperfect information and insufficient input information may distort the analysis. Finally, the analysis is too deterministic and does not account for uncertainty.

CONCLUSIONS

This chapter suggested ways of conceptualizing microsocial accounting and ways of measuring and valuating the environmental effects of organizational behavior. A tentative conceptual framework is presented as a way of conceptualizing microsocial accounting. This framework rests on proposed objectives, concepts, and qualitative characteristics of microsocial accounting. The measurement of the environmental effects of organizational behavior rests on measurement of social costs and social benefits. Various ways of measuring social costs and benefits are presented. The evaluation of social programs rest on two established techniques, namely, cost-benefit analysis and cost-effectiveness.

What is conveyed in this chapter is, firs, that a conceptual framework for socioeconomic accounting is feasible and, second, that techniques of measurement evaluation of the environmental effects of organizational behavior are available. What remains to be accomplished by corporate firms and interest groups is a trial implementation and "legitimization" of microsocial accounting.

NOTES

1.   Meinoff Dierkes and Raymond A. Bauer, *Corporate Social Accounting* (New York: Praeger), p.xi.

2.   Kavassen V. Ramanthan, "Toward a Theory of Corportate Social Accounting," *Accounting Review* (July 1976), pp. 519-521.

3.   Ibid., pp.520-521.

4.   Ibid., pp. 522-523.

5.   Ibid.

6.   Financial; Accounting Standards Board, "Qualitative Charachteristics: Criteria for Selecting and Evaluating Financial Accounting and Reporting Policies," Exposure draft (Stamford, Conn.: FASB, 1979).

7.   American Accounting Association, *A Statement of Basic Accounting Theory* (Evanston, III.: AAA, 1966), p.9.

8.   American Accounting Association, Committee on Concepts and Standards for external Financial Reports, *Statement of Accounting Theory and Theory Acceptance* (Sarasota, Fla.: AAA, 1977), p. 16.

9.   American Accounting Association, *A Statement of Basic Accounting Theory,* p. 10.

10.   "Conceptual Framework for Financial Accounting and Reporting: Elements of Financial Statements and their Measurements," FASB Discussion Memorandum (Stamford, Conn.: FASB, 1976), p.1.

11.   Robert H. Haveman, "On Estimating Environmental Damage: A Survey of Recent Research in the United States," in Organization for Economic Cooperation and Development, *Environmental Damage Costs* (Paris: OECD, 1976), p. 102.

12.   Alien V. Kneese, Robert U. Ayres, and Ralph C. d'Arge, *Economics and the Environment: A Materials Balance Approach* (Baltimore: Johns Hopkins University Press, 1970).

13.   Ibid., p. 107.

14.   Office of Service and Technology, "Cumulative Regulatory Effects on the Cost of Automotive Transportation (RECAT): Final Report of the *ad hoc* Committee" (Washington D.C.: Office of Service and Technology, February 28, 1972). Programmers Analysis Unit, *Economic and Technical Appraisal of Air Pollution in the United Kingdom* (Chilton: Berkes, 1971).

15.   R.C. Ridker, *Economic Costs of Air Pollution* (New York: Praeger, 1967); P. G. Lave and N. T. Seskin "Air Pollution and Human Health," *Science* 169 (1968), p. 723.

16.   R. T. Stickney, N. P. Mueller, and A. S. Spence, "Pollution vs. Rubber," *Rubber Age* 45 (September 1971); Midwest Research Institute, *Systems Analysis of the Effects of Air Pollution on materials* (Chicago: Midwest Research Institute, January 1970).

17.   Ridke also attempted to estimate soiling and deterioration damages by relying on two other approaches: survey of consumers, and survey of the cleaning industry.

18.   P. Benedict, M. Miller, and T. Olson, *Economic Impact of Air Pollution Plants in the United States* (Standford, Calif.: Stanford Research Institute. November 1971); S. Millecan, *A Survey and Assessment of Air Pollution Damage to California Vegetation in* 1970 (Sacramento: California Department of Agriculture, June 1971).

19.   T. Landau, "Statistical Aspects of Air Pollution as It Applies to Agriculture." Paper presented at the 1971 meeting of the Statistical Societies. Fort Collins, Colo.

20.   R. Diffey, "An Investigation into the Effect of High Traffic Noise on House Prices in a Homogeneous Submarket." Paper presented at a Seminar on House Prices and the Micro-economics of Housing, London School of Economics, December 1971.

21.   P. Plowden, *The Cost of Noise* (London: Metra Consulting Group, 1970).

22.   R. E. Wyzga, "A Survey of Environmental Damage Functions," in *Environmental Damage Costs* (Paris: Organization for Economic Co-Operation and Development, 1974).

23.   M. Clawson and J. L. Knetsch, *Economics of Outdoor Recreation* (Baltimore: Johns Hopkins University Press, 1971).

24. Organization for Economic Co-Operation and Development, *Economic Measurement of Environmental Damage* (Paris: OECD, 1976), p. 6.

25. Ibid., p. 52.

26. A. Myrick Freeman III., *The Benefits of Environmental Improvement: Theory and Practice* (Baltimore: John Hopkins University Press, 1979), p. 4.

27. Ibid., p. 82.

28. M. Kurtz, "An Experimental Approach to the Determination of the demand for Public Goods," *Journal of Public Economics* 3 (1974), pp. 329-348; Peter Bolrun, "An Approach to the Problem of Estimating Demand for Public Goods," *Swedish Journal of Economics* I (March 1971), pp. 94-105.

29. H. R. Bowen, "The Interpretation of Voting in the Allocation of Economic Resources," *Quarterly Journal of Economics* 58 (1963), pp.27-48.

30. James L. Barr and Otto A. Davis, "An Elementary Political and Economic Theory of the Expenditures of Local Government," *Southern Economic Journal* 33 (October 1996), pp. 149-165; T. E. Borcherding and R. T. Deacon, "The Demand for Services of Nonfederal Governments," *American Economic Review* 67 (December 1972), pp. 891-901; T. C. Bergstorm and R. P. Goodman, "Private Demands for Public Goods," *American Economic Review* 63 (June 1973), pp. 280-296.

31. Ridker, *Economic Costs of Air Pollution,* p. 25.

32. A. R. Prest and r. Turvey, "Cost-Benefit Analysis: A Survey," *Economic Journal* (December 1965), pp. 683-735.

33. PPBS rests essentially on cost-benefit analysis.

34. Another test for potential Pareto improvements is that everyone in society could be made better off by means of a costless redistribution of the net benefits.

35. Otto Eckstein, "A Survey of the Theory of Public expenditure Criteria," in James M. Buchanan, ed., *Public Finances: Needs, Sources and Utilization* (Princeton: Princeton University Press, 1961).

36. Jesse Burkhead and Jerry Miner, *Public Expenditure* (Chicago: Aldine-Atherton, 1971), p.225.

37. R. N. McKean, Efficiency in Government through Systems Analysis (New York: Wiley, 1958), ch. 8.

38. George A. Steiner. "Probems in Implementing Program Budgeting," in David Novick, ed., *Program Budgeting* (Cambridge: Harvard University Press, 1965), pp. 87-88.

39. William J. Baumol, "On the Discount Rate for Public Projects," in Robert Haveman and Julius Margolis, eds., *Public Expenditures and Policy Analysis* (Chicago: Markham, 1970), p. 274.

40. Burkheads and Miner, *Public Expenditure,* p. 232.

41. U.S. Bureau of the Budget, *Standards and Criteria for formulating and evaluating Federal Water Resources Development* (Washington, D.C.: U.S. Government, 1961), p.67.

42. A. C. Pigou. *The Economics of welfare,* 4th ed. (London: Macmillan, 1932).

43. R.A. Musgrave, *Fiscal Systems* (New Haven: Yale University Press, 1969), pp. 797-806.

44. Prest and Turvey, "Cost-Benefit Analysis," pp. 729-731.

45. U.S. House of Representatives, Committee on Interstate and Foreign Commerce, Subcommittee on Oversight and Investigations, *Federal Regulation and Regulatory Reform*, 94th Cong., 2d sess., 1976, ch. 15 (subcommittee print).

46. Michael S. Baram, "Cost-Benefit Analysis: An Inadequate Basis for Health Safety, and Environmental Regulatory Decision Making," *Ecology Law Quarterly* 8 (1980), pp. 473-531.

47. Barry G. King, "Cost-Effectiveness Analysis? Implications for Accountants," *Journal of Accountancy* (May 1970), p. 43.

48. M.C. Houston and G. Ogawa, "Observations on the Theoretical Basis of Cost effectiveness," *Operations Research* (March-April 1966), pp. 242-266.

49. King, "Cost-Effectiveness Analysis" p. 44.

50. William A. Niskanen, "Measures of effectiveness," in Thomas A. Goidman, ed., *Cost-Effectiveness Analysis* (New York: Praeger, 1967), p.20.

51. Neil M. Singer, *Public Microeconomics* (Boston: Littler, Brown, 1976), p. 320.

52.   King, "Cost-Effectiveness Analysis" p. 48-49.

SELECTED READINGS
Toward a Theory of Microsocial Accounting

Beams, Floyd A., and Paul E. Fertig. "Pollution Control through Social Cost Conversion." *Journal of Accountancy* (November 1971), pp. 37-42.

Bendock, C. M. "Measuring Social Costs." *Management Accounting* (January 1975), pp. 13-15.

Chanstain, Clark E. "Corporate Accounting for Environmental Information." *Financial Executive* (May 1975), pp. 45-50.

Churchill, Neil C. "Toward a Theory for Social Accounting." *Sloan Management Review* (Spring 1974), pp. 1-16.

Churchman, C. W. "On the Facility, Felicity and Morality of Measuring Social Change." *Accounting Review* (January 1971).

Linowes, David F. "The Accountant' enlarged Professional Responsibilities." *Journal of Accountancy* (February 1973), pp. 47-57.

Mason, Alister K. "Social Costs: A New Challenge for Accountants." *Canadian Chartered Accountant Magazine* (June 1971), pp. 390-395.

Ramanathan, Kavassen V. "Toward a Theory of Corporate Social Accounting." *Accounting Review* (July 1976), pp. 516-528.

Ronen, J. "Accounting for Social Costs and Benefits." In J.J. Cramer, Jr., and G. H. Sorter, eds. *Objectives of Financial Statements* (New York: American Institute of Certified Public Accountants, May 1974), pp. 317-342.

Sawin, Henry S. "The CPA's Role in Restoring the Ecological Balance." *Management Advisor* (March-April 1971), pp. 23-29.

Shulman, James S., and Jeffrey Gale. "Laying the Groundwork for Social Accounting." *Financial Executive* (March 1972), pp. 38-52.

Evaluating Social Programs: Cost-Benefit Analysis

Anderson, Lee G., and Russel F. Settle. *Benefit-Cost Analysis: A Practical Guide* (Lexington, Mass.: Heath, 1977).

Bailey, Duncan, and Charles Schotta. "Private and Social Rates of return to the education of Academicians." *American Economic review* (March 1972).

Baram, Micheal S. "Cost-Benefit Analysis: An Inadequate basis for Health, Safely, and Environmental Regulatory Decision Making." *Ecology Law Quarterly* 8 (1980), pp. 473-531.

Baumol, William J. "On the Discount Rate for Public Projects." In Robert Haveman and Julius Margolis, eds. *Public Expenditure and Policy Analysis* (Chicago: Markham, 1970).

--------. "On the Social Rate of Disocunt." *American Economic Review* (September 1968).

Eckstein, Otto. "A Survey of the Theory of Public Expenditure Criteria." In James M. Buchanan, ed. *Public Finances, Sources and Utilization* (Princeton: Princeton University Press, 1961).

Gramlich, Edward M. *Benefit-Cost Analysis of Government Programs* (Englewood Cliffs, N.J.: Prentice-Hall, 1981).

Hanke, Steve H. "On the Feasibility of Benefit-Cost Analysis." *Public Policy* 29, no. 2 (Spring 1981), pp. 147-157.

Kendall, M. G., ed. *Cost Benefit Analysis* (New York: American Elsevier, 1971).

McKean, R. N. *Efficiency in Government through Systems Analysis* (New York: Wiley, 1958).

Mishan, E.J. *Cost-Benefit Analysis* (New York: Praeger, 1976).

Novick, David, ed. *Program Budgeting* (Cambridge: Harvard University Press, 1965).

Prest, A. R., and R. Turvey. "Cost-Benefit Analysis: A Survey." *Economic Journal* (December 1965), pp. 683-735.

Sassone, Peter G., and William A. Schaefer. *Cost-Benefit Analysis: A Practical Guide* (Lexington, Mass.: Heath. 1977).

Weisbrod, Burton A. "Costs and Benefits of Medical Research: A Case Study of Poliomyelitis." *Journal of Policaital Economy* (May-June 1971); pp. 527-544.

Evaluating Social Program: Cost-Effectiveness Analysis

Committee on Accounting for Not-for-Profit Organizations. "Report if the Committee." *Accounting Review,* supplement, 46 (1971), pp. 81-164.

Committee on Measures of Effectiveness for Social Programs. "Report of the Committee." *Accounting* Review, supplement, 47 (1972), pp. 337-398.

Committee on Nonfinancial Measures of Effectiveness. "Report of the Committee." *Accounting* Review, supplement, 46 (1971), pp. 165-212.

Committee on Not-for-Profit Organizations, 1972-73. "Report of the Committee." *Accounting* Review, supplement, 49 (1974), pp. 225-249.

Goidman, Thomas A. *Cost-Effectiveness Analysis* (New York: Praeger, 1967).

Heuston, M. C., and G. Ogawa. "Observations on the Theoretical Basis of Cost Effectiveness." *Operations Research* (March-April 1966), pp. 242-266.

King, Barry G. "Cost-Effectiveness Analysis: Implications for Accountants." *Journal of Accounting* (May 1970).

Singer, Neil M. *Public Microeconomics* (Boston: Little, Brown, 1976).

Sorenson, James E., and Hugh D. Grove. "Cost-Outcome and Cost-Effectiveness Analysis: Emerging Nonprofit Performance Evaluation Techniques." *Accounting Review* (July 1977), pp. 658-675.

Measurement in Microsocial Accounting

Barr, James L., and Otto A. Davis. "An Elementary Political and Economic Theory of the Expenditures of Local Government." *Southern Economic Journal.* (October 1966), pp. 149-165.

Bergstorm, T. C., and R. P. Goodman. "Private Demands for Public Goods." *American Economic Review* 63 (June 1973), pp. 280-296.

Bohn, Peter. "An Approach to the Problem of Estimating Demand for Public Goods." *Swedish Journal of Economics* I (march 1971), pp. 94-105.

Borcherding, T. E., and R. T. Deacon, "The Demand for Services of Nonfederal Governments." *American Economic Review* 67 (December 1972), pp. 891-901.

Bowen, H. R. "The Interpretation of Voting in the Allocation of Economic Resources." *Quarterly Journal of Economics* 58 (1963), pp. 27-48.

Clawson, M., and J. L. Knetsch. *Economics of Outdoor Recreation* (Baltimore: Johns Hopkins University Press, 1971).

Feenberg, D., and E. S. Mills. *Measuring the Benefits of Water Pollution Abatement* (New York: Academic Press, 1980).

Freeman, A. Myrick III. *The Benefits of environmental Improvement: Theory and Practice* (Baltimore: Johns Hopkins University Press, 1979).

--------. "On Estimating Air Pollution Control Benefits from land Value Studies. *Journal of Environmental Economics and Management* I (May 1974), pp. 74-83.

Hause, John C. "The Theory of Welfare Cost Measurement." *Journal of Political Economy* 6 (December 1975), pp. 1145-1182.

Kapp, K William. *Social Costs of Business Enterprise* (New York: Asia Publishing House, 1963).

Kneese, Alien V.; Robert U. Ayres; and ralph C. d'Arge. *Economics and the environment: A Materials Balance Approach* (Baltimore: John Hopkins Univeristy Press, 1970).

Kurtz, M. "An Experimental Approach to the Determination of the Demand for Public Goods." *Journal of Public Economics* 3 (1974), pp. 329-348.

Organization for Economic Co-Operation and Development. *Economic Implication of Pollution Control* (Paris: OECD, 1974).

--------. *Economic Measurement of Environmental Damage* (Paris: OECD 1976).

--------. *Economic Damage Costs* (Paris: OECD 1974).

Plowden, P. *The Cost of Noise* (London: Metra Consulting Group, 1970).

Ridker, R. G. *Economic Costs of Air Pollution* (New York: Praeger, 1967).

Part 2- LEASING

Chapter 1
Analysis of the Lease-or-Buy Decision

Leasing has recently become an important source of financing for many types of assets. The lessee acquires the use of an asset while the title is retained by the lessor. More specifically, a lease is a contract between an owner (the lessor) and another party (the lessee) that grants the lessee the right to use the lessor's property under certain conditions and for a specified period of time. Because of the contractual nature of lease obligation, a lease should be considered a financing device and an alternative to debt financing. Both the lease rental payments and the payments of principal and interest on debt are fixed obligations. Any default in the payment of either obligation can create serious problems.

The decision to lease an asset is generally evaluated by comparing it with a borrowing decision necessary for an outright purchase of the same asset; different valuation models have been proposed, and any choice can be challenged because of the controversial issues surrounding a given model and its corresponding variables and parameters. The main purpose of this chapter is to explain leasing arrangements and the main issues in financing leasing, and to provide a methodology for analysis.

The lease as a new form of financing undergoes constant change, as shown by the number and variations of the sources of leasing arrangements. Financial institutions involved in leasing differ mainly in their degree of specialization and include independent leasing companies, service leasing companies, lease brokers, commercial brokers, and insurance companies.

TYPES OF LEASING ARRANGEMENTS

Although it is possible to describe major forms of lease arrangements, the options, terms, and conditions may vary from contract to contract, giving a firm great flexibility in an adaptation of leasing as a financing method.

Operating versus Financial Leases

The first distinction to be made in leasing is between *operating and financial leases.* Under both contracts, the lessee agrees to make periodic rental payments. An operating lease is a short-term contract that is cancelable given proper notice at the option of the lessee, whereby the lessor gives the lessee the use of property in exchange for rental payments and at the same time retains the usual ownership risks (such as obsolescence) and rewards (such as a gain from appreciation in value at the end of the lease period). To compensate the lessor for assuming the ownership risks, the periodic rental payments of an operating lease will include a return on investment plus most ownership costs, such an maintenance, taxes, depreciation, obsolescene, casualty losses, and so forth. Examples of operating leases include car rentals, apartment rentals, telephone service, and space rental in shopping centers.

A financial lease is a comparatively long0term contract that is non-cancelable by the lessor, who assumes little or no ownership costs. As a result, the periodic rental payments include only a return on investment, and the lessee may be required to pay most of the ownership costs. At the termination of the lease, options may exist allowing the lessee to acquire the asset at either a nominal cost or no cost at all. The financial lease allows the lessor to recover the investment and even realize a profit through the lessee's continuous rental payments over the period specified by the contract. The financial lease gives the lessee continuous use of the asset at a certain cost and, consequently, is a means of financing the use (but not the ownership) of the asset. In other words, the difference between the operating and financial lease lies mainly in the cancellation and financing options. As opposed to an operating lease, a financial lease is noncancelable, and it can be perceived as a financing instrument.

Sale and Leaseback, Direct leasing, and Leverage Leases

Another important distinction in lease financing is made between the sale and leaseback and direct lease arrangements. The difference lies in the nature of the prior ownership of the asset to be leased. Under the sale and leaseback arrangement, a firm sells an asset it owns to another party, which in turn leases it back to the previous owner. Under this popular arrangement, a company in need of liquidity receives cash from the sale of the asset while retaining the economic use of the asset during the lease period.

Under direct leasing, the lessee acquires the use of an asset it did not previously own. The lessee can enter into the leasing arrangements with a manufacturer, independent leasing company, or financial institution.

With the advent of direct leasing through commercial banks in 1963, a new lease arrangement speared, called a leverage lease. This is a tripartite arrangement whereby the lessor finances a portion of the acquisition of the asset (50 to 80 percent of the purchase price) from a lender (commercial bank), securing the loan by a mortgage of the leased property as well as by the assignment of the lease and lease payments. The leverage lease is a popular instrumental for special-purpose leasing companies and partnerships of individuals in high tax brackets because of the tax benefits provided by the accelerated depreciation charges, the investment tax credit, the interest on debt, and the favorable return on the equity participation by the lessor. From the point of view of the lessee, the leverage lease is similar to any other lease and, consequently, does not affect the method of variation.[1]

Leverage leasing involves at least four parties: a lessee, a manufacturer (or distributor), a lessor, and a lender. Arrangements are complex, and the parties enter into the agreement primarily for tax and financial cost savings rather than convenience. The lessee is able to obtain financial leasing from the lessor at a cost lower than the usual cost of capital; the lessor, being of a high income tax bracket, gains an investment tax credit (or capital cost allowance) benefit resulting in reduced taxes. The lessor passes on some of this benefit to the lessee though reduced lease costs. Direct leasing, sale and leaseback, and leverage leasing are illustrated later in Exhibit 1.1

Maintenance, Nonmaintenance, and Net Leases

The assignment of responsibility for the maintenance of the asset during the life of a lese takes three forms: maintenance lease, nonmaintenance lease, and net lease.

A *maintenance lease* assigns responsibility for the maintenance of the leased asset's good working order to the lessor. The lessor is required to incur the maintenance and repair expenses and the local and state to incur the maintenance and repair expenses and the local and state taxes, and to provide insurance for the leased asset. The maintenance lease is preferable when the lessor is better equipped to provide low-cost repair than the lessee in terms of technology and skills. It is used mostly in rentals of automobiles, trucks, and specialized equipment, like computers, requiring a highly qualified maintenance staff.

A *nonmaintenance lease* assigns the responsibility for the maintenance of a leased asset to the lessee. The lessee is required to pay for all maintenance and repair costs and the local and state taxes, and to provide insurance. The nonmaintenance lease occurs principally in long-term leasing of land and buildings.

A *net lease* assigns total responsibility for an asset's maintenance to the lessee to the point that the lessee may be required to absorb all losses incurred by the sale of the asset at the end of the life of the lease, which is typical in fleet leasing of vehicles. In car leasing the net lease is sometimes referred to as an open-end lease: In return for a slightly lower monthly lease fee, the lessee agrees to make up the price differential if the leased car sells for less than the prearranged price when the lease expires because of excess mileage, poor maintenance, or any other reason.

ADVANTAGES OF LEASING
Shifting the Risks of Ownership

A firm that purchases an asset is subject to the risk of obsolescence due to innovation in the field. Generally, in the decision to lease or buy an asset subject to a high rate of obsolescence, the leasing alternative will appear more appropriate. Through leasing rather then buying the asset, the lease can shift the risk of obsolescence and of ownership to the lessor. The argument in favor of leasing relies heavily on the assumption that the lessor is not aware of the rate of obsolescence and innovation in the field. In most cases, however, the lessor is very knowledgeable and is in a better position to anticipate the rate of obsolescence than the lessee. The lessor, well aware of the risks of ownership, will attempt to recover the investment plus interest over the leases period and will probably include the implicit charge for obsolescence in the computation of the rental payments. Only when the lessor inaccurately estimates the rate of obsolescence does the lessee benefit from shifting the risks of ownership. If the asset becomes obsolete more rapidly than the lessor anticipated, the leasing alternative will be beneficial to the lessee. The lessor can keep the rental payments low by spreading the risk of obsolescence over many lease contracts. The diversification in this case will benefit both the lessor and the lessee.

Avoidance of Restrictions Associated with Debt

Leasing is assumed to offer fewer restrictions than debt and, consequently, to provide more flexibility. Most loan agreements are bond indentures include protective covenant restrictions, but similar limitations are not as common in leasing. One usual restriction accompanying leasing is in the use of the leased property. For example, the use of the leased equipment may be limited in terms of the number of hours per day. Changes and adjustments in the lease equipment may also be prohibited unless authorized by the lessor.

The advantage of fewer restrictions with leasing than with debt financing will probably disappear in the near future. Most lenders impose restrictions on the amount to be leased for firms financed heavily by debt. Because leasing is becoming more and more accepted as a form of financing, protective covenants will probably be drafted for both leasing and bond indentures.

Effect on Cash Borrowing Capacity

It is often said that leasing allows a firm to conserve cash and raise more funds than debt financing. This is based on the following claims- some supportable and some unsupportive- made on behalf of leading.

People often argue that leasing allows the optimal use of cash leading to an improvement in a firm's total earning power. Thus, it is maintained, the capital intended for the purchase of fixed assets with low turnover is tied up for the acquisition of current assets with high turnover. Retailers most often are advised to rent their premises and allocate their capital to inventory and accounts receivable. Although seemingly attractive, this claims on behalf of leasing is the result of confusion about the relationship between the investment and financing decisions. It assumes that the financing method is a determinant of the mix of assets. A firm actually decides first on the optimal mix of assets necessary for its line of business and then decides on the proper way of financing this mix by comparing the costs of buying and leasing. The firm can decide either to borrow or lease. In either case it decides to use the optimal mix of assets effectively and efficiently.

People also argue that leasing permits a firm not only to avoid buying an asset, but also to finance up to 100 percent of the cost of the asset. What is the impact on a firm's borrowing capacity? Does leasing provide more funds? The usual assumption is that leasing has no effect on a firm's borrowing power and a positive effect on its borrowing capacity. However, this line of reasoning is misleading. Given the fixed obligatory nature of the lease, it should be considered equivalent to an implicit loan of 100 percent of the funds needed. The borrowing capacity is definitely reduced, and the borrowing power must be compared with debt financing. The erroneous assumption that leasing provides more funds results from the conventional accounting treatment, whereby lease obligations are not shown by liabilities on the balance sheet. This situation has changed, and accounting treatments now tend to favor to capitalization of long-term leases.

Leasing permits the financing of capital additions on a piecemeal basis. To be practical, long-term debt financing must usually be arranged on a much larger scale than lease financing, which can be adjusted to each individual unit of property acquired. This can be a valid reason for using lease financing to make occasional asset acquisitions spaced over a period of time. However, this justification lost its validity when the total amount of capital additions over a given period is large enough to justify a debt issue. Long-term debt adapted to the timing of expenditures, either through the use of interim bank borrowing with subsequent refunding or by a direct placement of securities with institutional investors, providing for a series of takedowns.[2]

Tax Advantages

A common argument in the lease-or-buy controversy is whether leasing offers tax advantages over ownership. Under present tax laws, rental payments are considered an operating expense and can be deducted from taxable income. This gives rise to two basic differences in the tax effects of leasing as compared with ownership:

1. Leasing makes it possible, in effect, to write off the depreciable portion of property over the basic term of a lease, which is generally shorter than the period that would be permitted for depreciation. The result is not a tax savings but a shift in the timing of deductions and tax payments similar to the effects of accelerated depreciation. To the extent the tax payments are deferred, the company benefits by having the use of these funds for the additional period.
2. Leasing makes it possible, in effect, to write off land value against taxable income, which is not allowed for depreciation purposes. The effect can be very significant when land represents a substantial portion of the total investments in urban department store properties. Although leasing provides a way to recover part of the investment in land during the basic periods of the lease, it also deprives the company of 100 percent of this value at the end of the period- which still leaves a net loss of 48 percent. Furthermore, if past trends in land value are any indication of future trends, the loss could be considerably greater.[3]

Another cost implicitly packaged in the terms of any leasing contract is corrected with the federal income tax deduction. One of the frequently cited advantages of equipment leasing is that a leasing contract permits the lessee to enjoy a more advantageous stream of income tax expense deductions than would be possible with outright ownership of the equipment, where only depreciation and interest could be deducted. In fact, there may be some advantage if the lease payments are scheduled so they are higher in the earlier years of the lease than the sum of depreciation and interest and, conversely, lower in later years. Under these conditions, present value of the tax deductions is greater than under outright ownership. This advantage can be achieved in another way under financial leases. The agreement can be made for a relatively short initial term-say five years. During this time the lessor recovers the entire cost of the equipment: If the lessee purchased the equipment directly, it would have to be depreciated over a longer time span- say, seven to ten years.[4]

The Economic Recovery Tax Act of 1981 allows companies to transfer the tax benefits of tax credits and of the Accelerated Cost Recovery System (ACRS) on new plants and equipment bought between January 1 and August 13, 1981, through what is called safe-harbor leasing. Such transactions are safe as long as the letter of the Internal Revenue Service regulations is followed. This is possible in two cases:

1. Under a reciprocal lease-sublease, the seller of the tan benefits (the lessor-sublessee) acquires new equipment for its own use and, within three months of purchase, leases it to the buyer of the tax credits (the lessee-sublessor). The seller transfers tax credits to the buyer via the lease, and the buyer simultaneously sublease the property back to the seller (the user) without those credits. The rentals payable by the buyer exceed the rentals to be received by the buyer. This differential is effectively the purchase price of the tax credits transferred.
2. Under a sale leaseback, the seller of the tax benefits (the seller and lessee of the property) acquires new equipment for its own use and, within three months of purchase, sells it to the buyer of the tax benefits (the buyer and lessor of the property). This enables the seller to transfer to the buyer and tax benefits related to the equipment. The consideration is composed of a cash down payment of at least

10 percent of the original cost of the property and a note for the remainder. The buyer than leases the property back to the seller for a lease term that is equal to the term of the note. If the rentals under the lease are equal to the payments on the note (principal and interest), the buyer's initial investment (the down payment) is the purchase price of the tax benefits. The seller continues to be the user of the property. The seller may retain title to the property or reacquire title at the end of the lease term for a nominal amount, such as $1.[5]

The intent of the legislation is that tax leases will allow firms that do now owe taxes or are unable to realize certain tax benefits to realize those benefits by making them transferable. Instead of receiving the benefits directly as a reduction of income taxes payable, firms not owing taxes can realize them by selling the right to those benefits to other firms that can use them to reduce taxes payable.

Shortly after the passage of the act, Ford Motor Company announced that it was selling to International Business machines Corporation (IBM) its investment tax and depreciation deductions on "under $1 billion" worth of machinery, equipment, and tools acquired so far in 1981. Similarly, Bethlehem Steel Corp. and R. R. Donnelley & Sons Co. entered into a safe-harbor lease transaction that involved the exchange of tax credits. Donnelley will buy steel manufacturing equipment from Bethlehem and lease it back to the steel maker.

A NORMATIVE MODEL FOR LEASE EVALUATION

Any model for lease evaluation is determined on a cash flow basis. The treatment of the variable in the model differs, depending on whether it is the lessee's or the lessor's model.

Lessor's Analysis

The lessor attempts to determine a rental payment amount that will insure that the present value of rental payments plus the present value of the salvage value of the asset equals or exceeds the original cost of the asset. The discount rate the lessor chooses will be adjusted for the recovery of both the cost of capital of the lessor and other ownership costs before taxes. The lessee may have the option of paying the rental payments at the beginning or the end of each year. Both cases will be examined using the following sample problem.

Assume a firm has decided to lease an asset under the following conditions:

Purchase price of the asset (A_0) = $30,000

Expected salvage value of the asset (S) = $10,000

Before-tax rate of return (K_1) = 8 percent

Salvage value discount rate (K_s) = 20 percent

Lease period (n) = 5 years.

To compute the rental payment, proceed as follows:
1. The present value of the salvage value (Spv) *is*

$$S_{PV} = \frac{S}{(1 + K_s)^n} = \frac{\$10,000}{(a + 0.20)^5} = \$4,018.$$

2. The rental (R_j) if paid in advance is

$$A_0 - S_{PV} = R_1 + \sum_{j=2}^{5} \frac{R_j}{(1+K_L)^{j-1}}$$

$$= R_1 + \sum_{j=2}^{5} \frac{R_j}{(1+0.08)^{j-1}}$$

$30,000 - $4,018 = R_j (1 + 3.31213)$

$R_j = $6,025$

3. The rental (R_j) if paid at the end of period is

$$A_0 - S_{pv} = \sum_{j=1}^{n} R_j \frac{1}{(1+K_L)^j}$$

$$\$30,000 - \$4,018 = \sum_{j=1}^{n} R_j \frac{1}{(1+0.08)^j}$$

$$= R_j (3.99271)$$

$$R_j = \$6,507$$

Lessee's Analysis

The lessee's approach concentrates on how the asset is to be acquired, leaving to more conventional capital budgeting techniques the prior decision on whether the asset is to be acquired at all. Thus, the question the lessee examines is whether to borrow and buy or to lease. The answer is found by comparing the respective costs of both alternatives. The summary measure used for the comparison can be either the net present value advantage of leasing (*NAL*) or the pretax interest rate on the lease (X_i). The *NAL* measure is expressed as follows:

$$NAL = A_0 - \sum_{j=1}^{n} \frac{R_j}{(1+X_1)^j} + \sum_{j=1}^{n} \frac{TR_j}{(1+X_2)^j} - \sum_{j=1}^{n} \frac{TD_j}{(1+X_3)^j} - \sum_{j=1}^{n} \frac{TI_j}{(1+X_4)^j}$$

[1] [2]   [3]   [4]   [5]

$$+ \sum_{j=1}^{n} \frac{O_j(1-T)}{(1+X_5)^j} - \frac{V_n}{(1+K_s)^j}$$

[6]   [7]

The variable included in the *NAL* equation are defined as follows:

A_0 = Purchase price of the asset

R_j = Lease payment in period j

D_j = Depreciation charge in period j

V_n = Expected after-tax salvage value of the asset = $S_j - (S_j - B_j) T_g$

S_j = Salvage value in period j

B_j = Book value in period j

X_i = Discount rate to apply to the various cash flow streams of the equation

T_g = Tax rate applicable to gains and losses on the disposal of fixed assets

T = Corporate income tax rate

n = Number of years covered by the lease agreement

I_j = Interest component of the loan payment

K_s = Salvage value discount rate

O_j = Incremental operating costs of ownership in period t

The interpretation of the *NAL* equation is influenced by the treatment of the key variables in the lease evaluation decision. The seven terms in the *NAL* equation can be interpreted as follows:

1. The purchase price of the asset is an unavoidable cost of purchasing.
2. The present value of the rental payments is a cost of leasing.
3. The present value of the tax shield provided by the rental payments is a benefit of leasing and, consequently, an opportunity cost of purchasing.
4. The present value of the tax shield provided by the depreciation expense is a benefit of purchasing.
5. The present value of the tax shield provided by the interest expense on a "loan equivalent" to a lease is another benefit of purchasing.
6. The present value of the after-tax operating cost is a burden of ownership.
7. The present value of the after-tax residual value is a benefit of ownership.

Summarizing the seven terms, the basic equation provides the net present value advantage of leasing. Setting *NAL* equal to zero and solving for X_i provides the pretax interest rate on the lease. The *NAL* equation can also be explained as follows:
1. The present value of the borrow-and-buy alternative is

$$A_0 - \sum_{j=1}^{n} \frac{TD_j}{(1 + X_3)^j} - \sum_{j=1}^{n} \frac{TI_j}{(1 + X_4)^j} + \sum_{j=1}^{n} \left[\frac{O_j(1 - T)}{(1 + X_5)^j}\right] - \frac{V_n}{(1 + K_s)^j)}$$

2. The present value of leasing is
3. *NAL* = present value of borrowing and buying – present value of leasing. Two problems in the applicability of the *NAL* equation lie in the choice of the appropriate discount rates to be used and the computation of the loan equivalent to the lease.

The discount rates X_1, X_2, X_3, X_4, and X_5 are those applied by the market to evaluate the streams of distribution of R_j, TR_j, TD_j, TI_j, and $O_j(1-T)$. Possible alternative are a single discount rate or an appropriate rate for each stream. We will first use the after-tax cost of debt as a single discount rate for all streams; later in the chapter, the other alternatives proposed in the literature will be discussed. Thus, the after-tax cost of debt will be used for each cash flow stream except V_n, which will be discounted as its own rate (K_s = 20 percent) due to the uncertainty associated with this "estimated" value.

The loan equivalent decision also generated a debate in the literature. This chapter will propose a first alternative and later present other proposed alternatives. For the first alternative, it assumed that

$P_0 = A_0,$
$P_0 = \sum_{j=1}^{n} \frac{L_j}{(1+r)_j},$
where

P_0 = Present value of the loan equivalent
L_j = Loan payment at the end of each period j
R = Pretax interest rate on term loans "comparable" to the lease

To illustrate the lessee's analysis, the same problem presented in the lessor's analysis will be used. The data required are as follows:

A_0 = \$30,000
S = \$10,000
R_j = \$6,025 (at the beginning of each period)
R_j = \$6,507 (at the end of each period)
D_j = Straight-line depreciation at period $j = \frac{A_0 - S}{n} = \$4,000$
O_j = \$2,000
$B = 0$
T_s = 10 percent
$V_n = S - [(S - B)T_g] = \$9,000$
r = 6 percent
T = 50 percent
n = 5 years
K_u = 20 percent
The lessee's analysis proceeds as follows:
1. For the loan payment computation, it has been assumed in this analysis that $P_0 = A_0$, and
$$P_0 = A_0$$
$$P_0 = \sum_{j=1}^{n} \frac{L_j}{(1+r)^j},$$
Given a 6 percent interest rate on loans, the amount of the annual loan payment at the end of each year is found by solving the following equation for L_j:
$$P_0 = \sum_{j=1}^{5} \frac{L_j}{(1+0.06)^j}.$$
$L_j = \$7,122.$
2. When the rental payments are made in advance, the lease evaluation analysis proceeds by the computation of the *NAL* as follows:

$$NAL = \$30,000 - \left[\$6,025 + \sum_{j=1}^{4} \frac{\$6,025}{(1+0.03)^j} \right] + \sum_{j=1}^{5} \frac{(\$6,025)(0.5)}{(1+0.03)^j} - \sum_{j=1}^{5} \frac{(\$4,000)(0.5)}{(1+0.03)^j}$$

$$- \left[\frac{\$800\,(0.5)}{(1+0.03)^1} + \frac{\$1,480\,(0.5)}{(1+0.03)^2} + \frac{\$1,142\,(0.5)}{(1+0.03)^3} + \frac{\$783\,(0.5)}{(1+0.03)^4} + \frac{\$403\,(0.5)}{(1+0.03)^5} \right]$$

$$+ \sum_{j=1}^{5} \left[\frac{\$2,000\,(1-0.5)}{(1+0.03)^j} \right] - \frac{\$9,000}{(1+0.20)^5}$$

= \$30,000 – (\$6,025 + \$22,396) + \$13,796 - \$9,159 - \$2,130 + \$4,580 - \$3,617

= \$5,048   = *NAL* when rental payments are made in advance.

3. The lease evaluation analysis when the rental payments are made at the end of the period is as follows:

$$NAL = \$30,000 - \sum_{j=1}^{5} \frac{\$6,057}{(1+0.03)^j} + \sum_{j=1}^{5} \frac{(\$6,507)(0.5)}{(1+0.03)^j} - \sum_{j=1}^{5} \frac{(\$4,000)(0.5)}{(1+0.03)^j}$$

$$- \left[\frac{\$800\,(0.5)}{(1+0.03)^1} + \frac{\$1,480\,(0.5)}{(1+0.03)^2} + \frac{\$1,142\,(0.5)}{(1+0.03)^3} + \frac{\$783\,(0.5)}{(1+0.03)^4} + \frac{\$403\,(0.5)}{(1+0.03)^5} \right]$$

$$+ \sum_{j=1}^{5} \left[\frac{\$2,000\,(1-0.5)}{(1+0.03)^j} \right] - \frac{\$9,000}{(1+0.20)^5}$$

= \$30,000 - \$29,800 + \$14,900 - \$9,159 - \$2,130 + \$4,580 - \$3,167

= \$4,774 = *NAL* when rental payments are made at the end of the period.

These computations show the lease alternative to be preferable to the purchase alternative. Several points should be further emphasized:

1. Changing the depreciation method from straight-line to accelerated depreciation may change the outcome.
2. The timing of the rental payments has an impact on the *NAL*.
3. The analysis assumes that the acquisition price of the asset is equal to the principal of the loan.
4. All the cash flow streams except for the salvage value are discounted at the after-tax cost of debt.
5. It is assumed that the investment decision has been deemed acceptable. Only the financing decision remains to be evaluated in terms of a choice between borrowing and leasing.

ALTERNATIVE CALCULATIONS

The Johnson and Lewellen Approach

R. W. Johnson and W. G. Lewellen examined (1) whether the financing and investment decisions should be mixed in appraising lease possibilities and (2) which discount rate should be used.[6] (See Exhibit 1.1 for all of the approaches to lease evaluation.)

Johnson and Lewellen pose the decision problem as a lease-or-buy rather than a lease-or-borrow decision, since a lease contract is simply an arrangement for the long-term acquisition of service, which does not differ in financing terms from the alternative acquisition-of-service arrangement called purchase. Hence the inclusion of a charge for interest as a "cost" of owning is viewed as a deficiency of current models for lease evaluation, and the concept of a loan equivalent is not necessary in the lease evaluation model.

The issue of the appropriate rate to use in discounting the cash flows relevant to the decision has been investigated by Johnson and Lewellen. They emphasize the following ideas:

1. The after-tax cash flows with predictability matching that associated with a firm's debt service obligations should be capitalized at the firm's after-tax borrowing rate (after-tax cost of debt). This will include the obligations incurred under the lease contract, such as lease payments and their respective tax savings.
2. The after-tax cash flows with uncertainty like the general risks faced by the firm in its line of business should be discounted at the firm's cost of capital. This will include the depreciation tax shield, the after-tax operating costs, and the salvage value.

The Johnson and Lewellen model now can be presented. It states

$$\Delta NPV = NPV(P) - NPV(L) = \sum_{j=1}^{n} \left[\frac{D_j T - O_j(1-T)}{(1+K)^j} \right]$$
$$+ \frac{V_n}{(1+K)^j} - A_0 + \sum_{j=1}^{n} \frac{R_j(1-T)}{[1+r(1+T]}$$

where

ΔNPV = Change in the firm's net present value
$NPV(P)$ = The net present value of borrowing and buying
$NPV(L)$ = The net present value of leasing
K = Cost of capital at 12 percent

A positive value of NPV would imply that purchasing the asset is economically superior to leasing it. This would occur if the net salvage value exceeded after-tax operating costs or if the purchase price less depreciation tax savings were less than the burden of lease payments. Using the data savings in the previous illustration, the Johnson and Lewellen model proceeds as follows:

1. If the rental payments are made at the beginning of the period,

$$\Delta NPV = \sum_{j=1}^{5} \left[\frac{\$2,000 - \$1,000}{(1+0.12)^j} \right] + \frac{\$9,000}{(1+0.12)^{-5}} - \$30,000 + \left[\$6,025 + \sum_{j=1}^{4} \frac{\$6,025}{1.03^j} \right] - \sum_{j=1}^{5} \left[\frac{\$6,025(1-0.5)}{(1+0.03)^j} \right]$$
$$= \$(6,664).$$

Thus, leasing is preferred.

2. If the rental payments are made at the end of the period,

$$\Delta NPV = \sum_{j=1}^{5}\left[\frac{\$2,000 - \$1,000}{(1 + 0.12)^j}\right] + \frac{\$9,000}{(1 + 0.12)^{-5}} - \$30,000 + \sum_{j=1}^{5}\frac{\$6,507}{1.03^j} - \sum_{j=1}^{5}\left[\frac{\$6,507(1 - 0.5)}{(1 + 0.03)^j}\right] = \$(6,388).$$

Leasing is preferred in this case as well.

As a result of discounting the costs of financing at r(1- T) and the ownership cash flows at K, the Johnson and Lewellen approach in this case creates a bias in favor of leasing. R. S. Bower contested the choice:

Johnson and Lewellen's selection of K as the discount rate is understandable but unappealing. It is understandable because K is the rate used in discounting depreciation shelters in conventional capital budgeting, where the shelter is part of the cash flow calculation. The selection of K is unappealing, though, because it involves discounting some of the tax shelter given up in leasing at a high rate, K, and discounting all of the tax shelter that comes with leasing at a low rate, $r(1-T)$. It is difficult to avoid the conclusion that a higher discount rate for the shelter element of lease cost does a great deal more to bias the analysis in favor of leasing than it does to recognize any real difference in risk.[7]

The Roenfeldt and Osteryoung approach expanded on the Johnson and Lewellen approach by categorically separating the investment decision from the financing decision.[8] The methodology used consisted of (1) determining the desirability of the investment decision, and (2) given that the investment decision was deemed desireable, evaluating the financing decision by comparing the after-tax cost of borrowing (r_b) with the after-tax cost of leasing (r_l). Using the data from the illustration in the previous section, the Ronefeldt and Osteryoung approach proceeds as follows.

Step 1: The Investment Decision

The investment decision is made of the basis of a net present value or internal rate of return approach following traditional capital budgeting techniques (see chapter 5). The computation of a net present value or internal rate of return involves estimating the annual sales generated by the asset and computing the resulting net cash flows, as follows:

The Roenfeldt and Osteryoung Approach

Exhibit 1.1
Approaches to Lease Evaluation

Approach	Summary measure	Excluded flows or other comments	Equivalent Loan calculations	X2	X3	X4	X5	X6	X7
Breechy [1,3]	i	tL_j is used instead of tR_j in the 3rd term of the equation.	$P_0 = A_0$ $B_0 = \sum_{j=0}^{n}(R_j/(1+r)^j)$ $L_j = R_j(P_0/B_0)$	i	i	i	i	i	i
Bower, Herringer, Williamson [4]	NAL		$P_0 = A_0$ $B_0 = \sum_{j=0}^{n}(R_j/(1+r)^j)$ $L_j = R_j(P_0/B_0)$	r	k	k	k	k	k
Doenges [5] Mitchell [8] Wyman [12]	i(1-t)	I_j is excluded. Wyman provides a probability distribution of rates.	None	i(1-t)	i(1-t)	i(1-t)	-	i(1-t)	i(1-t)
Findlay [6]	NAL	Certainly equivalents of O_j and V_n are used in the 6th and 7th terms.	$P_0 = \sum_{j=0}^{n}(R_j/(1+r)^j)$ $L_j = R_j$	r	r(1-t)	r(1-t)	r(1-t)	r(1-t)	r(1-t)
Johnson and Lewellen [7]	NAL	I_j is excluded.	None	r(1-t)	r(1-t)	k	-	k	k
Roenfeldt and Osteryoung [10]	i(1-t)	I_j is excluded. Certainly equivalents of O_j and V_n are used in the 6th and 7th terms.	None	i(1-t)	i(1-t)	i(1-t)	-	i(1-t)	i(1-t)
Vancil [11]	NAL		$P_0 = A_0$ $L_j = R_j$	r	k	k	k	k	k

*Only the first two or three equations required to produce the equivalent loan flows are shown in each box. The remaining equations are the same for each approach. The full set of equations for Beechey's approach is:

$$P_0 = A_0$$

$$B_0 = \sum_{j=0}^{n}(R_j/(1+r)^j)$$

$$L_j = R_j(P_0/B_0)$$

$$I_j = rP_{j-1}$$

$$Q_j = L_j - I_j$$

$$P_j = P_{j-1} - Q_j.$$

Source: R. S. Bower, "Issues in Lease Fianncing," *Financial Management* (Winter 1973), p. 27. Reprinted with permission, Financial Management Association, College of Business Administration #3331, University of South Florida, Tampa, FL 33620-5500, 813-974-2084.

	0	1	2	3	4	5
				Year		
1. Sales (Assumed)		$20,000	$20,000	$20,000	$20,000	$20,000
2. Depreciation		4,000	4,000	4,000	4,000	4,000
3. Cash Operating Costs		2,000	2,000	2,000	2,000	2,000
4. Taxable Income (Line 1 – Line 2 – Line 3)		14,000	14,000	14,000	14,000	14,000
5. Tax Liability (4 X T)		7,000	7,000	7,000	7,000	7,000
6. Net cash Flow (Line 1 – Line 5 – Line 3)		11,000	11,000	11,000	11,000	11,000
7. Salvage Value (V_n)						9,000
8. Discount Factor ($K = 12$)						3.605
9. Discount Factor ($K_s = 20$)						0.402
10. Present Value of Cash Flow						39,655
11. Present Value of V_n						3,618
12. Total Present Value (Line 10 + Line 11)						$43,273

Thus, the net present value is equal to $13,273, or $43,273 - $30,000, and the investment is deemed desirable.

Step 2: The Financing Decision

The financial decision – to borrow or to lease – is made on the basis of a criterion of least cost by comparing the after-tax cost of borrowing (r_b) to the after-tax cost of leasing (r_l). To compute r_b, the rate that equates the after-tax interest payments and amortization of the principal to the loan amount, the following formula is used:

$$A_0 = \sum_{j=1}^{n} \frac{L_j - I_j T}{(1 + r_b)^j}$$

$$\$30,000 = \sum_{j=1}^{5} \frac{\$7,122 - [0.5(I_j)]}{(1 + r_b)^j}.$$

The numerator (the net costs of borrowing) is computed as follows:

Year	Loan Payment	Interest	Interest Tax Shield ($I_j T$)	Net cost of Borrowing
1	$7,122	$1,800	$900.00	$6,222.00
2	7,122	1,480	740.00	6,382.00
3	7,122	1,142	571.00	6,551.00
4	7,122	783	391.00	6,730.50
5	7,122	403	201.50	6,920.50

Solving for r_b yields $r_b = 3$ percent. To compute r_i, the rate that equates the adjusted rental payments to the cost of the asset (A_0), Roenfeldt and Osteryoung make the following changes:

1. The rental payments are reduced by the amount of any operating costs assumed by the lessor.
2. The depreciation tax shield and after-tax salvage value are added to the cost of leasing.
3. Certainly equivalents are introduced into the operating and residual cash flows to adjust for risk.

The following formula is then used

$$V_0 = \left(\sum_{j=1}^{n} \frac{[L_j - \alpha_j O_j](1-T) + D_j T}{(1+r_1)^n} \right) + \left[\frac{\partial_n S_n - (\alpha_n S_n - B)T_g}{(1+r_l)^n} \right]$$

where

α_j = Certainty equivalent for the operating costs
α_n = Certainty equivalent for the salvage value

Assuming $\alpha_j = 0.6$ and $\alpha_n = 0.99$, the cost of leasing (r_l) can be computed as follows:
1. If the rental payments are made at the end of the period,

$$\$30,000 = \left\{ \sum_{j=1}^{5} \frac{[\$6,507 - 0.6(\$2,000)](1 - 0.5) + [(\$4,000)(0.5)]}{(1+r_1)^n} \right\}$$
$$+ \left\{ \frac{0.99(\$10,000) - [0.99(\$10,000) - 0](0.10)}{(1+r_l)^n} \right\}$$
$$= \sum_{j=1}^{5} \left[\frac{\$4,653.5}{(1+r_1)^n} \right] + \left[\frac{\$8,910}{(1+r_1)^5} \right]$$

r_1 = 2 percent, and leasing is preferable to borrowing.

2. If the rental payments are in advance,

$$\$30,000 = \left\{ \sum_{j=1}^{5} \frac{[\$6,507 - 0.6(\$2,000)](1 - 0.5) + [(\$4,000)(0.5)]}{(1+r_1)^n} \right\} + \left[\frac{\$8,910}{(1+r_1)^5} \right]$$

r_1 = 2.1 percent, and leasing is preferable to borrowing.

Issues in Lease Financing

Bower summarized the following points of agreement and disagreement in the differing approaches to the lease-or-buy decision.[9] All the models require inputs that include the purchase price of the asset to be lease (A_0), lease payments at the end or at the beginning of the period (R_j), a depreciation charge relevant for tax payments at the end of the period (D_j), a cash operating cost expected to occur in period I if the asset purchased but not if it is leased (O_j), an expected after-tax salvage value of the asset at the end of the last period covered by the lease agreement (V_n) a pretax interest rate on the loan equivalent to the lease (r), an after-tax cost of capital for the corporation (k), a corporate income tax rate (T), and the number of periods covered by the lease agreement (n).

The points of disagreement relating to the lease-or-buy analysis included the following:

1. The choice of a summary measure, either the pretax interest rate on a lease (I) or the net advantage to a lease (NAL).
2. The inclusion or exclusion of some of the terms previously presented in the normative model.
3. The computation of the loan equivalent.
4. The choice of a discount rate for each of the cash flows included in the normative model.

The Bower Approach: A Decision Format

Bower has developed a decision format to reconcile the disagreements among the various approaches to the lease-or-buy analysis and still permit those interested to take advantage on the model's broad agreement on other points. The decision format examines the decision implications associated with different tax shelter discount rates.

The decision format uses the cost of capital (K) to calculate benefits that involve the purchase price, operating savings, and salvage value; it uses the appropriate interest rate (r) to calculate the present cost of the lease payments. The tax shelter effect is then calculated for rate of discount (X) from 0 to 14 percent.

The cost of purchasing (COP) depends on the purchase price, depreciation tax shelter, cash operating cost avoided by leasing, and salvage value:

$$COP = A_0 + \sum_{j=0}^{n} \left[\frac{TD_j}{(1+X)^j} \right] + \sum_{j=0}^{n} \left[\frac{O_j(1+T)}{(1+K)^j} \right] - \frac{V_n}{(1+K)^n}.$$

The cost of leasing (COL) depends on the purchase price, depreciation tax shelter, cash operating cost avoided by leasing, and salvage value:

$$COL = \sum_{j=0}^{n} \left[\frac{R_j}{(1+r)^j} \right] - \sum_{j=0}^{n} \left[\frac{TR_j}{(1+X)^j} \right] + \sum_{j=0}^{n} \left[\frac{TI_j}{(1+X)^j} \right].$$

An illustration example of Bower's decision format will be given using the data presented in the example in the "Lessor's Analysis" section. There is, however, one major change: The lease payments (R_j), as calculated in the lessor's analysis, will no longer be used. The equivalent loan is computed by Bower as follows:

$$\text{Loan equivalent } (P_0) = \sum_{j=1}^{n} \frac{R_j}{(1+r)^j},$$

where

R_j (Lease payment) = Loan payment (L_j).
r = Pretax interest rate on term loans "comparable" to the lease.

Although most of the data supplied in the original example applies here, assume that as an alternative to purchasing, the asset can be leased for five years for a payment of $7,962 per annum. In this case, the lease equivalent no longer equals the purchase price of the asset; instead, the following holds true:

$$\text{Loan equivalent } (P_0) = \sum_{j=1}^{n} \frac{\$7,962}{(1+0.06)^j} = \$33,538.$$

The loan equivalent is:

Year	Loan Payment	Loan Balance (Year Start)	Interest	Principal Repayment	Loan Balance (Year-End)
1	$7,962	$33,558	$2,012	$5,950	$27,588
2	7,962	27,588	1,655	6,307	21,281
3	7,962	21,281	1,277	6,685	14,596
4	7,962	14,596	876	7,086	7,510
5	7,962	7,510	452	7,511	0

The decision format is presented in Exhibits 1.2 and 1.3. The columns at the right in Exhibit 1.2 show that when the tax shelter is discounted at r(1-T)= 10 percent, the net advantage of purchasing is $49. At all discount rates above 9.65 percent, the lease has a net disadvantage. Therefore, if a decision maker analyzing a graph such as Exhibit 1.3 believes that the proper tax shelter discount rate lies well below the intersection point, the decision to lease rather than purchase would provide the greater financial benefit to the company.

In developing this decision format 'Bower has devised a composite approach to the lease-or-buy decision that enables the executive to make a judgment on the principle disagreement among academicians and on

how the proper tax shelter discount rate, r(1-T), may affect the ultimate cost of the decision.

CONCLUSION

A firm may enter into a leasing arrangement for many reasons. Some of the primary motivations follow:

1. Leasing enables a firm to take advantage of tax shelters.
2. A leasing arrangement conserves working capital.
3. Cash budgeting benefits, because leasing permits accurate predictions of cash needs.
4. Leasing allows a company to retain a degree of flexibility lost by debt financing (that is, bond indenture sometimes imposes restrictions on future financing).
5. A leasing arrangement provides convenience.

6. Leasing can provide an economical means of obtaining excellent servicing and maintenance of equipment if a maintenance lease is included.
7. An operating lease provides more flexibility than ownership if the asset becomes unprofitable; it avoids part or all of the risk of obsolescence; and it can provide for modern equipment from year to year.
8.

Exhibit 1.2 Decision Format Table

Year (t)	Purchase Price	Lease Payment	Tax Shelter			After-Tax Operating Saving	After-Tax Salvage
			Lease Payment	Depreciation	Loan Interest		
	A	R(t) = L(t)	TR(t)	TD(t)	TI(t)	O(1 - t)	V(n)
0	30,000						
1		7,962	3,981	2,000	1,006	1,000	
2		7,962	3,981	2,000	828	1,000	
3		7,962	3,981	2,000	638	1,000	
4		7,962	3,981	2,000	438	1,000	
5		7,962	3,981	2,000	226	1,000	9,000

Present Value at

k = 0.12	30,000					3,605	5,107
r = 0.06		33,538					

	TR(t)	TD(t)	TI(t)	Cost of Purchasing	Leasing
0	19,905	10,000	3,136	18,498	16,769
0.02	18,764	9,427	2,993	19,071	17,767
0.04	17,223	8,904	2,868	19,594	19,183
0.06	17,769	8,425	2,737	20,073	19,506
0.08	15,895	7,985	2,624	20,513	20,267
0.10	15,091	7,582	2,518	20,916	20,965
0.12	14,351	7,210	2,419	21,288	21,606
0.14	13,667	6,866	2,327	21,632	22,198

Exhibit 1.3
Decision Format Graph

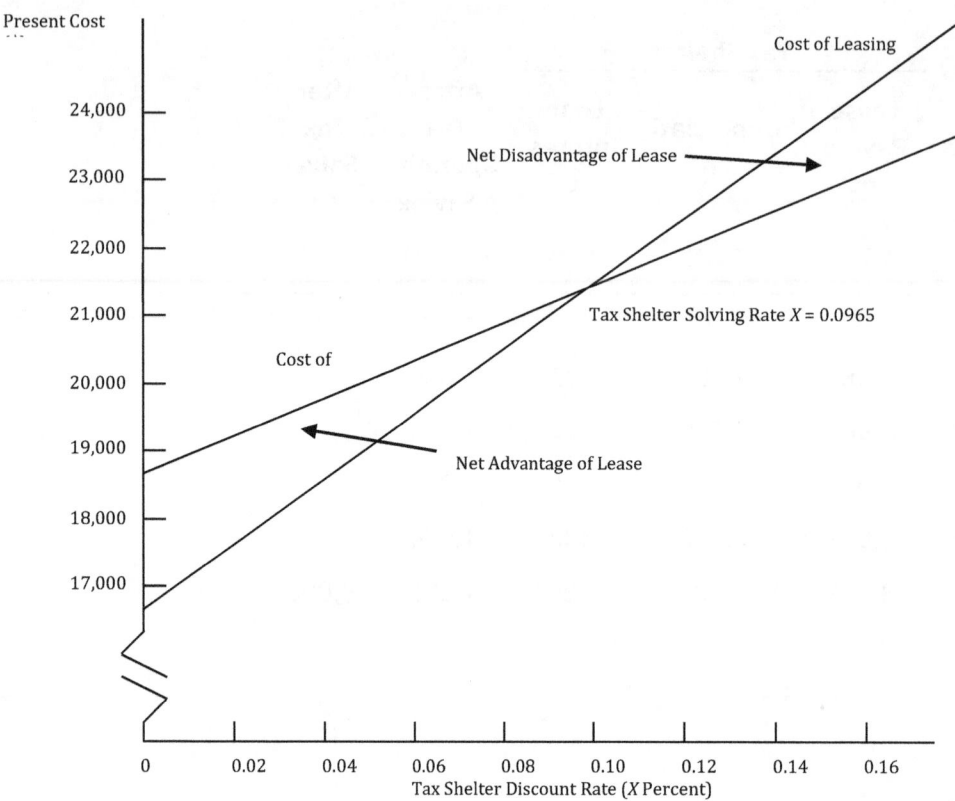

Most of the significant methods of analyzing lease-or-buy alternatives use the same basic formula for calculations, but there is considerable disagreement in the calculation methods. The disagreement lies with both relevant alternatives and the choice of the best summary measure of comparison. The relevant alternatives include the outstanding principal of the loan equivalent, the principal component, the present value of the lease claim, and the discount rates to be applied to cash flows in each category, which are intended to reflect opportunity cost. Summary measures are either the increment in net present value of owners, wealth, or the after-tax interest rate on the lease.

The disagreement is more significant in the treatment of the terms, including lease payments and the tax shelter acquired or given up if the lease is accepted. This is most obvious in the decision to include or lease is accepted. This is most obvious in the decision to include or exclude the tax deduction associated with interest on the equivalent loan.

Bower's decision form of lease analysis is the most appropriate method to use today. It is a composite of the factors agreed upon by other theorists, and it enables decision makers to choose the cost of capital and interest rate they feel is most appropriate during the relevant period for making their lease-or-buy decisions. Bower's decision format also anables decision makers to see the effects of their costs and rates and make their decisions in light of the uncertainty of these factors.

APPENDIX

QUESTIONS

1. Analysis of the Lease-or-Buy Decision: The Johnson and Lewellen Approach

The Holland Consulting Company is considering obtaining a piece of equipment having a five-year useful life and costing $15,000. As an alternative to purchasing, the company can lease the equipment for five years for a payment of $4,200 per annum. The equipment, which would be fully depreciated on a sum-of-the-years'-digits schedule, is expected to command a $1,500 cash salvage value at the end of year 5 and will require $1,000 more in annual (pretax) operating costs if it is owned rather than leased. The Holland Consulting Company is also assuming the corporate income tax rate to be 50 percent, the capital gains tax rate to be 30 percent, the cost of capital after taxes to be 12 percent, and the pretax effective interest rate to be 8 percent.

Required: Should Holland Consulting Company lease or buy the equipment? (Use the Johnson and Lewellen approach.)

2. Analysis of the Lease-or-Buy Decision: A Decision Format

Assume the same data as in question 1. This time, the Holland Consulting Company has decided to modify the Johnson and Lewellen approach as follows:

1. It will apply the cost of capital to the purchase price, after-tax operating savings, and after-tax salvage value.
2. It will apply the after-tax rate of interest to the lease payment, the lease payment tax shelter, and the depreciation tax shelter.
3. It will apply an after-tax rate of interest from 0 to 14 percent.

Required: Should the Holland Company lease or buy equipment?

3. Analysis of the Lease-or-Buy decision: Another Decision Format

Assume the same data as in question 1. This time, the Holland Consulting Company has decided to modify the Johnson and Lewellen approach as follows:

1. A loan equivalent is introduced in the evaluation. Findlay's loan equivalent formula is to be used.
2. The cost of purchasing depends on the purchase price, depreciation tax shelter, cash operating cost avoided by leasing, and salvage value.
3. The cost of leasing depends on the lease payment, lease tax shelter, and interest tax shelter lost by leasing.
4. The after-tax salvage an the after-tax operating savings are discounted at the cost of capital.
5. The lease payments are discounted at the pretax rate of interest.
6. The tax shelters are discounted at the rate of interest 0 to 14 percent.

Required:

1. Determine the loan equivalent schedule using Findlay's equivalent loan.
2. Compute the costs of purchasing and costs of leasing, and determine if the Holland Consulting Company should lease or buy the equipment.

4. Comparison of Lease Evaluation Models

The Richard Company is contemplating the addition of a truck to the commercial truck fleet. The truck costs $56,000, which does not include transportation costs of $4,000. The Richard Company has a policy of capitalizing freight in the determination of the acquisition cost. The truck has an estimated three-year useful life and a $2,000 residual value. Other relevant information for deciding whether to lease or buy the truck includes the following.

Borrowing rate: 6 percent
Cost of capital before taxes: 20 percent
Tax rate: 50 percent
Depreciation method: sum-of-the-years' – digits method
Rate of return on investment desired: 10 percent
Salvage value discount rate: 20 percent

Required:

1. From the lessor's perspective, determine the annual rental payment if paid in advance.
2. From the lessor's perspective, determine the annual rental payment if paid at the end of the period.
3. Present the normative model to be used by the lessee. What is required to express the model as an advantage to ownership?
4. Determine the loan payment on a loan equivalent to the lease.
5. From the lessee's perspective, should the Richard Company lease the equipment if the rental payment is made at the beginning of the period?
6. From the lessee's perspective, should the Richard Company lease the equipment if the rental payment is made at the end of the period?
7. Present the Johnson and Lewellen model that can be used by the lessee.
8. Repeat part 6 using he Johnson and Lewellen model.

ANSWERS

1. **Analysis of the Lease-or-Buy Decision: The Johnson and Lewellen Approach**
   To decide whether to lease or buy, the Holland Consulting Company should proceed as follows:

Year	(1) Tax Savings on Depreciation $(t\,D_j)$	(2) After Tax Added Operating Costs $Q\,(1-T)$	(3) Salvage Value Net of Taxes, V_n	(4) After Tax Lease Payment $L_i\,(1-t)$	(5) Present Value of (1)−(2)+(3) at 12%	(6) Present Value Of (4) at 4%
1	(.5) 5,000	(.5) 1,000		(.5) (4,200)	$1,786	$2,019
2	(.5) 4,000	(.5) 1,000		(.5) (4,200)	1,196	1,942
3	(.5) 3,000	(.5) 1,000		(.5) (4,200)	712	1,867
4	(.5) 2,000	(.5) 1,000		(.5) (4,200)	318	1,795
5	(.5) 1,000	(.5) 1,000	(.70) (1,500)	(.5) (4,200)	596	1,726
					$4,608	$9,349

Equipment Purchase = $15,000
Therefore $\Delta NPV = \$4,608 - \$15,000 + \$9,439 = -\$1,043$
Conclusion = leasing is better than purchase.

2. Analysis of the Lease-or-Buy Decision: A Decision Format

To decide whether to lease or buy, the Holland Consulting Company should proceed as follows:

Evaluation: The purchase price net of salvage an the operating expernses that will now be covered by the lessor are the benefits associated with leasing. The lease payments, less any net additional tax shelter they provide, are the costs of leasing. The benefits which are discounted at the cost of capital, are $16,206. The benefits in questions appear and are graphed in the following table:

			Tax Shelter			
Year	Purchase Price A_0	Lease Payment R_i	Lease Payment tR_i	Depreciation tD_i	After-Tax Operating Savings $O_i(1-t)$	After Salvage V_n
0	$15,000					
1		$4,200	$2,100	$2,500	$500	
2		4,200	2,100	2,000	500	
3		4,200	2,100	1,500	500	
4		4,200	2,100	1,000	500	
5		4,200	2,100	500	500	$1,050

PV K=.12	$15,000				$1,802	-$596

					Lease	
					Benefit	Cost
					$16,206	
					(@12%)	
.0		-$21,000	+$10,500	-$7,500		$18,000
.02		-19,797	+9,898	-7,164		17,063
.04		-18,698	+9,349	-6,852		16,201
.06		-17,692	+8,846	-6,564		15,410
.08		-16,769	+8,385	-6,296		14,680
.10		-15,921	+7,961	-6,046		14,006
.12		-15,140	+7,570	-5,813		13,383
.14		-14,119	+7,209	-5,596		12,806

$t = .5, k = .12, r = .08$

This table also shows the costs of the lease discounted at various rates; therefore, they satisfy preference for both present value and internal rate of return summary measures.

This lease has a net disadvantage at after-tax interest rates below .0399 and a net advantage at rates above this figure. At .04, the after-tax interest rate provided in the case, the net advantage is $5. The decision format indicates a borderline choice in favor of the lease or, more pragmatically, a choice that should make very little difference to the owners of the lessee corporation even if the executives are using 8 percent as the appropriate pre-tax borrowing rate when the rate is correctly 6 percent or 10 percent.

In conclusion, this format offers to the executive table and a graph (Exhibits 1.2 and 1.3) which took the cost of capital as given in calculating the benefits of leasing and assumed that tax shelters should be discounted at the after-tax rate of interest and allows the executive to examine the decision implication associated with different interest rates.

3. Analysis of the Lease-or-Buy decision: Another Decision Format

A. The loan is calculated as Findley's loan equivalent. The loan schedule is:

Year	Loan Balance, Beginning of Year	Interest At 8%	Principal	Loan Balance Year End
1	$16,769	$1,342	$2,858	$13,911
2	13,911	1,113	3,087	10,823
3	10,823	866	3,334	7,489
4	7,489	599	3,601	3,888
5	3,888	311	3,889	

B. The decision format applied to this problem appears as follows:

Tax Shelter

Year	Purchase Price A_0	Lease Payment R_i	Lease Payment tR_i	Depreciation tD_i	Loan Interest* tI_i	After-Tax Operating Savings $O_i(1-t)$	After Salvage V_n
0	$15,000						
1		$4,200	$2,100	$2,500	$671	$500	
2		4,200	2,100	2,000	556	500	
3		4,200	2,100	1,500	433	500	
4		4,200	2,100	1,000	300	500	
5		4,200	2,100	500	156	500	$1,050

t= .5, k=.12, r=.08

PV*						Cost of	
K=.12	$15,000					Purchasing	Leasing
r=.08	$16,769						
.0		$10,500	$7,500	$2,116	$8,706	$8,385	
.02		9,898	7,164	2,019	9,042	8,890	
.04		9,349	6,852	1,929	9,354	9,349	
.06		8,846	6,564	1,846	9,642	9,769	
.08		8,385	6,296	1,768	9,910	10,152	
.10		7,961	6,046	1,697	10,160	10,505	
.12		7,570	5,813	1,630	10,393	10,829	
.14		7,209	5,596	1,567	10,610	11,127	

*The loan is calculated as Findlay's equivalent loan. The loan schedule is:

Year	Loan Balance, Beginning of Year	Interest At 8%	Principal	Loan Balance Year End
1	$16,769	$1,342	$2,858	$13,911
2	13,911	1,113	3,087	10,823
3	10,823	866	3,334	7,489
4	7,489	599	3,601	3,888
5	3,888	311	3,889	

* PV of After-Tax Operating Savings = \$1,802
* PV of After-tax Salvage Value   = \$ 596

4. Comparison of Lease Evaluation Models

A. The lessor determines first the present value of the residual as follows:

$$S_{PV} = \frac{S}{(1+R)^{-t}}$$
$$= \frac{2,000}{(1+.20)^{-3}} = \$1,158$$

Then, the rental (X), if paid in advance

$$C - S = X_1 + \sum_{t=2}^{3} \frac{X_t}{(1+R)^{t-1}}$$

$$= \$60,000 - 1,158 = X_1 + \frac{X_2}{(1+.10)} + \frac{X_3}{(1+.10)^2}$$

$$X = \$21,056$$

B. The rental (X), if paid at end of period, may be computed as follows:

$$C - S = \sum_{t=1}^{n} \frac{X_t}{(1+R)^t} \quad or \quad \$60,000 - \$1,158 = \sum_{t=1}^{n} \frac{X_t}{(1+.10)^t}$$

$$X = \$23,660$$

C. The normative model to be used by the lessee is as follows:

$$NAL = \sum_{t=1}^{n} \frac{P - (I_t - D_t)T_c}{(1+K_d)^t} + \frac{O_t(1-T_c)}{(1+K_d)^t} - S - \frac{(S-B)T_g}{(1+K_s)}$$

$$- \sum_{t=1}^{n} \frac{L_t(1-T_c)}{(1+K_d)^t}$$

Where:
P = the loan payment: interest and amortization of principal
L_t = the rental payment in period t
I_t = interest payment in period t
D_t = depreciation in period t
O_t = incremental operating costs of ownership in period t
T_c = ordinary corporate tax rate
T_s = tax rate applicable to gains and losses on the disposal of fixed assets
S_n = expected cash value of asset in period N
B = book value of asset in period N
K_d = explicit after-tax cost of new debt capital
K = weighted average cost of capital, after tax
K_s = discount rate applied to residual values

D. The loan payment is found by:

$$\$60,000 = \sum_{t=1}^{n} \frac{L_t}{(1+.06)^t}$$

$L_t = \$22,447$

The loan schedule is as follows:

Year	Payment (L_t)	Interest (I_t)	Principal	Balance
1	$22,447	$3,600	$18,847	$41,153
2	22,447	2,469	19,978	21,175
3	22,447	1,270	21,175	-

E. Lessee's analysis when rental payments are made in advance:

Year	0	1	2	3	Explanations
1. Loan Payment		$22,447	$22,447	$22,447	
2. Interest		3,600	2,469	1,270	
3. Depreciation		29,000	19,140	9,860	
4. Tax Deduction (2+3)		32,600	21,609	11,130	
5. Tax Shield (4X.50)		16,300	10,804	5,565	
6. Net Ownership (1-5)		6,147	11,643	16,882	
7. After Tax Lease Cost	$10,753	10,753	10,753		
8. Advantage to Ownership	10,753	4,606	(910)	{(16,882)2,000}	(Salvage Value)
9. Discount Factor (K_d = 3%)		.971	.943	{.915,.579}	K_s = 20%
10. Present Value of Owner	10,753	4,472	(858)	{(15,4771,158)}	
11. Advantage of Ownership				78	

F. Lessee's analysis when rental payments are made at end of period:

Year	0	1	2	3	Explanations
Row 1 to 6 are similar to the previous lessee's analysis					
7. After Tax Lease Cost	-	$11,830	$11,830	$11,830	
8. Advantage of Ownership	-	5,683	187	(5,052)	
8a. S				2,000	(Salvage Value)
9. Discount Factor (K_d=3%)		.971	.941	.915	
9a. (K_s=20%)				.579	

10. Present Value
    of Owning $5,518   179   (4,623)

10.a S 1,158

11. Advantage to
    Ownership   2,229

G. Johnson and Lewellen's model states:

$$\Delta NPV = NPV(P) - NPV(L) = \sum_{t=1}^{n} \frac{D_t T - O_t(1-T)}{(1+K)^t} + \frac{S - T_g(S-B)}{(1+K)^n}$$
$$- A_o + \sum_{t=1}^{n} \frac{L_t(1-T)}{(1+K_d)^t}$$

Where
ΔNPV = change in the firm's NPV
$NPV (P)$ = the NPV of borrow and buy
$NPV (L)$ = the NPV of leasing

H. The lessee's analysis using Johnson and Lewellen's model proceeds as follows:

Year	0	1	2	3	Total
1. Depreciation Tax Shield	-	$14,500	$ 9,570	$ 4,930	
2. Salvage				2,000	
3. After-Tax Lease Cost		11,830	11,830	11,830	
4. Discount Factor ($K = 10\%$)		.909	.826	.751	
5. Present Value of Ownership		13,180	7,904	3,702 / 1,502	$26,288 (Salvage)
6. Discount Factor ($K_d = 3\%$)		.971	.943	.915	
7. Present Value of Leasing		11,487	11,156	10,824	33,467

Therefore, ΔNPV = $26,288 - $60,000 + $33,467 = ($245). Leasing is preferred.

NOTES

1. For a discussion of leverage leasing, see Robert C. War, "Economic Implications of Multiple Rates of Return in the Leverage Lease Context," *Journal of Finance* (December 1973), pp. 275-286; and E. Richard Packham, "An Analysis of the Risks of Leverage leasing," *Journal of Commercial Bank Lending* (March 1975), pp. 2-29.
2. D. R. Grant, "Illusion in lease Financing," *Harvard Business Review* (March-April 1959), p. 129.
3. Ibid., p. 126.
4. R. V. Vamco, "lease or Borrow: New Method of Analysis," *Harvard Business Review* (September-October 1961), p. 127.
5. Financial Accounting Standards Board, *Accounting for the Sale or Purchase of Tax Benefits through Tax Leases, Exposure Draft* (Stemford, Conn: FASB, November 30, 1981), p. 11.
6. R. W. Johnson and W. G. Lewellen, "Analysis of the Lease or Buy Decision," *Journal of Finance* (September 1972), pp. 815-823.
7. R. S. Bower, "Issues in Leasing Financing," *Financial Management* (Winter 1973), p. 129.
8. R. L. Roenfeldt and J. S. Osteryoung, "Analysis of Financial Leases," *Financial Management* (Spring 1973), pp. 74-87.
9. Bower, "Issue in Lease Financing," p. 27.

SELECTED READINGS

Beechy, T. H. "The Cost of Leasing: comment and Correction." *Accounting Review* (October 1970), pp. 769-773.

Beechy, T. H. "Quasi-Debt Analysis of Financial Leases." *Accounting Review* (April 1969), pp. 375-381.

Billiam, Phillip L. "Lease versus Purchase: A PArtical Problem." *Cost and Management* (September-October 1974), pp. 32-36.

Bower, R. S., F. C. Herringer, and J. P. Williamson. "Lease Evaluation." *Accounting Review* (April 1966), pp. 257-265.

Burns, Jane O. and Kathleen Bindon. "Evaluating Leases with LP." *Management Accounting* (February 1980), pp. 48-53.

Chapter 2
Accounting for Long-Term Leases: Part I

INTRODUCTION

Leasing is quickly becoming one of the most popular ways of financing fixed asset acquisitions, producing funds for about a third of the external purchased capital equipment in the United States. As defined in the Financial Accounting Standards Board's (FASB) *Statement No. 13 as Amended and Interpreted through January 1990,* a lease is an agreement convening the right to use property, plant, or equipment (land or depreciable assets or both) usually for a stated period of time.[1] The lessor is the owner giving up the right to use the property, plant and equipment and the lessee is the one acquiring the right.

Up to the 1960s, firms had the option of reporting the lease information in the notes or disclosing nothing. Other options included either capitalizing the lease if it conveys some ownership rights and privileges, or expensing the lease payment if it does not convey these rights and privileges. The capitalizing proposals included various views such as capitalize those leases similar to installment purchases, capitalize all long-term leases,[2] and capitalize firm leases when the penalty for non-performance is substantial.[3] The FASB voted for the capitalization approach when the lease transfers substantially all the risks and benefits of the ownership, representing in substance a purchase by the lessee and a sale by the lessor, The capitalization applied to noncancellable leases. The capitalization of the present value of future rental payments dictates that the lessee recognizes an asset (leased equipment) and a liability (lease obligation), and the lessor recognizes a receivable (net lease receivable) and a credit to equipment. More entries that are required depending on the complexity of the situation are treated in the remainder of this chapter.

ADVANTAGES OF LEASING

The popularity and growth of leasing is best explained by its advantages. They include:

1. *Financing advantage* in the form of 100 percent financing at fixed rates and without a down payment and more flexible than debt agreements.
2. *Reduction of the risk of obsolescence* to the lessee that may include in some cases the transfer of the risk in residual value to the lessor.
3. *Tax advantages* though the deduction of the lease payments or a write-off of the full cost of the asset.
4. *Alternative minimum tax problems* may turn the alternative minimum tax (AMT) to our advantage. As explained by Donald Kieso and Jerry Weygandt: "under the AMT rules, a portion of accelerated depreciation deductions are considered tax preference items that are added to a company's regular taxable income to arrive at the alternative minimum taxable income (AMTI). The company must pay whichever is higher, the regular tax or the AMT. Since ownership of equipment can't contribute to an increased AMTI and, ultimately, to an alternative minimum tax liability in access of the regular tax liabilities, companies often find leasing a way to avoid the owners alternative tax provisions."[4]
5. *Balance sheet advantages* are realized through the absorption of an operating lease rather than a capitalized lease and therefore not adding a liability to the balance sheet and preserving a good borrowing capacity, a hood rate of return, current ratio, and ratio of debt to stockholders' equity.[5] The expensing of an operating lease constitutes a good form of "off-balance-sheet financing."

TYPES OF LEASES OF PERSONAL PROPERTY AND CRITERIA FOR CAPITALIZATION

As stated earlier, the lease that transfers substantially all the risks and benefits of ownership is essentially capitalized as an asset by the lessee and a sale by the lessor. FASB No. 13 identified four criteria applicable to both lessor and lessee and two criteria applicable only to the lessee to help in the classification of personal property leases. The capitalization criteria applicable to both lessee and lessor are:

1. The lease transfers ownership of the property to the lessee.
2. There is a bargain purchase option in the lease contract.
3. The lease term is equal to 75 percent of the estimated economic life of the leased property.
4. The present value of the minimum lease payments (excluding executor costs) equals or exceeds 90 percent of the fair value of the leased property of the lessor.[6]

The capitalization criteria applicable to the lessor only are:

1. The collectability of the minimum lease payments is reasonably predictable.
2. No important uncertainties surrounded the amount of unreimbursable costs yet to be incurred by the lessor under the lease.

Given the criteria, the classification of the lessee is one of the following:

1. An *operating lease* if the lease does not meet any of the four criteria applicable to both lessee and the lessor.
2. A *capital lease* if the lease meets ant of the four criteria applicable to both the lessee and lessor.

The classification by the lessor is one of the following:

1. A *sales-type lease* if (a) the lease meets one or more of the four criteria applicable to bot the lessee and lessor, (b) the lease meets both of the criteria applicable to lessor only and, (c) there is a manufacturer's or dealer's profit (or loss) to the lessor measured by the difference between the fair value of the leased property at the inception of the lease and the lessor's cost or carrying value (book value).
2. A *direct financing lease* if (a) the lease meets one or more of the four criteria applicable to both the lessee and lessor, (b) the lease meets both or all criteria applicable to the lessor only, and (c) there is no manufacturer's or dealer's profit (or loss) to the lessor.
3. 3. *An operating lease* if the lease does not met any of the four criteria applicable to both lessee and lessor and does not meet both the criteria applicable to the lessor.

ACCOUNTING FOR CAPITAL LEASE BY THE LESSEE

Important Elements of a Capital Lease

The computation and entries required in a capital lease depend on a good understanding of the following four key elements:

1. *Minimum lease payments:* They are the payments accepted or required to be paid by the lessee to the lessor. They include the following:
    - A. *Minimum rental payments,* which are the minimum required payments by the lessee under the lease terms.
    - B. *Guaranteed residual value,* which is an estimated residual value of the leased property as guaranteed by the lessee or a third party, unrelated to the lessor. It is the amount that the lessor has the right to require the lessee to purchase the asset that the lessor is guaranteed to realize. [7]
    - C. *Penalty on failure to renew or extend* the lease that is sometimes required of the lessee.
    - D. *Bargain purchase option,* which is an option at the inception of the lease, to purchase the lease property at the end of the lease them at a fixed price sufficiently below the expected fair value to make the purchase reasonably assured.

2. *Executory costs,* which are the ownership type costs, such as insurance, maintenance, and tax expenses, to be excluded, if borne by the lessee, from the computation of present value of the minimum lease payments.
3. *The discount rate,* which is used in the computation of the present value of the minimum lease payments and included after:
   A. *The lessee's incremental borrowing rate,* defined as "the rate that, at inception of the lease, the lessee would have incurred to borrow the funds necessary to buy the leased asset on a secured loan with repayment terms similar to the payment schedule called for in the lease,"[8] or
   B. *The lessor's interest rate implicit in the lease* if known by the lessee and it is less than the lessee's incremental borrowing rate. It is the discount rate that equates the present value of the minimum lease payments and any unguaranteed residual value acquiring the lease to the fair value of the leased property to the lessor.[9]

Capital Lease by the Lessee Illustrated

This case is a lease without a purchase or bargain purchase option (annuity due basis). The Zribi (lessor) Company and the Alvertos (lessee) Company sign a lease agreement on January 1, 1996, calling for the Zribi Company to lease restaurant equipment to the Alvertos Company beginning January 1, 1996. The relevant information is as follows:

1. The lease term is five years. The lease is noncancelable and requires equal payments of $14,990.81 at the beginning of each year.
2. The equipment has a fair value and cost of $50,000, estimated life of five years, and a zero residual value.
3. The Alvertos Company agrees to pay the executor costs of $3,000 per year,which is included in the annual payments to the Zribi Company.
4. There are no renewal or purchase options, with the equipment reverting to the Zribi Company.
5. The Alvertos' incremental borrowing rate is 11 percent per year, the Zribi's implicit lease rate is 10 percent and is known to the Alvertos Company.

The lease meets two criteria for a classification as a capital lease – namely, (1) a lease term of five years equal to the equipment's economic life, and (2) a present value of lease payments of $50,000 (assigned below) that is higher than 90 percent of fair value of the equipment ($50,000). The capitalized amount as an asset is the present value of the minimum lease payments. It is computed as follows:

$$\text{Capitalized amount} = (\$14,990.81 - \$3,000) \times 4.16986 \text{ (the present value of an annuity due to \$1 for 5 periods at 10\%)} - \$11,990.81 \times 4.16986 = \$50,000.$$

All the relevant information is computer in Exhibit 2.1. The journal entries are as follows:
   1. Recording of the capital lease on January 1, 1996:

Leased Equipment Under Capital Leases	$50,000	
Obligation Under Capital Leases		$50,000

The entry recognizes an asset and an obligation at the present value of rental payments ($50,000) rather than the total annual rental payments of $74,954.05 ($14,990.81 × 5).

Exhibit 2.1
Alvertos Company: Lease Amortization Schedule (Annuity Due Basis)

Date	Annual Lease Payment (a)	Executory Costs (b)	Interest at 10% On Unpaid Obligations (c)	Reduction of Lease Obligation (d)	Balance of Lease Obligation Liability (e)
1/1/96					$50,000.00
1/1/96	$14,990.81	$3,000	$------0------	$11,990.81	$38,009.19
1/1/97	$14,990.81	$3,000	$3,800.919	$ 8,189.891	$29,819.299
1/1/98	$14,990.81	$3,000	$2,981.929	$ 9,008.881	$20,810.418
1/1/99	$14,990.81	$3,000	$2,081.041	$ 9,909.769	$10,900.700
1/1/100	$14,990.81	$3,000	$1,090.064	$10,900.700	$------0------
	$74,954.05	$15,000.00	$9,953.953	$50,000.00	

(a)   Required lease payments

(b)   Executory costs paid by the lessee and included in rental payments

(c)   Columns (e) at the beginning of the year X 10% except for 1/1/96

(d)   (a) – (b) – (c)

(e)   Preceding balance – (d)

2. Recording the first rental payments in advance on January 1, 1996:

Property Taxes Expenses	$30,000.00	
Obligations Under Capital Lease	$11,990.81	
Cash		$14,990.81

This entry recognizes (a) the executor costs of $3,000, (b) the principal (or reduction of the lease obligation) or $11,990.81, and (c) zero interest expenses since no interest has accrued.

3. Recognition of accrued interest as December 31, 1996:

Interest Expense	$3,800.919	
Accrued Interest on Obligation Under Capita Lease (or Interest Payable)		$3,800.919

The interest expense is recognized in the year it is accrued as a result of the applicable of the accrual concept.

4.

Deprecation Expense-Capital Leases	$10,000	
Accumulated Depreciation-Capital Leases		$10,000

($50,000/5 years)

5. At the end of the year, the Obligation Under Capital Leases on the Balance sheet is divided into its current and noncurrent portion as follows:

A. *Current Liabilities*

Interest Payable	$3,800.919
Obligations Under Capital Leases	$8,185,891

B. *Noncurrent Liabilities*

Obligations Under Capital Leases	$29,819.891

Exhibit 2.2
Alvertos Company: Charges to Operations – Capital lease Versus Operating Lease

	Capital Lease				Operating Lease Charges	Difference
Year	Depreciation	Executory Costs	Interest	Total Charge		
1996	$10,000.00	$3,000.00	$3,800.919	$16,800.919	$14,900.81	$1,810.109
1997	$10,000.00	$3,000.00	$2,981.929	$15,981.929	$14,900.81	$991.119
1998	$10,000.00	$3,000.00	$2,081.041	$15,081.041	$14,900.81	$90.231
1999	$10,000.00	$3,000.00	$1,090.064	$14,090.064	$14,900.81	$(907.746)
2000	$10,000.00	$3,000.00	$------0------	$13,000.000	$14,900.81	$(1,990.81)
	$50,000.00	$15,000.00	$9,953.953	$74,954.05	$74,954.05	$------0------

6. Recording the second rental payment in advance January 1, 1997:

Property Tax Expenses	$3,000.000	
Accrued Interest on Obligation		
Under capital Lease	$3,800.919	
Obligation Under Capital Lease	$8,189.851	
Cash		$14,990.81

7. The same pattern of entries is followed though the year 2000.

Operating Method of the Lessee Illustrated

If the capital lease between the Zribi Company and the Alvertos Company was in fact an operating lease, only the rental payments will be recorded at the beginning of each year as follows:

Rent Expense	$14,990.81	
Cash		$14,990.81

No rent asset or corresponding liability is recognized in the balance sheet. Only rent expense is recognized in the income statement, and a note disclosure is required for all operating leases that have noncancelable leases in excess of one year.

A comparison of the charges under the lease approach and the operating lease approach, as shown in Exhibit 2.2, indicated that the total charges are the same, and the charges are higher in the earlier years and lower in the later years under a capital lease. The choice of capitalization under capital lease rather than expensing under an operation lease results in:

1. Higher short- and long-term debt because of the recognition of Obligations Under Capital Lease,
2. Higher fixed assets because of the recognition of Leased Equipment Under Capital Leases, and
3. Lower income in the earlier years and higher income in the later years of the life of the lease.

ACCOUNTING FOR LEASES BY THE LESSOR

The lessor's interest in leases is related to the following three benefits:
1. *Interest Revenue.* Leasing is a form of financing, therefore financial institutions and leasing companies find leasing attractive because it provides competitive interest margins.
2. *Tax Incentives.* In many cases, companies find leasing attractive because it provides them with an opportunity to transfer such tax benefits to another party (the lessor) in return for a lower rental rate on the leased asset.
3. *High Residual Value.* Another advantage to the lessor is the reversion of the property at the end of the lease term. Residual values can produce large profits.[10]

As explained earlier, the classification of leases by the lessor results in one of three types of leases: operating, sales-type, or direct financing.

Direct Financing Leases by the Lessor: Key Concepts

As explained earlier, a direct financing lease is one that meets one or more of the criteria applicable to both lessee or lessor; meets both of the criteria applicable to the lessor only, and there is no profit or loss to the lessor. Because there is no profit or loss in a direct financing lease, the net receivable to the lessor must equal the cost of carrying value of the property. Three accounts need to be defined:

1. *Lease Payments Receivable or Minimum Lease Payments Receivable:* This is the gross investment. It is equal to the sum of:
     a. The undiscounted minimum lease payments to be received by the lessor plus
     b. The unguaranteed residual value accruing to the lessor.

Note that:
     a. The "minimum lease payments" include: (1) rental payments (excludes executor costs), (2) a bargain purchase option (if any), (3) a guaranteed residual value (if any), and (4) penalty for failure to renew (if any).
     b. The lease payments receivable includes either guaranteed or unguaranteed residual value with the guaranteed residual value included in the minimum lease payments and the unguaranteed residual value included as a second item.
2. *Unearned Interest Revenue or Unearned Interest-Leases:* This is the difference between the gross investment or lease payment receivable and the cost or carrying value of the lease property.
3. *Net Investment to the Lessor:* This is the difference between the gross investment and the unearned interest revenue. Generally the balance sheet treats the unearned interest revenue as a contra receivable to yield the "net investment to the lessor."

Direct Financing by the Lessor: Illustrated
Returning to the previous example between the Zribi Company and the Alvertos Company, the following information is relevant:
1. The five-year uncancelable label beginning January 1, 1996, requires equal rental payments of $14,990.81 that include $3,000 of property costs.
2. The equipment has a cost and a fair value of $50,000, an estimated life of five years, and no residual value.
3. No initial direct cost and no renewable options are included with the property returning to the Zribi Company at the end of the lease.
4. Collectibility of payments is assumed and no unreimbursable costs are expected.
5. The interest rate implicit in the lease is 10 percent. It is the rate that, when applied to the gross receivable, will discount that amount to a present value that is equal to the next receivable. The annual rental payments charged to the lessor are computed as follows:

Annual payments: Known Present Value equal to the Cost of Equipment
                    Present Value of an Annuity due to $1 for 5 periods at 10 percent

= $$\frac{\$50,000}{4.16986}$$

= $11,990.81

6. The lease meets the criteria for a direct financing lease classification. It is a direct financing lease rather than a sales-type lease because the fair value (present value) of the property is equal to its cost.
7. The Lease Payments Receivable is equal to the minimum lease payments minus executor costs paid by the lessor plus the undescended unguaranteed residual value accruing to the lessor. Therefore: Lease Payments Receivable = [($14,990.81 - $3,000) × 5] + $0 = $59,954.05.

155

8. The Unearned Interest Revenue is equal to the minimum lease payment receivable minus the cost or carrying value of the leased equipment. Therefore: Unearned Interest Revenue = $59,954.05 – 450,000 = $9,954.05.

9. The Net Investment to the lessor is equal to $50,000, the minimum lease payments receivable of $59,954.05 minus the Unearned Interest Revenue of $9,954.05.

10. The accounting entries based on the lease amortization schedule shown in Exhibit 2.3 are as follows:

A. Initial recording of the lease on January 1, 1996
Lease Payments receivable $59,954.05
    Equipment $50,000
    Unearned Interest Revenue-
    Leases $9,954.05
B. Collection of first year's lease payment in January 1, 1996
Cash $14,990.81
    Lease Payment Receivable $11,990.81
    Property tax Expense/Property
    Taxes Payable $3,000.00
C. Recognition on December 31, 1996, of interest revenue earned during the first year:
Unearned Interest Revenue-Leases $3,800.919
    Interest revenue-Leases $3,800.919

The unearned interest revenue is amortized by the use of the effective interest method. At the end of the year 1996 the lease payments receivable is disclosed as both current and noncurrent assets as follows:

1. The net investment at the end of 1996 is equal to $441,810.109 (the balance of 1/1/96 of $38,009.19 plus the interest receivable for 1996 of $3,800.919).
2. The current portion ($14,990.81) is the net investment to be received in 1997 of $8,189.891 plus the interest of $3,800.919.
3. The noncurrent portion is the $29,819.299 [lease payments] receivable of $35,972.43 ($11,990.81 × 3) minus unearned interest revenue of $6,153.054 ($1,090.064 + $2,081.041 + $2,981.919).
D. Collection of second year's lease payments:
Cash $14,990.81
    Lease Payments Receivable $11,990.81
    Property tax Expense/Payable $3,000.00
E. Recognition of December 31, 1997, interest revenue earned during the year:
Unearned Interest Revenue-Leases $2,981.929
    Interest Revenue-Leases $2,981.929
F. The entries should be similar through the year zero.

Operating Method of the Lessor: Illustrated

Exhibit 2.3
Zribi Company: Lease Amortization Schedule (Annuity Due Basis)

Date	Annual Lease Payment (a)	Executory Costs (b)	Interest on Net Investment at 10% (c)	Net Investment Recovery (d)	Net Investment (e)
1/1/96					$50,000.00
1/1/96	$14,990.81	$3,000.00	$------0------	$11,990.81	$38,009.19
1/1/97	$14,990.81	$3,000.00	$3,800.919	$8,189.891	$29,819.299
1/1/98	$14,990.81	$3,000.00	$2,981.929	$9,008.881	$20,810.418
1/1/99	$14,990.81	$3,000.00	$2,081.041	$9,909.769	$10,900.700
1/1/00	$14,990.81	$3,000.00	$1,090.064	$10,900.700	$------0------
	$75,954.05	$15,000.00	$9,953.953	$50,000.00	

(a)   Required lease payments producing 10% return on net investment

(b)   Executory costs paid by the lessee and included in rental payments

(c)   Columns (e) at the beginning of the year X 10% (except for 1/1/96)

(d)   (a) – (b) – (c)

(e)   Preceding balance minus (d)

The lessor using the operating method proceeds by recording every rental payments as a rental revenue, recording a depreciation expense for the leased equipment, and recording either additional costs as expense. Returning to the previous example between the Zrili Company and the Alvertos Company, the following entries are made:

A. Collection of Rental Payment on Operating Lease on 1/1/96
   Cash $14,990.81
       Rental Revenue $14,990.81
B. Recognition of Annual Depreciation expense on 12/31/96
   Depreciation Expense-Leased
   Equipment $5,000.00
       Accumulate Depreciation-
       Leased Equipment $5,000.00

CONCLUSIONS

Accounting for long-term leases involves either expensing or capitalizing the rental expenses. FASB Statement No. 13, which is the main subject of this chapter, outlines explicitly the techniques to be used under specific conditions by the lessee and the lessor. More advanced techniques are examined in Chapter 3.

NOTES

1.	"Accounting for Leases," *FASB Statement No. 13 as Amended and Interpreted through January 1990* (Norwalk, Conn.: FASB, 1990), Sec. 1.10.101
2.	John H. Myers, "Reporting of Leases in Financial Statements," *Accounting Research Standard No. 4* (New York: American Institute of Certified Public Accountants, 1964).
3.	Yuri, Ijiri, *Recognition of Contractual Rights and Obligations,* Research Report (Stamford, Conn.: FASB, 1980).
4.	Donald E. Kieso, and Jerry J. Weygandt, *Intermediate Accounting,* 4th ed. (New York: John Wiley, 1993), p.1123.
5.	E. A., Imhoff, Jr., R. C. Lipe, and D. W. Wright, "Operating leases: Impact of Constructive Capitalization," *Accounting Horizons* (March 1991).
6.	*FASB Statement No. 13,* par. 7.
7.	Sometimes the lessee is required to make up a *residual value deficiently* resulting from unusal events. Such deficiency is not included in the minimum lease payments but is recognized as period costs when incurred, as suggested by "Lessee Guarantee of the Residual Value of Leased Property," *FASB Interpretation No. 19* (Stamford, Conn: FASB, 1977), par. 3.
8.	*FASB Statement No. 13,* par. 5(1).
9.	Ibid., par 5(k).
10.	Kieso and Weygandt, *Intermediate Accounting,* p. 1133.

SELECTED READING
"Accounting for Leases." *FASB Statement No. 13 as Amended and Interpreted through January 1990* (Norwalk, Conn: FASB, 1990).

Chapter 3
Accounting for Long-Term Leases: Part II

This chapter introduces more advanced techniques for accounting for leases.

IMPACT OF RESIDUAL VALUES
Residual value, which is the estimated fair value of the leased asset at the end of the lease, can be either guaranteed or unguaranteed by the lessee. As stated earlier, guaranteed residual values are included in the minimum lease payments. Both guaranteed and unguaranteed residual values affect accounting by the lessee and lessor. For the lessor the determination of the lease payments with a residual value is also different. For example, let's suppose that the Zribi Company from chapter 2 expected the restaurant equipment to have a residual value of $2,500. It would compute the lease payments as shown in Exhibit 3.1.

The Case of a Guaranteed Residual Value
The guaranteed residual value is included in the minimum lease payments, which require that the lessee capitalizes the present value of the amount guaranteed. To illustrate let's return to the Zribi Company as the lessor and the Alvertos Company as the lessee example and assume that the Alvertos Company agrees to guarantee the entire amount of the residual value of $2,5000. The capitalized amount for the Alvertos Company is as follows:
1. Recognition of the annual depreciation of leased equipment on 12/31/96
   Depreciation Expense-Capital
   Leases $9,500.00
      Accumlated Depreciation-Cap-
      ital Leases $9,500.00
      [($50,000 - $2,500)/ 5 years]
2. At the end of the year 1996, the Obligation Under Capital Leases in the balance sheet is divided into its current and noncurrent portions as follows:
   A. Current liabilities
      Interest Payable $3.838.145
      Obligations Under Capital
      Leases $7,780.398
   B. Noncurrent Liabilities
      Obligations Under Lease $30,601.059
3. Recording the second rental payments in advance 1/1/97
   Property Tax Expense $3,000.00
   Obligations Under Capital leases $7,780.398
   Accrued Interest on Obligations
   Under Capital leases $3,838.398
      Cash $14,618.543
4. The same patterns of entries are followed through the year zero.

The Case of an Unguaranteed Residual Value
The lessee does not recognize the unguaranteed residual value in the computation of the minimum lease payments and the capitalization of the leased asset under obligation. To illustrate, let's return to the Zribi Company as the lessor and the Alvertos Company as the lessee example and assume that the Alvertos Company

Exhibit 3.1
Zribi's Computation of Lease Payments in the Case of Residual Value (Lessor's Computation, Annuity Due Basis)

1.	Fair market Value of Equipment of the Zribi Company	$50,000.00
2.	Less Present Value of Residual Value ($2,5000 X 0.62092)	$ 1,552.30
3.	Amount to be recovered by the Zribi Company	--------------
	Through the Lease Payments	$48,447.70
4.	Five Periodic Payments ($48,447.70/4.16986)	$11,618.543

1. Present value of five annual rental payments discounted at 10 percent ($11,618.543 × 4.16986) ... $48,447.70

Plus

2. Present value of a single sum of $2,500 (the guaranteed residual value) discounted at 10 percent ($2,500 × 0.62092) ... $1,552.30
   ----
3. Present value of minimum lease payments ... $50,000.00

The Alvertos Company lease amortization schedule is shown in Exhibit 3.2. It is basis for the following entries:

5. Capitalization of lease on 1/1/96

Leased Equipment Under Capital Leases	$50,000	
Obligation Under Capital Leases		$50,000

6. First Rental payment on 1/1/96

Property Tax Expense	$3,000.00	
Obligations Under Capital Leases	$11,618.543	
Cash		$14,618.543

7. Recognition of accrued interest on 12/31/96

Interest Expense	$3,838.145	
Interest Payable (or Accrued Interest Obligation Under Capital Leases)		$3,838.145

Exhibit 3.2
Alvertos Company Lease Amortization Schedule (Lessee's Computation, Annuity Due Basis) and Guaranteed Residual Value (GRV)

Date	Annual Lease Payment (a)	Executory Costs (b)	Interest on Net Investment at 10% (c)	Net Investment Recovery (d)	Net Investment (e)
1/1/96					$50,000.00
1/1/96	$14,618.543	$3,000	$------0------	$11,618.543	$38,381.457
1/1/97	$14,618.543	$3,000	$3,838.145	$7,780.398	$30,601.059
1/1/98	$14,618.543	$3,000	$3,060.105	$8,558.438	$22,042.621
1/1/99	$14,618.543	$3,000	$2,204.262	$9,414.281	$12,628.34
1/1/00	$14,618.543	$3,000	$1,262.834	$10,355.709	$ 2,272.631
12/31/00	$2,500.000		$ 227.263	$2,272.03*	$------0------
	$75,592.715	$15,000	$10,592.609*	$50,000.00*	

*rounded

(a)   Required lease payments producing 10% return on net investment

(b)   Executory costs paid by the lessee and included in rental payments

(c)   Columns (e) at the beginning of the year X 10% (except for 1/1/96)

(d)   (a) – (b) – (c)

(e)   Preceding balance minus (d)

does not agree to guarantee the entire amount of the residual value of $2,500. The capitalized amount for the Alvertos Company is as follows:
1. Present value of five annual rental payments discounted at 10 percent
    (11,681.543 × 4.16986) $48,447.70
Plus
2. Unguaranteed residual value of $2,500 not capitalized
                              $----0----
3. Present value of minimum lease payments
                              $48,447.70

The Alvertos Company lease amortization schedule is shown in Exhibit 3.3. It is the basis for the following entries:

Exhibit 3.3

Alvertos Company Lease Amortization Schedule (Lessee's Computation, Annuity Due Basis) and Unguaranteed residual Value

Date	Annual Lease Payment (a)	Executory Costs (b)	Interest on Net Investment at 10% (c)	Net Investment Recovery (d)	Net Investment (e)
1/1/96					$48,447.70
1/1/96	$14,618.543	$3,000	$------0------	$11,618.543	$36,829.152
1/1/97	$14,618.543	$3,000	$3,682.915	$7,935.628	$28,893.529
1/1/98	$14,618.543	$3,000	$2,889.352	$8,729.191	$20,164.338
1/1/99	$14,618.543	$3,000	$2,016.433	$9,602.11	$10,562.228
1/1/00	$14,618.543	$3,000	$1,056.222	$10,562.22*	$------0------
	$73,092.715	$15,000	$9,644.922	$48,447.70	

* Rounding error

1. Capitalization of lease on 1/1/96
   Leased Equipment Under Capital
   Leases $48,447.70
       Obligations Under Capital
       Leases $48,447.70
2. First Rental payment on 1/1/96
   Property Tax Expense $3,000.00
   Obligations Under Capital Leases $11,618.543
       Cash $14,618.543
3. Recognition of accrued interest on
   12/31/96
4. Recognition of annual depreciation
   expense on 12/31/96
   Depreciation Expense-Capital
   Leases $9,689.54
       Accumlated Depreciation-Cap-
       ital Leases $9,689.54
   [($48,447.70/5 years]
5. At the end of the year 1996, the Obligation Under Capital Leases in the balance sheet is divided into its
   current and noncurrent portions as follows:
   C. Current liabilities
       Interest Payable $3,682.915
       Obligations Under Capital
       Leases $7,935.628
   D. Noncurrent Liabilities
       Obligations Under Lease $28,893.529
6. Recording the second rental pay-
   ments in advance 1/1/97
   Property Tax Expense $3,000.00
   Obligations Under Capital leases $3,682.915
   Accrued Interest on Obligations
   Under Capital Leases $7,935.628
       Cash $14,618.543
7. The same patterns of entries are followed through the year zero.

The Case of a Residual Value for the Lessor

For the lessor the assumption is that the residual value will be realized whether it is guaranteed or unguaranteed. Returning to the previous example of the Zribi Company as the lessor and the Alvertos Company as the lessee and the residual value of $2,500 (whether guaranteed or unguaranteed), the following information is relevant to the lessor.

1. Gross Investment: ($11,618.543 × 5) + $2,500 = $60,592.715
2. Unearned Interest Revenue: $60,592.715 - $50,000 = $10,592.715
3. Net Investment = $60,592.715 - $10,592.715 = $50,000.00

The lease amortization for the lessor is illustrated in Exhibit 3.4. It is the basis of the following entries:
1. Initial recording of the lease as its
   Inception on 1/1/96

Lease Payments Receivable	$60,592.715	
Equipment		$50,000.00
Unearned Interest Revenue-Leases		$10,592.715

1. Recording of the first rental payment on 1.1.96

Cash	$14,618.543	
Lease Payments Receivable		$11,618.543
Property Tax Expense/Property Tax Payable		$3,000.00

2. Recognition of accrued interest on 12/31/96

Unearned Interest Revenue-Leases	$3,838.145	
Interest Revenue-Leases		$3,838.145

SALES-TYPE LEASES: ACCOUNTING FOR THE LESSOR

The major difference between a direct financing lease and a sales-type lease is the presence of a manufacturer's or dealer's profit or loss in a sales-type lease and the accounting for initial direct costs. This profit or loss is equal to the difference between:
1. The present value of the minimum lease payments (net of executor costs) computed at the interest rate implicit in the lease (i.e., the sales price), and
2. The cost or carrying value of the asset plus any initial direct costs less the present value of the unguaranteed residual value accruing to the benefit of the lessor.

To illustrate a sales-type lease, let's assume the same example as in direct financing where (1) the residual value is $2,500 (with a present value of $1,553.30), (2) the equipment had a cost $40,000 to the lessor, the Zribi Company, and (3) the fair market value of the residual value is $1,000.
A. The following information is relevant to the lessor in case the residual value is a guaranteed residual value:
1. Gross Investment: ($11,618.543 × 5) + $2,500 = $60,952.715
2. Unearned Interest Revenue: $60,592.715 - $50,000 = $10,592.715
3. Sale Price of the Asset: ($48,447.70 + 1,552.30) = $50,000.00
4. Cost of Good Sold: $40,000
5. Gross Profit: ($50,000 - $40,000) = $10,000
B. The following information is relevant to the lessor in case of an unguaranteed residual value:

1. Gross Investment: ($11,618,543 × 5) + $2,500 = $60,592.715
2. Unearned Interest Revenue: $60,592.715 - $50,000 = $10,592.715
3. Sale Price of the Asset: $48,447.70
4. Cost of Good Sold: $40,000 - $1,552.30 = $38,447.70
5. Gross Profit: ($48,447.70 + $38,447.70) = $10,000.00

Exhibit 3.4
Zribi Company Lease Amortization Schedule (Lessor's Computation, Annuity Due Basis) and Guaranteed Residual Value

Date	Annual Lease Payment (a)	Executory Costs (b)	Interest on Net Investment at 10% (c)	Net Investment Recovery (d)	Net Investment (e)
1/1/96					$50,000.00
1/1/96	$14,618.543	$3,000	$------0------	$11,618.543	$38,381.457
1/1/97	$14,618.543	$3,000	$3,838.145	$7,780.398	$30,601.059
1/1/98	$14,618.543	$3,000	$3,060.105	$8,558.438	$22,042.621
1/1/99	$14,618.543	$3,000	$2,204.262	$9,414.281	$12,628.34
1/1/00	$14,618.543	$3,000	$1,262.834	$10,355.709	$ 2,272.631
12/31/00	$2,500.000		$ 227.263	$2,272.03*	$------0------
	$75,592.715	$15,000	$10,592.609*	$50,000.00*	

*rounded

3. Required lease payments producing 10% return on net investment

(f)   Executory costs paid by the lessee and included in rental payments

(g)   Columns (e) at the beginning of the year X 10% (except for 1/1/96)

(h)   (a) – (b) – (c)

(i)   Preceding balance minus (d)

C. The entries assuming guaranteed residual value are:
1. Initial recording of the
   sales-type lease on 1/1/96

Minimum Lease Receivable	$60,592.715	
Cost of Goods Sold	$40,000.00	
Sales Revenue		$50,000.00
Equipment Held for Lease		$40,000.00
Unearned Interest Leases		$10,592.715

2. Collection of annual payment
   Of the 1/1/96

Cash	$14,618.543	
Minimum Lease Receivable		$11,618.543
Property Expense/ Payable		$3,000.00

3. Recognition of interest
   revenue on 12/31/96

Unearned Interest-Leases	$3,682.915	
Interest Revenue		$3,682.915

4. Collection of second annual
   payment for 1/1/97

Cash	$14,618.543	
Minimum Lease Receivable		$11,618.543
Property Expense/ Payable		$3,000.00

5. Recognition of interest
   revenue as of 12/31/97

Unearned Interest-Leases	$2,889.352	
Interest Revenue		$2,889.352

6. Recognition of residual
   value at the end of lease
   term
   (12/31/00)

Equipment	$1,000.00	
Cash	$1,500.00	
Lease Payment Receivable		$2,500.00

D. The entries assuming an unguaranteed residual value are:
1. Initial recording of the
   sales-type lease on 1/1/96

Minimum Lease Receivable	$60,592.715	
Cost of Goods Sold	$38,447.70	
Sales Revenue		$48,447.70

	Equipment		$40,000.00
	Unearned Interest Revenue		$10,592.715

2. Collection of annual payment for 1/1/96

	Cash	$14,618.543	
	Minimum Lease Receivable		$11,618.543
	Property Tax Expense/ Payable		$3,000.000

3. Recognition of interest revenue on 12/31/96

	Unearned Interest-Leases	$3,682.915	
	Interest Revenue		$3,682.915

4. Collection of second annual payment for 1/1/97

	Cash	$14,618.543	
	Minimum Lease Receivable		$11,618.543
	Property Expense/ Payable		$3,000.000

5. Recognition of interest revenue as of 12/31/97

	Unearned Interest-Leases	$2,889.352	
	Interest Revenue		$2,889.352

6. Recognition of residual value at the end of lease term(12/31/00)

	Equipment	$1,000.00	
	Cash	$1,500.00	
	Lease Payment Receivable		$2,500.00

ACCOUNTING FOR INITIAL DIRECT COSTS BY THE LESSOR

Initial direct costs have been redefined in FASB Statement No. 91.[1] Basically the initial direct costs of a lease transaction include two types as follows:

1. Incremental direct costs are the costs resulting from and are essential to the lease transaction
2. Internal direct costs are the costs related to the evaluation of the lessee's personal condition, and other costs of the activities performed by the lessor.

The accounting treatment for initial direct costs is different for each type of lease:

1. For an operating lease, the initial direct costs are recorded as prepaid assets and allocated over the lease term as an expense proportionally to the rental receipts.
2. For a direct financing lease, the initial direct costs are deferred and added to the net investment in the leases and amortized over the life of the lease as a yield adjustment.
3. For a sales-type lease, the initial direct costs are expensed in the same period.

ACCOUNTING FOR SALE-LEASEBACK

A sale-leaseback occurs when the owner of the asset sells the asset to another and simultaneously leases it back from the buyer (1) to benefit from better financing and (2) to derive a tax advantage from deducting the entire lease payment. Two situations are possible:

1. If the lease meets the condition for a capital lease, the profit from the transaction is deferred and amortized over the lease term by the lessee in proportion to the amortization of the leased asset.
2. If the lease does not meet the conditions for a capital lease, it is considered an operating lease and the profit is amortized proportionally to the rental payments.

Any loss, however, is recognized immediately. To illustrate a sale-leaseback transaction, assume that the Lessee Corporation, on January 1, 1996, sells a ship having a book value of $2,460,000 to the Lessor Corporation for $10,460,000 and simultaneously leases it back under the following conditions:

1. The term of the lease is four years, noncancelable
2. The payments at the beginning of every year are $3,000,000.
3. The fair value of the ship is $10,460,000 on 1/1/96 with a four-year economic life.
4. The lessor's rate is 10 percent.

Assuming the lease is a capital lease, the entries based on exhibit 3.5 are as follows:

1. Sale of ship by the lessee to the lessor on 1/1/96

Cash	$10,460,000	
Ship		$2,460,000
Unearned Profit on Sale-Leaseback		$8,000,000

2. Initial recording of sale-leaseback on 1/1/96

Leased Ship Under Capital Leases	$10,460,000	
Obligations Under Capital Leases		$10,460,000

3. Recording of first lease payment on 1/1/96

Obligations Under Capital Leases	$3,000,000	
Cash		$3,000,000

4. Recoding of depreciation expense on 12/31/96

Depreciation expense	$2,615,000	
Accumulated Depreciation ($10,460,000/4)		$2,615,000

Exhibit 3.5
Lessee's lease Amortization Schedule

Date	Annual Rental Payment	Interest of 10%	Reduction of Balance	Balance
1/1/96				$10,460,000
1/1/96	$3,000,000.00	$------0------	$3,000,000	$7,460,000
1/1/97	$3,000,000.00	$746,00	$2,254,000	$5,206,000
1/1/98	$3,000,000.00	$520,000	$2,480,000	$2,726,000
1/1/99	$3,000,000.00	$272,000	$2,726,000	$------0------

5. Amortization of unearned profit on
sales-leaseback on 12/31/96

Unearned Profit on Sale-leaseback	$2,000,000	
Realized Profit on Sale-Leaseback		$2,000,000
(or Depreciation Expense-Leased Ships)		
($8,000,000/4)		

6. Recognition of interest expense on
12/31/96

Interest Expense	$746,000	
Interest Payable		$746,000

To the lessor the entries are as follows on 1/1/96

1. Ship	$10,460,000	
Cash		$10,460,000
2. Lease Payments Receivable		
($3,000,000 × 4)		$12,000,000
Ship		
Unearned Interest Revenue		
3. Cash	$3,000,000	
Lease payments Receivable		$3,000,000

ACCOUNTING FOR LEASES INVOLVING REAL ESTATE

There are specific issue for accounting for leases involving real estate that include lease of land only, lease of both land and buildings, and lease of real estate and equipment.

1. If the lease involves land only, the lease for the lessee is a capital lease if (a) there is a transfer of ownership, and (b) there is a bargain purchase options, otherwise it is an operating lease. For the lessor the lease is either a sale-type or a direct financing lease if it meets the ownership conditions, the bargain purchase option conditions, and the collectability and uncertainty tests. Otherwise it is an operating lease.
2. If the lease involves both land and buildings and meets the ownership conditions and the bargain purchase option conditions, it is capital lease for the lessee and either a sale-type lease or a direct financing lease for the lessor, depending on the existence of a profit or loss.
3. If the lease involved both land and buildings, does not meet the ownership conditions, the bargain purchase option conditions, and the fair value of the land is less than 25 percent of the fair value of both land and buildings, the land portion is ignored and the lease is classified on the basis of the buildings' characteristics.
4. If the lease involves both land and buildings, does not meet the ownership condition and the bargain purchase option condition, and the fair value of the land is more than 25 percent of the fair value of both land and buildings, both the lessee and the lessor account for the land as an operating lease and the buildings as a capital lease if it meets the necessary requirements.
5. If the lease involves both real estate and equipment, the portion of the minimum lease payments application to the equipment portion of the lease should be estimated by whatever means are appropriate. The classification of the equipment is done separately from the real estate. The accounting for the real estate portion proceeds as described in the preceding section. For a leased property that is part of a large building, reasonable estimates of the lease property's fair value might

be objectively determined by referring of an independent appraisal of the lease property or to estimated replacement cost information.

LEVERAGED LEASES
Definition of Leverage Leases

The use of leverage leases for the financing of capital equipment has reached an annual value of $6.5 billion. The leverage lease allows a boost to the tax benefits to the lessor, who has to come up with a small percentage of the purchase price and finance the rest while keeping 100 percent of the ownership of the asset.

A leveraged lease is defined as one having all of the following characteristics:

1. It meets the definition of a direct financing lease while the 90 percent of fair value criterion does not apply.
2. It involves at least three parties:
   a. Owner-lessor (commonly called equity participant)
   b. A lessee (commonly called user of the asset)
   c. A long-term creditor (commonly called debt participant)
3. The amount of the financing is sufficient to provide the lessor with a substantial "leverage" in the transaction.
4. The leverage debt provided by the long-term creditor (60 percent to 80 percent) is nonrecourse as to the general credit of the lessor. It is secured by the lessee's payment and a security interest in the property. Therefore, the interest rate depends on the credit rating of the lessee rather than the lessor.
5. The lessor buys the asset from the manufacturer using his capital and the capital provided by the long-term creditor. He or she leases the asset to the lessee. The lessor uses the lease payments to make debt service payments (interest and principal) and keeps the remaining difference. The lessor benefits from (a) the lease payments, and (b) the income tax deductions from accelerated depreciating expenses, interest expenses, and other possible expenses. In general, the lessor's net investment declines during the early years once the investment has been completed and rises during the later years of the lease before its final elimination.

Accounting for Leveraged Leases

The lessee should treat the leveraged lease in the same manner as the nonleveraged lease. The lessor's treatment is more complex. The lessor records the investment in the leveraged lease net of the nonrecourse debt. The net of the balances of the following accounts represents the initial and continuing investment in leveraged leases.

A. Rentals receivable, net of that portion of the rental applicable to the principal and interest on the nonrecourse debt.
B. A receivable for the amount of the investment tax credit to be realized on the transaction.
C. The estimated residual value of the leased asset.
D. Unearned and deferred income consisting of (i) the estimated pretax lease income (or loss), after deducting initial direct costs, remaining to be allocated to income over the lease term and (ii) the investment tax credit remaining to be allocated to income over the lease term.

The investment in leveraged leases less deferred taxes arising from differences between pretax accounting income and taxable income shall represent the lessor's net investment in leveraged leases for purposes of computing periodic net income from the lease.[2]

To illustrate the accounting for leveraged leases, let's consider the following example. The lessor company and lessee company sign a lease agreement dated January 1, 1975, that calls for the lessor company to lease equipment to the lessee company until the beginning of January 1, 1990. The terms and provisions of the lease agreements and other pertinent data are as follows:

Costs of leased asset (equipment)	$1,000,000
Lease term	15 years, dating from January 1, 1975
Lease rental payments	$90,000 per year (payable last day of each year)
Residual value	$200,000 estimated to be realized one year after lease termination. In the eleventh year of the lease the estimate is reduced to $120,000.

Financing:

Equity investment by lessor	$400,000
Long-term nonrecourse debt	$600,000, bearing interest at 9 percent and repayable in annual installments (on last day of each year) of $74,435.30.
Depreciation allowable to lessor for Income tax purposes	Seven-year ADR life using double-declining balance method for the first two years (with half-year convention election applied in the first year) and sum-of-years digits method for remaining life, depreciated to $100,000 salvage value.
Lessor's income tax rate (federal and state)	50.4 percent (assumed to continue in existence throughout the term of the lease)
Investment tax credit	10 percent of equipment cost or $100,000 (realized by the lessor on last day of first year of lease)
Initial direct costs	For simplicity, initial direct costs have not been included in the illustration.

Given the above terms and provisions, the cash flow analysis by years and the allocation of annual cash flow to investment and income are presented in Exhibit 3.6 and 3.7. The journal entries for lessor's initial investment and first year of operations are as follows:

JOURNAL ENTRIES FOR YEAR ENDING
DECEMBER 31, 1975

LESSOR'S INITIAL INVESTMENT

Rentals receivable (exhibit 3.6, total of column 1 less residual value, less totals of columns 2 and 6)	$233,470	
Investment tax credit receivable (exhibit 3.6 column 7)	$100,000	
Estimated residual value (given)	$200,000	
Unearned and deferred income (Exhibit 3.7, totals of columns 5 and 7)		$133,470
Cash		$400,000
First Year Operation		
Cash	$15,565	
Rentals receivable (Exhibit 3.6, column 1 less columns 3 and 6)		$15,565
(Collection of 1st years' net rental)		
Cash*	$100,000	
Investment tax credit receivable (Exhibit 3.6 column 7)		$100,000
(Receipt of investment tax credit)		
Unearned and deferred income	$9,929	
Income from leveraged leases (Exhibit 3.7, column 50)		$9,929
(Recognition of first year's portion of pretax income allocated in the same proportion as the allocated of total income $[34,588/116,601] \times 33,470 =$ 9,929) Unearned and deferred income	$29,663	
Investment tax credit recognized (Exhibit 3.7, column 7)		$29,663

Exhibit 3.6
Cash Flow Analysis by Years

	1 Gross lease rentals and residual value	2 Depreciation (for income tax purposes)	3 Loan interest payments	4 Taxable income (loss) (col. 1 - 2 - 3)	5 Income tax credits (charges) (col. 4 × 50.4%)	6 Loan principal payments	7 Investment tax credit realized	8 Annual cash flow (col. 1 - 3 + 5 - 6 + 7)	9 Cumulative cash flow
Initial Investment	$-	$-	$-	$-	$-	$-	$-	$(400,000)	400,000
1	$90,000	$142,857	$54,000	$(106,857)	$53,856	$20,435	$100,000	$169,421	$(230,579)
2	$90,000	$244,898	$52,161	$(207,059)	$104,358	$22,274	$-	$119,923	$(110,656)
3	$90,000	$187,075	$50,156	$(147,231)	$74,204	$24,279	$-	$89,769	$(20,887)
4	$90,000	$153,061	$47,971	$(111,032)	$55,960	$26,464	$-	$71,525	$50,638
5	$90,000	$119,048	$45,589	$(74,637)	$37,617	$28,846	$-	$53,182	$103,820
6	$90,000	$53,061	$42,993	$(6,054)	$3,051	$31,442	$-	$18,616	$122,436
7	$90,000		$40,163	$49,837	$(25,118)	$34,272	$-	$(9,553)	$112,883
8	$90,000		$37,079	$52,921	$(26,672)	$37,357	$-	$(11,108)	$101,775
9	$90,000		$33,717	$56,283	$(28,367)	$40,719	$-	$(12,803)	$88,972
10	$90,000		$30,052	$59,948	$(30,214)	$44,383	$-	$(14,649)	$74,323
11	$90,000		$26,058	$63,942	$(32,227)	$48,378	$-	$(16,663)	$57,660
12	$90,000		$21,704	$68,296	$(34,421)	$52,732	$-	$(18,857)	$38,803
13	$90,000		$16,957	$73,043	$(36,813)	$57,478	$-	$(21,248)	$17,555
14	$90,000		$11,785	$78,215	$(39,420)	$62,651	$-	$(23,856)	$(6,301)
15	$90,000		$6,145	$83,855	$(42,263)	$68,290	$-	$(26,698)	$(32,999)
16	$90,000	$100,000	$-	$100,000	$(50,400)	$-	$-	$149,600	$116,601
Totals	$1,550,000	$1,000,000	$516,530	$33,470	$(16,869)	$600,000	$100,000	$116,601	

Source: "Accounting for Leases," *FASB Statement No. 13 as Amended and Interpreted Through May 1980* (Stamford, Conn: FASB, 1980), Schedule 2. Required with permission.

Exhibit 3.7
Allocation of Annual Cash Flow to Investment and Income

	1	2	3	4		5	6	7
		Annual	Cash	Flow		Component	of	Income[2]
Year	Lessor's net investment at beginning of year	Total (from Schedule 2, col. 8)	Allocated to Investment	Allocated to income[1]		Pretax income	Tax effect of pretax income	Investment tax credit
1	$400,000	$169,421	$134,833	$34,588		$9,929	$(5,004)	$29,663
2	$265,167	$119,923	$96,994	$22,929		$6,582	$(3,317)	$19,664
3	$168,173	$89,769	$75,227	$14,542		$4,174	$(2,104)	$12,472
4	$92,946	$71,525	$63,488	$8,037		$2,307	$(1,163)	$6,893
5	$29,458	$53,182	$50,635	$2,547		$731	$(368)	$2,184
6	$(21,177)	$18,616	$18,616	$-		$-	$-	$-
7	$(39,793)	$(9,553)	$(9,553)	$-		$-	$-	$-
8	$(30,240)	$(11,108)	$(11,108)	$-		$-	$-	$-
9	$(19,132)	$(12,803)	$(12,803)	$-		$-	$-	$-
10	$(6,329)	$(14,649)	$(14,649)	$-		$-	$-	$-
11	$8,320	$(16,663)	$(17,382)	$719		$206	$(104)	$617
12	$25,702	$(18,857)	$(21,079)	$2,222		$637	$(321)	$1,906
13	$46,781	$(21,248)	$(25,293)	$4,045		$1,161	$(585)	$3,469
14	$72,074	$(23,856)	$(30,088)	$6,232		$1,789	$(902)	$5,345
15	$102,162	$(26,698)	$(35,532)	$8,834		$2,536	$(1,278)	$7,576
16	$137,694	$149,600	$137,694	$11,906		$3,418	$(1,723)	$10,211
Totals		$516,601	$400,000	$116,601		$33,470	$(16,869)	$100,000

[1] Lease income is recognized as 8.647% of the unrecovered investment at the beginning of each year in which the net investment is positive. The rate is that rate which when applied to the net investment in the years in which the net investment is positive will distribute the net income (net cash flow) to those years. The rate for allocation used in this Schedule is calculated by a trial and error process. The allocation is calculated based upon an initial estimate of the rate as a starting point. If the total thus allocated to income (column 4) differs used the estimated rate from the net cash flow (Schedule 2, column 8) the estimated rate is increased or decreased, as appropriate, to derive a revised allocation. This process is repeated until a rate is selected which develops a total amount allocated to income that is precisely equal to the net cash flow. As a particular matter, a computer program is used to calculate Schedule 3 under successive iterations until the correct rate is determined.

[2] Each component is allocated among the years of positive net investment in proportion to the allocation of net income in column 4.

Source: "Accounting for Leases," *FASB Statement No. 13 as Amended and Interpreted Through May 1980* (Stamford, Conn: FASB, 1980), Schedule 3. Required with permission.

(Recognition of first year's portion of
investment tax credit allocation in the
same proportion as the allocation of total

income [34,588/116,601] × 100,000
= 29,6630)

Cash (Exhibit 3.6, column 5)	$53,856	
Income tax expense (Exhibit 3.7, column 6)	$5,004	
Deferred taxes		$58,860

To record receipt of first year's tax credit from lease operation, to charge income tax expense for tax effect of pretax accounting income, and to recognize as deferred taxes the tax effect of the difference between pretax accounting income and the tax loss for the year, calculated as follows:

---

*Receipts of the investment tax credit and other tax benefits are shown as cash receipts for simplicity only. Those receipts probably would not be in the form of immediate cash inflow. Instead, they likely would be in the form of reduced payments of taxes on other entities whose operations are joined with the lessor's operations in a considered tax return.

Tax loss (Exhibit 3.6, column 4)	$(106,857)
Pretax accounting income	9,929
Difference	$(116,786)
Deferred taxes ($116,786 × 50.4%)	$58,860

The financial statements including the footnotes at the end of the year are as follows:

1. BALANCE SHEET

ASSETS				LIABILITIES		
	December 31,				*December 31,*	
	1976	*1975*			*1976*	*1975*
Investment in leveraged leases	$334,708	$324,207	Deferred taxes arising from leveraged leases		$58,860	$116,535

2. INCOME STATEMENT

(ignoring all income and expense items other than those relating to leveraged leasing)

	1976	**1975**
Income from leveraged leases	$ 6,582	$ 9,929
Income before taxes and investment tax credit	6,582	9,929
Less: Income tax expense*	(3,317)	(5,004)
	3,265	4,925

Investment tax credit recognized*	19,664	29,663
Net Income	$22,929	$34,588

3. FOOTNOTES

Investment in Leveraged Leases

*These two items may be netted purposes of presentation in the income statement, provided that the separate amounts are disclosed in a note to the financial statements.

The Company is the lessor in a leveraged lease agreement entered into in 1975 under which mining equipment having an estimated economic life of 18 years was leased for a term of 15 years. The Company's equity investment represented 40 percent of the purchase price; the remaining 60 percent was furnished by third-party financing in the form of long-term debt that provides for no recourse against property. At the end of the lease term, the equipment is turned back to the Company. The residual value at that time is estimated to be 20 percent of cost. For federal income tax purposes, the company receives the investment tax credit and has the benefit of tax deductions for depreciation on the entire leased asset and for interest on the long-term debt. Since during the early years of the lease those deductions exceed the lease rental income, substantial excess deductions are available to be applied against the company's other income. In the later years of the lease, rental income will excess the deductions and taxes will be payable. Deferred taxes are provided to reflect this reversal. The company's net investment in leveraged lease is composed of the following elements:

	December 31,	
	1976	1975
Rentals receivable (net of principal and interest on		
The nonrecourse debt)	$202,340	$217,905
Estimated residual value of leased assets	200,000	200,000
Less: Unearned and deferred income	(67,632)	(93,878)
Investment in leveraged leases	334,708	324,027
Less: Deferred taxes arising from leveraged leases	(166,535)	(58,860)
Net investment in leveraged leases	$168,173	$265,167

If we assume a revision in the estimated residual value of the leases asset in the eleventh year of the lease from $200,000 to $120,000, then the revised allocation of annual cash flow to investment and income, the balance in investment accounts at the beginning of the eleventh year before revised estimate, and the adjustments of investment of accounts will be as in Exhibit 3.8, 3.9, and 3.10. Finally, the journal entries will be as follows:

Exhibit 3.8
Allocation of Annual Cash Flow to Investment and Income, Revised to Include New residual Value Estimates

Year	1 Lessor's net investment at beginning of year	2 Total	3 Allocated to Investment	4 Allocated to income[1]	5 Pretax loss	6 Tax effect of pretax income	7 Investment tax credit
		Annual Cash Flow			Components of Income		
1	$400,000	$169,421	$142,458	$26,963	$(16,309)	$8,220	$35,052
2	$257,542	$119,923	$102,563	$17,360	$(10,501)	$5,293	$22,568
3	$154,979	$89,769	$79,323	$10,446	$(6,319)	$3,184	$13,581
4	$75,656	$71,525	$66,425	$5,100	$(3,085)	$1,555	$6,630
5	$9,231	$53,182	$52,560	$622	$(377)	$190	$809
6	$(43,329)	$18,616	$18,616	$-	$-	$-	$-
7	$(61,945)	$(9,553)	$(9,553)	$-	$-	$-	$-
8	$(52,392)	$(11,108)	$(11,108)	$-	$-	$-	$-
9	$(41,284)	$(12,803)	$(12,803)	$-	$-	$-	$-
10	$(28,481)	$(14,649)	$(14,649)	$-	$-	$-	$-
11	$(13,832)	$(16,663)	$(16,663)	$-	$-	$-	$-
12	$2,831	$(18,857)	$(19,048)	$191	$(115)	$58	$248
13	$21,879	$(21,248)	$(22,723)	$1,475	$(892)	$450	$1,917
14	$44,602	$(23,856)	$(26,862)	$3,006	$(1,819)	$916	$3,909
15	$71,464	$(26,698)	$(31,515)	$4,817	$(2,914)	$1,469	$6,262
16	$102,979	$109,920	$102,979	$6,941	$(4,199)	$2,116	$9,024

Total						
s	$476,921	$400,000	$76,921	$(46,530)	$23,451	$100,000

[1]The revised rate is 6.741%

Source: "Accounting for Leases," *FASB Statement No. 13 as Amended and Interpreted Through May 1980* (Stamford, Conn: FASB, 1980), Schedule 5. Required with permission.

Exhibit 3.9
Balances in Investment Accounts Before Revised Estimate of Residual Value

	1	2	3	4	5	6	7
				Unearned Defered Income			
	Rentals Receivable (1)	Estimated Residual Value	Investment Tax Credit Receivable	Pretax Income (Loss) (2)	Investment Tax Credit (3)	Defered Taxes (4)	Net Investment (col. 1 + 2 + 3) less (col. 4 + 5 + 6)
Initial Investment	$233,470	$200,000	$100,000	$33,470	$100,000	$-	$400,000
Changes in Year of Operation							
1	$(15,565)	$-	$(100,000)	$(9,929)	$(29,663)	$58,860	$(134,833)
2	$(15,565)	$-	$-	$(6,582)	$(19,664)	$107,675	$(96,994)
3	$(15,565)	$-	$-	$(4,174)	$(12,472)	$76,308	$(75,227)
4	$(15,565)	$-	$-	$(2,307)	$(6,893)	$57,123	$(63,488)
5	$(15,565)	$-	$-	$(731)	$(2,184)	$37,985	$(50,635)
6	$(15,565)	$-	$-	$-	$-	$3,051	$(18,616)
7	$(15,565)	$-	$-	$-	$-	$(25,118)	$9,553
8	$(15,564)	$-	$-	$-	$-	$(26,672)	$11,108
9	$(15,564)	$-	$-	$-	$-	$(28,367)	$12,803
10	$(15,565)	$-	$-	$-	$-	$(30,214)	$14,649

Balances, beginning of eleventh year	$77,822	$200,000	$-	$9,747	$29,124	$230,631	$8,320

(1) Schedule 2, column 1, excluding residual value, less column 3 and 6.
(2) Schedule 3, column 5.
(3) Schedule 3, column 7.
(4) 50.4% of difference between taxable income (loss), Schedule 2, column 4, and pretax accounting income (loss), Schedule 3, column

Exhibit 3.10
Adjustment for Investment Accounts for Revised Estimates of
Residual Value in the Eleventh Year

	1	2	3	4	5	6
			Unearned & Defered Income			**Net Investment**
	Rentals Receivable	**Estimated Residual Value**	**Pretax Income (loss)**	**Investment Tax Credit**	**Defered Taxes**	**(col. 1 + 2) less (col. 3 + 4 + 5)**
Balances, beginning of eleventh year (Schedule 6)	$77,822	$200,000	$9,747	$29,124	$230,631	$8,320
Adjustment of Estimated Residual Value and Unearned and Defered Income (Schedule 7 - journal entry 2)	$-	$(80,000)	$(19,686)	$(7,764)	$-	$52,550
Adjustment of Defered Taxes for the Cumulative Effect on Pretax Accounting Income (Schedule 7 - journal entry 2)	$-	$-	$-	$-	$(30,398)	$30,398
Adjusted balances, beginning of eleventh year	$77,822	$120,000	$(9,939)	$21,360	$200,233	$(13,832)

Adjusted Balance, Column 6:
Schedule 5, column 1.

JOURNAL ENTREIS- REDUCTION IN RESIDUAL VALUE IN ELEVENTH YEAR

1. JOURNAL ENTRY 1

Pretax income (or loss)		$60,314
Unearned and deferred income		$27,450
Pretax income (loss):		
Balance at end of 10th year	$9,747[1]	
Revised balance	$(9,939)[2]	
Adjustment	$(19,686)	
Deferred investment tax credit:		
Balance at end of 10th year	$29,124[3]	
Revised balance	$21,360[4]	
Adjustment	$(7,764)	
Investment tax credit recognized		$7,764
Estimated residual value		$80,000
To record:		
(i) The cumulative effect on pretax income and the effect on future income resulting from the decrease in estimated residual value:		
Reduction in estimated residual value		$80,000
Less: portion attributed to future years (unearned and deferred income)		$(19,686)
Cumulative effect (charged against current income)		$60,314

(ii) The cumulative and future effect of the change in allocation of the investment tax credit resulting from the reduction in estimated residual value.

[1] Exhibit 3.9, column 4
[2] Exhibit 3.8, total of column 5 less amounts applicable to the first 10 years.
[3] Exhibit 3.9, column 5.
[4] Exhibit 3.8, total of column 7 less amounts applicable to the first 10 years.

2. JOURNAL ENTRY 2

Deferred taxes	$30,398	
Income tax expense		$30,398

To recognize deferred taxes for the Difference between pretax accounting Income (or loss) and taxable income (or loss) for the effect of the reduction in estimated residual value.

    Pretax accounting loss per journal

entry 1	$(60,314)
Tax income (or loss)	
Difference	$(60,314)
Deferred taxes ($60,314 × 50.4%)	$(30,398)

NOTES

1. "Accounting for Nonrefundable Fees and Costs Associated with Originating or Acquiring Loans and Initial Direct Costs of Leases," *Statement of Financial Accounting Standards No. 91* (Stamford, Conn.: FASB, 1987).

2. "Accounting for Leases," *FASB Statement No. 13 as Amended and Interpreted Through May 1980* (Stamford, Conn.: FASB, 1980), par. 43.

SELECTED READING

"Accounting for Leases," *FASB Statement No. 13 as Amended and Interpreted Through January 1990* (Norwalk, Conn: FASB, 1990)

Chapter 4
Issues in Accounting for
Long-Term Leases

INTRODUCTION

Accounting for leases is very controversial because of the availability of different alternatives, including capitalization or expensing. Either one of them can be achieved by designing the leasing contract to include covenants permitting one of the alternatives. Therefore if firms attempt to escape the capitalization alternative and apt for the operating one, the user is left with the task of reconstructing the balance sheet to determine the new capital structure as if the firm had adopted the capitalizing alternative. In addition, the capitalizing alternative creates economic consequences and data with potential predictive ability. Accordingly, this chapter examines these issues as a way of assessing the merits of capitalization versus expensing.

LEASE ACCOUNTING RULES

Accounting for leases has always been a controversial accounting issue examined by various standard-setting bodies. The first effort started by the Committee on Accounting Procedures resulted in the publication of the *Accounting Research Bulletin* No. 38, *Disclosure of Long-Term Leases in Financial Statement of Lessees* in 1949. This publication was followed by a second effort of the Accounting Principles Board (APB), resulting in the publication of Accounting Principles Board Opinion No. 5, *Reporting of Leases in Financial Statements of Lessee.* The opinion required that noncancelable leases be capitalized if they are deemed to be clearly in substance installment purchases of property. Needless to say, firms managed to write leasing contracts with covenants more compatible with noncapitalization. The Securities and Exchange Commission (SEC) and the APB intervened again in 1973 to require more detailed footnote disclosures in the APB Opinion No. 31, *Disclosure of Lease Commitments by Lessees* and Accounting Series Release (ASR) No. 147, *Notice of Adoption of Amendments to Regulation S-X Requiring Improved Disclosure of Leases (1973).* For example, ASR no. 147 called for (1) disclosure of a schedule of cash flow commitments for all noncancelable, noncapitalized leases whether financing operating (a) for each of the five years following the date of the last balance sheet, (b) for each of the following three five-year periods, and (c) for the term of the lease remaining after the next 20 years; and (2) disclosure of present values of noncancelable financing leases and average and range of discount rates used in computing those present values.

The SEC indicated at the same time that the FASB needed to address the issue, which led to the issuance in November 1976 of Statement No. 13 distinguishing between capital leases and operating leases (see Chapters 2 and 3).

MEASUREMENT OF THE CURRENT PORTION OF LONG-TERM OBLIGATION

The requirement of Statement No. 13 is to record the capital lease as an asset and an obligation with the stipulation that the obligations shall be separately identified in the balance sheet as obligations in classifying them with current and noncurrent liabilities in classified balance sheets. There is, however, no guideline for the measurement of the current portion of long-term obligations or receivables.[1] The two alternatives considered in most textbooks are the change in present value approach (CPV), and the present value of next year's payment approach (PVNYP). This results in different amounts being reflected as the current portion of a long-term obligation. The differences in the approaches can be described as follows.[2]

A. The CPV approach defines the current portion (CP) as

$$CP = L(1 + r)^{-n}$$

Where

CP = capital portions of long-term obligation

L = constant lease payment

r = interest rate
N = number of time periods until the last lease payment

    B. The PVNYP approach defines the current portion as:
$$CP = L(1 + r)^{-1}$$
        As example let's assume a lease with $10,000 lease payment where n = 2 and r = 10 percent. The current portion of long-term obligation is measured

    A. Using the CPV approach as:
$$CP = \$20,000(1.10)^{-2} = \$16,528.81$$
    B. Using the PVNYP as:
$$CP = \$20,000(1.10)^{-1} = \$18,182.586$$

The difference between the two amounts- $1,653.776- does not seem material. However if n was equal to 20 years, then the current portion of long-term obligation using the CPV approach is:

$$CP = \$20,000 (1.10)^{-20} = \$2,972.818$$

The present value of next year's payment calculations is $18,182.586. Given this awkward situation, Robert Sweringa recommends the following measure. "Given the potential significance of the current and non-current portion of lease obligations as well as other long-term receivables and payables in classifying balance sheets, perhaps the FASB should consider how these portions should be calculated and provide some guidelines."[13]

Given the problem raised by the existence of the two alternatives to the measurement of the current portion of long-term lease obligations, and the absence of FASB guidelines, there is obviously need for an investigation of actual practices on the matter. Accordingly, A. W. Richardson examined a sample of 170 companies randomly selected from a list of 1,461 companies on the New York Stock Exchange, showing that the change in present value approach appears to be dominant in current financial reporting proactice.[4] In addition, the evidence showed that the adjustment of the reported financial statement numbers to those that would be obtained by the present value of next year's payments approach does not affect the ranking of companies by a number of financial measures. Accordingly, Richardson concludes:

> The results obtained for this randomly selected sample suggest that a uniform approach to determining the current portion of capital lease obligations exists in practice and the changing this approach would not have a significant effect on the ranking of companies in financial analysis. Consequently, it is not clear that the FASB should expend the resources to study this problem and issues guidelines as suggested by Sweringa (1984).[5]

CONSTRICTIVE CAPITALIZATION

A lot of annual reports of large corporations are reporting very large noncancelable operating lease commitments. The deliberate choice of treating those leases as operating leases creates serious understatements of the asset and liability sides of their balance sheets and major distortions in key statement financial ratios. These operating leases are in fact de facto off-balance sheet investing/financing instruments with serious impacts on the risk and return measures used by users of financial accounting information in the evaluation of the financial soundness of these firms. The way to correct for the limitations associated with annual reports loaded with very large noncancelable operating lease commitments is to reconstruct their balance sheets as if the operating leases have been capitalized as financing leases, a method known as constructive capitalization.[6]

Constructive capitalization consist of changing the recording of leases as rented arrangements (operating leases) to asset purchases (capitalized leases) at their inception, and therefore showing the estimated unrecorded liability and assets. To illustrate the application of constructive capitalization, this section relies on the example used in E. A. Imhoff, R.C. Lipe, and D. W. Wright's study.[7] The example examined leasing instructions in the 1988 annual report of McDonald's Corporation, the world's largest chain of fast food restaurants. The relevant data are shown in Exhibit 4.1. The problem is to estimate the present value of the schedule minimum operating lease cash flows totaling about $2,236 million. Various assumptions are made:

1. The examination of the debt footnote yielded a conservation measure for McDonald's historical interest rate averaging 10 percent.
2. The $1,402 million lump sum following 1993 is spread over 10 years resulting in an average cash flow per year beyond 1993 of $140.2 million per year ($1,402.357/10).

A capitalization of the cash flows using the annual 10 percent interest rate and 15-year average year remaining lease life is shown in Exhibit 4.2. It shows a present value of McDonald/s unrecorded liability for operating lease commitments of about $1,17 billion. Changing the interest rate (+2 percent) and the remaining life of the lease (+5 or +10 years) provided a range of estimates going from a low of $1.01 billion to a high of $1.31 billion for the unrecorded debt attributable to the operating leases.

The next step is to estimate the unrecorded amount, which depends on the scheduled cash flows, incremental borrowing rate, remaining life of the lease, an estimate of the weighted average total life of the leased assets, and our assumed depreciation method. Exhibit 4.3 is used as a mechanism for estimating the unrecorded asset after estimating the unrecorded liability. The table's percentages express the unauthorized unrecorded operating lease asset at a percentage of the remaining unrecorded operating lease liability at various stages of the asset's weighted average remaining useful life.[8]

Using the assumed weighted average total life of 30 years with 15 years remaining, and the 10 percent interest rate, the implied net book value of the unrecorded asset is 62 percent of the estimated unrecorded liability. If the assumed weighted average life is changed to 25 years with 15 years reaming, the implied net book value is now 72 percent of the estimated unrecorded liability. The authors settled on the value of 67 percent yielding a value of $785.8 million for McDonald's leased assets if the operating leases have been capitalized. The total effects of this constructive capitalization scenario are shown in Exhibit 4.4, with a 9 percent decrease in ROA (rate of return in assets) and a 30 percent increase in D/E (debt/equity). The same constructive capitalization scenario is used on seven pairs of firms from seven industries.[9] The results reported in Exhibit 4.5 show the constrictive capitalization of operating lease leads to a drastic and different financial picture, and may be essential for a sound financial analysis.

ECONOMIC CONSEQUENCES OF THE ADOPTION OF THE LEASE DISCLOSURE RULE

The previous example on constructive capitalization showed that the choice of capitalization increased the debt equity ratio by 30 percent from 1.35 times to 1.81 times. Therefore, firms may be motivated to move from capital leases to more operating leases as a way of reducing their leverage following the adoption

Exhibit 4.1
McDonald's Corporation Financial Statement Data and Leasing Footnote

Panel A

	($ in 000,000)
Reported Total Assets	$8,159
Reported Total Liabilities	$4,746
Reported Total Stockholders' Equity	$3,413
Reported Net Income	$ 646
Reported Effective Book Tax Rate	38.8%

Panel B

At December 31, 1988, the Company was lessee at 1,636 restaurant locations under ground leases (the Company leases the land and constructs and owns the buildings) and at 1,922 locations under improved leases (lessor owns the land and buildings). These leases are operating leases except for the building portions of 485 leases, which together with certain restaurant equipment leases, are capital leases. Land and building lease terms are generally for 20 to 25 years and, in many cases, provide for rent escalations and one or more five-year renewal options with certain lease providing purchase options. The Company is generally obligated for the rental occupancy costs which include property taxes, insurance and maintenances. In addition, the Company is lessee under noncancelable operating leases covering offices and vehicles.

At December 31, 1988, future minimum payments under capital leases and noncancelable operating leases, with initial terms of one year or more, are as follows:

(*In thousands of dollars*)	Capital leases	Operating leases Restaurant	Other	Total
1989	$17,047	$152,834	$28,289	$181,123
1990	15,209	151,897	26,422	178,319
1991	13,926	147,962	20,199	168,161
1992	10,214	143,556	13,864	157,420
1993	6,983	138,142	10,234	148,376
Thereafter	52,504	1,336,377	65,980	1,402,357
Total	115,883	$2,070,768	$164,988	$2,235,756
Less imputed interest	50,196			
Present value at December 31, 1986	$65,687			

Rent expense was as follows: 1988-$190 million; 1987-$160 million; and 1986-$143 million. Included in these amounts were percentage rents based on sales by the related restaurants in excess of minimum rents stipulated in certain capital and operating lease agreements as follows: 1988-$15 million; 1987-$12 million; and 1986-$11 million.

Exhibit 4.2
McDonald's Operating Leases: Equivalent Present Value ($ in millions)

Panel A: PV of Operating Leases

	Scheduled Cash Flows[a]	×	10% Present Value Factor	=	PV of Cash Flows
1989	181.1	×	.9091	=	$ 164.6
1990	178.3	×	.8264	=	147.3
1991	168.2	×	.7513	=	126.4
1992	157.4	×	.6830	=	107.5
1993	148.4	×	.6209	=	92.1
1994 to 2003	140.2[b]	×	3.8153[c]	=	534.9
					$1,172.8

$1,172.8   Estimated unrecorded debt.

[a] Rounded to the nearest $100,000, and assuming all payments occur at the end of each year.
[b] $1,402.357/10 years = $140.2 per year
[c] This factor is the present value of a 15 year annuity at 10% less the present value of a 5 year annuity at 10%, based on assumed $140.2 million at the end of each year from 1994-2003.

Panel B: Sensitivity Analysis

Assumptions as above except-	Estimated Unrecorded Debt
1. If interest rate is 8 percent (not 10 percent)	$1,311.0 million
2. If interest rate is 12 percent (not 10 percent)	$1,057.3 million
3. If total remaining life is 20 years (not 15 years)	$1,079.4 million
4. If total remaining life is 25 years (not 15 years)	$1,008.6 million

Source: Eugene A. Imhoff, Jr., Robert C. Lipe, and David W. Wright, "Operating Leases: Impact of Constructive Capitalization," *Accounting Horizons* (March 1991), p. 55. Reprinted with permission.

Exhibit 4.3
Constructive capitalization of Operating Leases: Relation Between Unrecorded Liability and Unrecorded Asset Over Time

Total Lease Life	Marginal Interest Rate	Ratio of Asset Balance to Liability Balance[a]							Point of Maximum Difference Between Asset And Liability
		% of Original Lease Life Expired							
		20%	30%	40%	50%	60%	70%	80%	
10	.08	93%	90%	87%	84%	81%	78%	75%	53%
15	.08	91	86	82	78	74	70	66	55%
20	.08	89	83	78	73	68	64	59	56%
25	.08	87	81	75	69	64	58	53	58%
30	.08	86	79	72	66	60	54	49	59%
10	.10	92	88	85	81	78	74	71	54%
15	.10	89	84	79	74	70	65	61	56%
20	.10	87	81	75	69	64	59	54	58%
25	.10	85	78	72	65	59	53	48	59%
30	.10	84	76	69	62	55	49	43	61%
10	.12	91	87	82	78	74	71	67	55%
15	.12	88	82	77	71	66	61	57	57%
20	.12	86	79	72	66	60	55	49	59%
25	.12	84	76	69	62	56	49	44	61%
30	.12	83	75	67	59	52	45	39	63%

*Ratio equals (RT/TL) times PV of annuity for TL at i%, divided by PV of annuity for RL at i%, where RL = remaining life, TL = total life and i% = marginal borrowing rate.

Source: Eugene A. Imhoff, Jr., Robert C. Lipe, and David W. Wright, "Operating Leases: Impact of Constructive Capitalization," *Accounting Horizons* (March 1991), p. 56. Reprinted with permission.

Exhibit 4.4
Impact of Constructive Capitalization of Operating Leases on McDonald's Balance Sheet and Financial Ratios

Panel A: Balance Sheet Impact

Balance Sheet
December 31, 1988
($ in millions)

Assets:	Liabilities:
	Unrecorded Lease Liabilities (See Table 2 Details) $1,172.8[a]
Unrecorded Lease Assets	Tax Consequences (.4 × $387) (154.8)[d]
(.67 × Liability) $785.8[b]	Net Liability Effect $1,018.0
	Stockholders Equity: Cumulative Effect on Retained Earnings Net of Tax Consequences ($1,172.8 - $785.8 = $387) × (1 - .4) (232.2)[c]
$785.8	$ 785.8

[a] Step 1- see table 2 calculation
[b] Step 2- using Table 3
[c] Step 3- based on combined total marginal tax rate of 40 percent
[d] Step 4 – either deferred income taxes or taxes payable depending on tax treatment of lease

Panel B: Impact on financial Ratios

	Assets (ROA) Return on	Total debt to Total equity (D/E)
1) As reported based on annual report	$\frac{\$646}{\$8,159} = 7.9\%$	$\frac{\$4,746}{\$3,413} = 1.39$ times
2) As revised per panel A adjustments to balance sheet only	$\frac{\$646}{\$8,945} = 7.2\%$	$\frac{\$5,764}{\$3,181} = 1.81$ times
3) Percentage change $(\frac{(1-2)}{1})$	9% Decrease in ROA	30% Increase in D/E

Source: Eugene A. Imhoff, Jr., Robert C. Lipe, and David W. Wright, "Operating Leases: Impact of Constructive Capitalization," *Accounting Horizons* (March 1991), p. 56. Reprinted with permission.

Financial Accounting Standard (FAS) No. 13. It is basically the hypothesis advanced and verified by Eugene Imhoff and Jacob Thomas that financial statement changed caused by FAS No. 13 increased the cost of using capital leases, thereby causing lessees to reduce the proportion of assets financed through capital leases.[10] They conclude as follows:

> Overall our results support the hypothesis that the financial statement effects of lease capitalization required by Statement of Financial Accounting Standard (SFAS) No. 13 had a significant impact on lessees. Capital leases as a source of financing declined sharply after the standard. The substantial amount of substitution into operating leases we observe suggests that renegotiation of lease contracts is a low-cost alternative, relative to other responses that potentially mitigate the financial statement effects of the standard. To the lesser extent, other capital structure changes were also selected in some instances, evidence by an increased use of nonlease financing (decreases in debt and increases in equity). Overall, most lessees apparently elected not to renegotiate contracts affected by lease capitalization nor to enter into technical default, and employed various capital structure changes instead.[11]

Given the above economic consequences in terms of the impact of the adoption of the disclosure rule mandated by SFAS No. 13 on the leverage portion of firms, the obvious research question is to determine the factors that affected managements' choices in accounting for leases prior to the implementation of SFAS No. 13. The research question, which fits well within the positive accounting paradigm, was examined by Samir El-Gazzar, Steve Lilien and Victor Pastena.[12]

The three explanations for nonsectional differences in the choices for accounting for leases were: debt convent constraint, compensation plans based on income, and political costs. Basically, a positive correlation between D/E and the operating method, between the increase in D/E and the operating method, between industry-adjusted D/E and the operating method, between the operating method and income-based compensation plans, and a negative correlation between sales and the operating method and between the effective tax rate and the operating method are expected. The results were generally in support of the positive impact of financial contracting and management bonus incentive variables. The political cost hypothesis was not supported while tax return considerations seem to influence management's lease accounting choice. The results from a positive accounting study point to the potential managerial concern for the balance sheet effect of lease capitalization. In fact, Mie Nakayma, Steve Lilien, and Martin Benis report that over 75 percent of the 176 companies opposing SFAS No. 13 explained their position by citing covenant violations or distortions of their debt-to-equity position.[13] This may explain why more firms renegotiated existing leases and modified the terms of new leases to avoid the capitalization required by SFAS No. 13. [14]

While most of the above studies focused on balance sheet effects, income effects seem to also argue for the adoption of the operating method. The point was illustrated by Ernst & Ernst[15] showing that reported income under the operating method is higher early in life of a lease, because the rental expense under the operating method is less than the sum of the initial interest and depreciation expenses under capitalization. While this advantage disappears at the end of the lease life, it continues if leasing activities continue to grow on a nominal basis. A complete examination of the economic consequences of the adoption of the disclosure rule prior to and following Statement No. 13 is provided by the following studies.

The effects of the lease capitalization in share prices by R. Bowman,[16] showed that prices behave as if financial leases are similar to other forms of debt. A number conclusion was reached by J. E. Finnerty, R. N. Fitzsimmons, and T. W. Oliver[17] showing that share prices are not affected by prescription of capitalization, even though some prior work by B.T. Ro[18] implied that the release of information had an adverse affect on security pricing. Other examinations of the economic consequences of the adoption of the disclosure rule prior to and

Exhibit 4.5
Impact of Constructive Capitalization of Operations Leases on Seven Industry Pairings

As reported ($ in millions)

Industry/ Company	Total Assets	Total Debt	Net Income	Reported ROA	Revised ROA	% Change	Reported D/E Multiple	Revised D/E Multiple	% Change
Home Furnishings									
Pier 1 Imports	$257.9	$163.8	$16.1	6.2%	4.0%	-55%	1.7	6.0	+243%
Rhodes, Inc.	261.5	152.0	11.9	4.6	4.1	-9	1.4	1.8	+30
Food Stores									
Winn-Dixie	1,417.7	678.3	112.3	7.9	5.3	-33	.9	2.8	+204
A&P (Great Atl. $ Pac.)	2,248.2	1,391.9	103.4	4.6	4.0	-14	1.6	2.5	+50
Fast Food									
Foodmaker (Jack-in-box)	470.5	352.9	13.9	2.9	2.4	-19	3.0	5.6	+85
Church's Fried Chicken	344.8	86.3	9.5	2.8	2.6	-4	.3	.4	+25
Semi-fast Food									
TGI Friday's	178.6	70.6	7.9	4.4	2.7	-38	.7	2.6	+302
Luby's Cafeteria	162.2	36.6	23.7	14.6	13.4	-8	.3	.4	+54
Clothing									
The Limited	1,587.9	858.8	235.2	14.8	9.6	-35	1.2	3.8	+222
Petrie Stores	1,134.3	595.8	47.5	4.2	3.5	-16	1.1	1.8	+64
Drug/Food Stores									
Walgreen Co.	1,362.0	739.6	103.5	7.6	5.6	-27	1.2	2.8	+134
American Stores	3,650.2	2,764.5	154.3	4.2	3.9	-9	3.1	4.0	+29
Airlines									
Delta	5,342.4	3,404.5	263.7	4.9	3.5	-29	1.8	4.4	+150
TWA	4,224.2	3,931.7	45.3	1.1	1.0	-9	13.3	23.8	+77
Average Percentage Changes									
High Lessee						-34%			+194%
Low Lessee						-10%			+47%

Excluding Extraordinary gains/Losses
Based on non-rounded ratio values: (Actual/Revised)/Actual.

Source: Eugene A Imhoff, Jr., Robert C. Lipe, and David W. Wright, "Operating Leases: Impact of Constructive Capitalization,"
   Accounting Horizons (March 1991), p.61. Reprinted by permission.

following Statement No. 13 are provided by A. R. Abdel-Khalik, R. B. Thompson, and T. W. Olivier[19] and by Abdel-Khalik.[20]

The first study focused on the impact of adoption ASR No. 147 *Notice of Adoption of Amendments to Regulation S-X Requiring Improved Disclosure of Leases*[21] and APB Opinion No. 31, *Disclosure of Lease Commitments by Lessees*[22] on the lessee's bond risk premium, and on the differences between the bond risk premiums of firms which utilize off-balance sheet lease financing and those of other firms that primarily finance through increase of capitalized long-term debt. The study is basically an evaluation of the impact of footnote disclosure of debt on the bond risk premium as a measure of the debt market's assessment of default risk. The results show that the disclosure of present values of noncapitalized leases does not appear to significantly influence bond risk premiums of firms affected by the disclosure ruling, and the mean bond risk premiums of some firms that finance through noncapitalized financing leases were significantly lower than mean bond risk premiums of the firms of similar risk profile. Abdel-Kjalik et al. concluded as follows:

> Taking these two findings together and assuming that (a) our samples are representative and (b) the bond risk premium is an appropriate measure of default risk, then it is arguable that some firms with material noncapitalized financing leases have enjoyed a relatively lower assessment of their default risk and that present value footnote disclosure has not altered this position. If our samples are not representative, then the same implications still apply but only to firms included in these samples. In either case, one may only speculate on what the impact of FASB Statement No. 13 might be on these types of firms. Since implementing Statement No. 13 will have the effect of moving the present values of these previously noncapitalized leases to long-term debt on the balance sheet, it is likely that we will observe a reassessment of default risk for these firms only if the implications drawn in this study are reasonably correct.[23]

The second study by Abdel-Khalik as the principal researcher focuses on the economic effects of lessees of FASB Statement No. 13.[24] Nine research questions were examined:

1. Does capitalization of leases have a major effect on the relationship of data within financial statements? The results showed, as expected, a decline in reported current ratio, an increase in debt/equity ratio, and a slight decrease in the accounting return on assets, especially for smaller companies with relatively significant leases tan for larger companies with relatively significant leases.
2. What are the kinds of decisions that appear to have been made at the company level following lease capitalization? The actions that may be caused by the capitalization of existing lease contracts may include:

(a) early retirement of debt, (b) conversion of bonds to equity shares, (c) financing acquisitions by issuing equity shares, (d) making discretionary accounting changes, (e) increasing investment outlays as measured by capital expenditures, (f) renegotiating terms of existing lease contracts so they would not satisfy the criteria for capital leases, or (g) creating unconsolidated finance subsidiaries to which lease contracts would be eassigned.[25]

The results showed that efforts have been made to structure the terms of new lease contracts or that capitalization could be avoided and that firms increased buying or constructing assets instead of leasing them. In addition, during a three-year period following the issuance of Statement No. 13 (1976-1978), the following unusual changes were examined: (a) increased retirements of long-term debt, (b) increased sales of equity shares, (c) decrease in outstanding convertible bonds, (d) decrease in the balance of treasury stock, (e) increased capital expenditures, (f) changes in the special items charged to income, and (g) increased acquisitions effected by issuing stocks. The observed unusual changed were in fact (a) sale of common stock and preferred stock, (b) retirement of long-term debt, and (c) conversions of bonds to stock.

3. Have preparers of financial statements of lessee companies been motivated by the accounting change required by Statement No. 13 to alter their economic decisions given the cosmetic nature of the change? Some of the reasons why management may do so include (a) dividing covenant violations, (b) beliefs and perceptions held by preparers of financial statements about the reaction of others, and (c) management's incentive compensation.

4. Do the capitalization of leases influence analysts' evaluations? The results showed that the analysts indicated no adverse effects on the evaluation of lessees supporting a concern of some preparers of financial statements that the evaluation of success indicator by users may be influenced by cosmetic accounting changes.[26]

5. What are the effects of capitalization of leases on the markets' assessment of risk and return on the securities of firms? This is done by examining (a) marker-based systematic risk of common stock, (b) bond ratings as a surrogate for systematic risk of common stock, (c) market-based unsystematic risk of common stock, (d) total variance of returns on common stock as a measure of total risk, (e) bond-risk premiums, (f) mean unexpected holiday returns on common stock, and (g) mean unexpected holiday returns on common bonds. The results indicate no significant association between the events leading up to the adoption of Statement No. 13 and the market-based measures.

6. How do users, preparers, and auditors of financial statements feel about the consistency between capitalization and the board objectives of financial statements? The responses disagreed with the ability to predict cash flow and the assessment of dividend-paying ability, and agreed with assessment of debt-paying ability.

7. What are the explicit negative views presented about the changes in lease disclosure requirements. The negative views focused on (a) the technical complexity and details of the standards, amendments, and interpretations of accounting for leases; (b) the arbitrary approach to determining the interest rate to be used in capitalization; (c) the administrative cost involved in compliance with the statement; (d) the negative effect on comparability of financial statements due to variation among companies in applying the rules; (e) the belief that the FASB has not demonstrated that disclosure under ASR 147 is inadequate compared with the alternative of capitalization; and (f) the elimination from disclosure of some data considered essential by financial analysts.[27]

8. How do users, preparers, and auditors of financial statements view certain possible changes in accounting for leases. The respondents were particularly in favor of (a) required footnote disclosure of a complete schedule of future cash flow commitments for all leases, and (b) continued measurement of annual expense charges as the amortization of the asset plus the interest on the debt.[28]

9. What are the lessons the researchers learned that could be of benefit to readers? The results indicate that (a) some of the actions that managers took were the results of conflict between the requirements of accounting standards and internal operating systems of their firms; (b) specifying a very tight set of criteria may lead to manipulation; (c) the perceptions, beliefs, and incentives of preparers play a major role in their action to accounting standards; (d) a withdrawal of data used by users leads to unfavorable reactions about the accounting standards; (e) accounting standards and methods seem to have outpaced many users' knowledge, creating a gap and a lot of frustration; and (f) auditors have huge expectations of the favorable impact of the concepted framework on the standard-setting process.[29]

PREDICTIVE ABILITY OF FINANCIAL RATIOS BASED ON THE LEASE DISCLOSURES RATE

Because the capitalization method advocated by SFAS No. 13 led to a better representation of both the liability and asset position of a firm, it should be expected that the financial ratios based on capitalization were a better predictive ability of economic events than the financial ratios based on the operating method. In fact, most of the predictive ability studies that followed the adoption of SFAS No. 13 managed to compute the leverage ratio but included the additional liability created by capitalization of the financial lease payments.[30] It is, however, appropriate to note that the one predictive ability study preceding the adoption of SFAS No. 13 did not support the hypothesis that addition of capitalization lease data to a firm's financial statements will increase the power of affected financial ratios for predicting firm bankruptcy.[31] Those results are not representative of the situation following the adoption of SFAS No. 13. As noted in the conclusion of the study: "This conclusion does not necessarily mean that leases should not be capitalized because lease data may be important for other uses of the financial statements not examined in this research. Additional research, employing other criteria, can produce more information about the effect of capitalized leases."[32] Although the study did not find differenced in the power of financial ratios to predict bankruptcy when ratios are computed with or without capitalizing long-term leases, the Zeta model developed by E. I. Altman, R. G. Haldeman, and P. Narayanaw,[33] which included a capitalization of all noncancelable operating and financial leases, resulted in a model that had better accuracy rates than the existing bankruptcy prediction models. Risk Elam's results are surprising since lease capitalization requirements do cause an apparent deterioration in firms' debt-equity ratios.[34,35] So, it is not surprising that Trevor Williams and Ian Zimmer,[36] in an experimental study evaluating the effects of alternative methods of accounting for leases, found that the reporting methods affected the behavior of financial analysts in projecting earnings but not in share valuations. Similarly, M. W. Dirsmith and J. B. Thies[37] relied on a survey of corporate executives to evaluate the impact of lessee accounting rules on management decisions. Their results show that (1) factors of economic substance have more of an impact on lease-purchase decision making than factors which primarily concern the form in which information is reported; and (2) reporting entities characterized as being financially weak consider form factors- that is, off-balance-sheet financing- to have a greater impact on lease-purchase decision making than do financially strong companies.[38]

CONCLUSION

This chapter examined some of the important issues associated with the adoption of Statement No. 13 in accounting for leases. The issues examined included (1) a history of the accounting rules, (2) the financial statement effect of the lease disclosure rule, (3) the measurement of the current portion of long-term lease obligation, (4) the constructive capitalization scenario, (5) the empirical studies in the economic consequences of the adoption of the disclosure rule, and (6) the predictive ability of financial ratios based on the lease disclosure rule.

NOTES

1. Harold E. Wyman, and Wesley T. Andrews Jr., "Classifying the Receivable in a Lease Transaction: A Dilemma," The *Accounting Review* (October 1975), pp. 905-908.
2. Robert J. Sweringa, "When Current Is Noncurrent and Vice Versa," *The Accounting Review* (January 1984), pp. 123-130.
3. Ibid., p. 130.
4. A. W. Richardson, "The Measurement of the Current Portion of Long-term Lease Obligations: Some Evidence from Practice," *The Accounting Review* (October 1985), pp. 744-752.
5. Ibid., p. 752.
6. E. A. Imhoff, Jr., R. C. Lipe, and D. W. Wright, "Operating Leases: Impact of Constructive Capitalization," *Accounting Horizons* (March 1991), pp. 51-63.
7. Ibid.
8. The following assumptions are made: (a) Straight line depreciation is the method used; (b) Both the unrecorded lease asset and the unrecorded lease liability are 100 percent of the percent value of future lease payments at the inception of each lease; (c) The unrecorded lease asset and the unrecorded lease liability are both zero after the lease payment is made for each lease.
9. The constructive capitalization relied on the following six uniform assumptions: (a) The interest rate for each firm is 10 percent; (b) The average remaining life of the operating leases is 15 years; (c) All the scheduled cash flows take place at year end; (d) The unrecorded asset is equal to 70

percent of the unrecorded debt; (e) The combined effective tax rate is 40 percent; (f) The effect on the current period's net income is zero.

10.   Eugene A. Imhoff and Jacob K. Thomas, "Economic Consequences of Accounting Standards: The Lease Disclosure Rule Change," *Journal of Accounting and Economics* (December 1988), pp. 277-310.

11.   Ibid., p. 305.

12.   Samir El-Gazzar, Steve Lilien, and Victor Pastena, "Accounting for Leases by Lessees," *Journal of Accounting and Economics* (October 1986), pp. 217-238.

13.   Mie Nakayma, Steven Lilien, and Martin Benis, "Due process and FAS No. 13," *Management Accounting,* 27, (1981), pp. 49-53.

14.   R. Abdel-Khalik, *Economic Effects on Lessees of FASB Statement No. 13: Accounting for Leases* (Stamford, Ct: FASB, 1981).

15.   Ernst & Ernst, *Accounting of Leases, Financial Reporting Developments,* Retrieval no. 38574 (New York: Ernst & Ernst, March 1977).

16.   R. Bowman, "Theoretical Relationship Between Systematic Risk and Financial (Accounting) Variables" *Journal of Finance* (June 1978).

17.   J. E. Finnerty, R. N. Fitzsimmons, and T. W. Oliver, "Lease Capitalization and Systematic Risk," *The Accounting Review* (October 1978), pp. 631-649.

18.   B. T. Ro. "The Disclosure of Capitalized Lease Information and Stock Prices," *Journal of Accounting Research* (Autumn 1978), pp. 315-340.

19.   A. R. Abdel-Khalik, R. B. Thompson, and R. E. Taylor, " The Impact of Reporting Lease off the blance Sheet on Bond Risk Premiums: Two Exploratory Studies," in *Economic Consequences of Financial Accounting Standards* (Stamford, CT: FASB, 1978), pp. 103-157.

20.   Abdel-Khalik, *Economic Effects on Lessees.*

21.   Securities and Exchange Commissions, *Notice of Adoption of Amendments to Regulation S-X Requiring Improved Disclosure of Leases, Accounting Series Release No. 147* (October 1973).

22.   American Institute of Certified Public Accountants, Accounting Principles Board, APB Opinion No. 31, *Disclosure of Leases Commitments by Lessees* (December 1973).

23.   Abdel-Khalik, Thompson, and Taylor, "The Impact of Reporting Leases off the Balance Sheet," pp. 151-152.

24.   Abdel-Khalik, *The Economic Effects on Lessees.*

25.   Ibid., p. 18.

26.   Ibid., p. 24.

27.   Ibid., p. 25.

28.   Ibid., p. 31.

29.   Ibid., p. 32.

30.   Ahmed Belkaoui, *Industrial Bond Ratings and the Rating Process* (Westport, CT: Greenwood Press, 1983).

31.   Rick Elam, "The Effect of Lease Data on the Predictive Ability of Financial Ratios," *The Accounting Review* (January 1975), pp. 25-43.

32.   Ibid., p. 41.

33.   E. I. Altman, R. G. Haldeman, and P. Narayanaw, "Zeta Analysis: A New Model to Identify Bankruptcy Risk of Corporations," *Journal of banking and Finance,* 1 (1997).

34.   D. C. Chamberlain, "Capitalization of Lease Obligations," *Management Accounting* (December 1975); and Elam, "The Effect of Lease Data."

35.   D. Palmon and M. Kwatinez, "The Significant Role Interpretation Plays in the Implementation of SFAS No. 13, "*Journal of Accounting, Auditing and Finance* (Spring 1980).

36.   Trevor Williams and Ian Zimmer, "The effects of Alternative methods of Accounting for Leases-An Experimental Study," *Abacus,* 15, 1 (1983), pp. 64-75.

37.   M. W. Dirsmith and J. B. Thies, "The Impact of Lessee Accounting Rules on Management Decisions," *Review of Business and Economic Research,* 5 (1976), pp. 26-35.

38.   Ibid., p. 34.

SELECTED READINGS

Abdel-Khalik, R. *Economic Effects on Lessees of FASB Statement No. 13: Accounting for Leases* (Stamford, CT: FASB, 1981).

Baker, C. R. "Leasing and Setting Accounting Standards: Mapping the Labyrinth." *Journal of Auditing Accounting and Finance* (Spring 1980).

Benjamin, J. J. "FASB Statement No. 13 in Retrospect and Prospect." *CPA Journal* (June 1977).

Elam, Erik. "The effect of Lease Data on the Predictive Ability of Financial Ratios." *The Accounting Review* (January 1975), pp. 25-43.

El-GAzzar, Samir, Steve Lilien, and Victor Pastena. "Accounting for Leases by Lessees." *Journal of Accounting an Economics* (October 1986), pp. 221-238.

Finnerty, J. E., R. N. FItzsimmona, and T. W. Oliver. "Lease Capitalization and Systematic Risk." *The Accounting Review* (October 1978).

Gritta, R. D. "The Impact of Capitalization of Leases on Financial Analysis." *Financial Analyst Journal* (March-April 1974).

Imhoff, E. A. Jr., and D. W. Wright. "Operating Leases: Impact of Constructive Capitalization." *Accounting Horizons* (March 1991).

Imhoff, E. A. Jr., andJacob K. Thomas. "Economic Consequences of Accounting Standards: The Lease Disclosure Rule Change." *Journal of Accounting and Economics* (December 1988), pp. 277-310.

Nakayman, Nie, Steve Lilian, and martin Benis. "Due Process and FAS No. 13." *Management Accounting* , 27 (1981), pp. 49-53.

Nelson, A. T. "Capitalizing leases- The Effect on Financial Ratios." *Journal of Accountancy*. (July 1963).

Richardson, A. W. "The Measurement of the Current Portion of Long-Term Lease Obligations: Some Evidence from Practice." *The Accounting Review* (October 1985).

Ro. B. T. "The Disclosure of Capitalized Lease Information and Stock Prices." *Journal of Accounting Research* (Autumn 1978).

Sweringa, Robert J. "When Current Is Noncurrent and Vice Versa." *The Accounting Review* (January 1984), pp. 123-130.

Williams, Trevor and Ian Zimmer. "The Effects of Alternative Methods of Accounting for Leases- An Ecperimental Study." *Abacus* (June 1983), pp. 64-75.

Wyman, Harold E. and Wesley T. Andrews, Jr. "Classifying the Receivable in a Lease Transaction: A Dilemma." *The Accounting Review* (October 1975), pp. 905-908.